Monetary and Fiscal Policy through

a DSGE Lens

Monetary and Fiscal Policy through a DSGE Lens

HAROLD L. COLE

OXFORD
UNIVERSITY PRESS

OXFORD
UNIVERSITY PRESS

Oxford University Press is a department of the University of Oxford.
It furthers the University's objective of excellence in research, scholarship,
and education by publishing worldwide. Oxford is a registered trade mark of
Oxford University Press in the UK and certain other countries.

Published in the United States of America by Oxford University Press
198 Madison Avenue, New York, NY 10016, United States of America.

Library of Congress Cataloging-in-Publication Data

Names: Cole, Harold Linh, 1957– author.
Title: Monetary and fiscal policy through a DSGE lens / Harold L. Cole.
Description: [New York, New York] : [Oxford University Press], [2020] |
Includes bibliographical references and index. |
Identifiers: LCCN 2019031801 (print) | LCCN 2019031802 (ebook) |
ISBN 9780190076030 (hardback) | ISBN 9780190076047 (paperback) |
ISBN 9780190076061 (epub)
Subjects: LCSH: Macroeconomics. | Equilibrium (Economics)
Classification: LCC HB172.5 .C643 2020 (print) | LCC HB172.5 (ebook) |
DDC 339.5—dc23 LC record available at https://lccn.loc.gov/2019031801
LC ebook record available at https://lccn.loc.gov/2019031802

CONTENTS

1

Introduction

Real scientific debate in economics largely takes place between researchers armed with different quantitative models or different parameterizations of the same model. The debate then revolves around discussing, and even arguing over, whose model is more plausible and whose implications we should therefore take seriously. If one of the models was "true," this should be fairly easy. Unfortunately, making a model tractable generally means seriously pruning the set of factors that can be considered. As a result, the models we deploy are never "true," and the process of developing better and better versions of a model to address key questions is really a series of successively better approximations. Understanding both the strengths and the weaknesses of any given model, especially with respect to the factors left out and the uncertainty with respect to the best parameter values to plug in, is a critical part of being able to use approximate models in an intelligent fashion. This is simply not possible without a fairly deep understanding of how the model works and how changes in various parameters affect the model's implications.

Most students will receive their economics diplomas without much exposure to and understanding of economic policy debates. Only those who go to graduate school and develop a high level of expertise are likely to get this exposure. This is really unfortunate, since our understanding of many models is sufficiently advanced that we have streamlined their analysis. Also, computational methods have been standardized too. The net result is that doing what once was hard is now surprisingly easy provided that one proceeds in a series of small steps.

Monetary and Fiscal Policy through a DSGE Lens. Harold L. Cole, Oxford University Press (2020).
© Oxford University Press. DOI: 10.1093/oso/9780190076030.001.0001

This text is designed to bridge the gap between standard undergraduate courses that teach students fairly standardized material without expecting them to deeply understand it or extend the analysis in any substantive fashion, and graduate courses in which one is expected to understand fully every arcane detail of extremely elaborate models. The goal of this text is to develop and extend various versions of a representative agent DSGE model from the 1980s to take on a wide range of topics in monetary and fiscal policy. We aim not only to have students analytically understand and analyze these models but also to develop computational code to quantitatively evaluate their implications. Armed with these quantitative models, students will be equipped to take part in the scientific debate on key policy questions.

The text starts with monetary policy and with examining the impact of inflation on welfare, which feeds into the determination of the optimal inflation rate. We will extend this analysis to incorporate a wide variety of features thought to be important. This includes the impact of price or wage frictions on the optimal policy.

Part 2 takes on fiscal policy and starts with examining the equilibrium response to different levels of labor and capital taxation. This naturally feeds into discussing optimal fiscal policy. We will extend this analysis to allow for some degree of heterogeneity because income heterogeneity is thought to be important in understanding the distributional consequences of fiscal policy.

The text is fairly sparse in the amount of data and historical context presented. One reason for this is that I have another text, *Finance and Financial Intermediation: A Modern Treatment of Money, Credit, and Banking*, which is more empirical than this one. Most of the students whom I teach with this text have already gone through the other text. If you feel like you need more background, please consult it or something like it.

The text also does not seek to cover every topic and tries explicitly to not go into the deep end of the pool where a serious graduate level of analysis would be needed. One reason is that there are already several very well-known and excellent graduate texts that cover first year graduate macroeconomics.[1] Instead, I try to stick closely to the standard representative agent neoclassical macro model, where money is introduced through a cash-in-advance constraint. This model was the backbone of macroeconomic analysis through the 1980s and has a lot of insights that are relevant for many policy questions. Also, understanding it well makes moving on to other and more complicated models a fairly easy step.

---

1. In particular, see Stokey, Nancy L., and Robert E. Lucas with Edward C. Prescott, *Recursive Methods in Economic Dynamics*, published by Harvard University Press. And, Ljungqvist, Lars, and Thomas L. Sargent, *Recursive Macroeconomic Theory*, published by the MIT Press.

In teaching this course, I have found it advantageous to do it the old-fashioned way: with chalk on blackboard, deriving everything as we go along. This means that at the start of every class, I typically put up the Lagrangian for the model we are discussing and go from there. This slows everything down to a comfortable pace and helps the students really learn and understand the derivations. This is made easy by the fact that so many of the fundamental derivations do not change as we move from model to model.

Writing your own code and doing the computations are fundamental to really understanding how quantitative modeling works. The first code is the big step, and after that, everything is just changing or adding an additional aspect. The text was originally designed with Matlab in mind as the computational language. This is obviously not necessary and one could readily imagine doing it with R or Python or Julia or Fortran or C++. One reason I like Matlab is that it is one of the easiest of these possibilities to get started in. One of the goals of my course and of this text is to make this material accessible not just to those who are extremely proficient in math and computation but also to those who are not. This is in large part because one of my fundamental takeaways from having been an economic researcher for a substantial period of time is that positive intellectual energy and the ability to ask interesting questions are typically much more important than analytic wizardry. However, Matlab is expensive and open source languages like Python or Julia are increasingly attractive. Moreover, Python is a much more general purpose programming language. For that reason, I include a number of examples of our basic code in Python at the end of the book. In addition, in the business cycle chapter, I show how one can use Dynare, an open source add-on to Matlab, to more readily code, compute and simulate the model by also providing an example of Dynare code in the appendix.

## PART 1

Money in a DSGE Model

The Cash-in-Advance
Model—First Step

To introduce money into a model you need a friction. This is because if barter is possible and efficient, it will generally be preferred to money, in which case, money will have no value other than the backing it gets directly, as in a commodity money arrangement. Moreover, it will not be used as a medium of exchange, since it is unnecessary. The simplest friction is to require that one have cash in order to buy goods.

To rationalize requiring cash, we will follow Robert Lucas's famous path and assume that when people meet to exchange goods, they do so in a goods market where it is hard to track people's identities; therefore, one cannot use fancy long-term contracts. Assume also that the structure of markets is such that exchanges take place through a sequence of meetings and that these meetings always involve people who want to buy a particular good and those who want to sell the same good. Hence, they cannot directly exchange goods for goods, so barter cannot occur. Instead, exchanges must be financed using a medium of exchange. Serving in this role will be an asset whose value can be readily understood. Assume that the only such good is money. Given these very stark assumptions, one must always use money to buy goods.[1]

---

1. A model with type of constraint was first developed in Lucas Jr, Robert E. "Interest rates and currency prices in a two-country world." Journal of Monetary Economics 10.3 (1982): 335–359. The timing of the model we present was originally developed in to Svensson, Lars EO. "Money and asset prices in a cash-in-advance economy." Journal of Political Economy 93.5 (1985): 919–944.

Monetary and Fiscal Policy through a DSGE Lens. Harold L. Cole, Oxford University Press (2020).
© Oxford University Press. DOI: 10.1093/oso/9780190076030.001.0001

Since we have essentially forced money's use here by assumption, this is a poor model for understanding the role of money. But that is not what we will be using this set-up for. We will be using it to understand the impact of changes in the supply of money and other exogenous variables. For this, we just need our assumptions about how money is used to be accurate enough to yield interesting predictions.

Formally, we will assume that in each period, a household can produce a particular type of good; call it good i, where i indexes all of the different possible goods, $i \in I$. So, the household, which is composed of two agents whom we will call the seller and the buyer, splits up, with the buyer taking the available cash off to the goods markets to buy all the different types of goods that the household does not produce, call them j, $\{j \in I : j \neq i\}$. At the same time, the seller heads off to the market for good i, where they sell some of their good i, saving the rest to consume themselves.

We will assume that each of the goods markets $i \in I$ has lots of buyers and sellers, and hence, the markets are competitive. By competitive we mean that each agent takes as given the market price at which they can sell or buy goods. To keep things simple we will assume that the supply of goods is symmetric (i.e., equal for all types i) and that the distribution of possible buyers is also symmetric. Hence, the prices that clear the market in each of these markets will all be identical. We can rationalize this assumption by adding an additional choice over the type of good one produces. Then everyone would choose the high-price goods and no one would choose the low-price goods. Hence, all goods have to have the same price.

Besides the goods market, we will also assume that there is an asset market. In the asset market, households will exchange money and financial assets. To keep things simple, we will assume that the only type of asset they exchange is a one-period pure discount bond. The presence of this bond will give us an interest rate that we can determine. It is in the asset market that the government will conduct monetary policy either by directly increasing the money supply (perhaps through transfer payments) or through buying or selling bonds for cash.

We will assume that each household produces the good at the beginning of each period using labor. The output of the good is given by

$$y_i = ZL, \tag{1}$$

where Z is the current productivity level of the economy and L is the amount of labor expended by the household.

We will assume that the households have the following preferences over their joint consumption within the period: They have a concave utility function over a composite of all the possible goods, or

$$u(C) \text{ concave, and } C = \left\{ \frac{1}{\#I} \sum_{i \in I} C(i)^{\rho} \right\}^{1/\rho}, \qquad (2)$$

where $\#I$ is the number of different goods and $\rho \in (0, 1)$. For now, the composite aspect doesn't matter much, except that households will optimally choose to consume the same amount of each good if prices are all the same.[2] The more important part is the concavity of u; specifically $u' > 0$ and $u'' < 0$. When we get a bit more formal, we will assume that u exhibits constant relative risk aversion (CRRA), or

$$u(C) = \frac{C^{1-\alpha}}{1-\alpha}.$$

The households also have a disutility of labor, so their total payoff for a period is

$$u(C) - v(L). \qquad (3)$$

We will assume that v is convex; specifically that $v' > 0$ and $v'' > 0$. So, the cost of additional effort is positive and increasing in the level of effort.

The timing of the model will end up mattering quite a bit. We graph the timing in figure 1, and spell it out more explicitly as follows.

Timing within Each Period
1. The household starts a period with M units of money
2. It exerts labor effort L to produce its good
3. The seller and buyer split up and go to their respective markets
4. The seller and buyer come back together in the asset market
5. They jointly consume the consumption good.
6. The period ends.

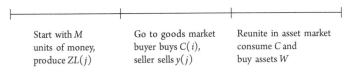

Start with M units of money, produce $ZL(j)$

Go to goods market buyer buys $C(i)$, seller sells $y(j)$

Reunite in asset market consume C and buy assets W

Figure 1. The Timeline of Events

2. Formally, this is a constant-elasticity-of-substitution (CES) aggregator.

1. THE HOUSEHOLD'S PROBLEM

We start with a simple, largely static version of the household's problem before moving on to dynamic versions.

1.1. Household's Within-Period Problem

Focus for the moment on the household's static consumption and labor effort choices. Assume that the household has initial money holdings M, which it can either spend this period on goods or carry over into the asset market, where it uses its money to buy assets or to hold as money for future purchases. For now, denote by $V(W)$ the future value of wealth. For simplicity we do not yet distinguish among the types of wealth.

The household can be thought of as choosing how much to consume of each of the different goods, $\{C(i)\}_{i\in I}$; how much to work to produce their production good $L(j)$; and how much wealth W for next period in order to maximize its payoff. This leads to the following formalization of the optimization problem for a household whose production type is j:

$$\max_{\{C(i)\}_{i\in I},L(j),W} u(C) - v(L(j)) + V(W) \text{ subject to}$$

$$M \geq \sum_{i\in I/j} P(i)C(i)$$

$$W \leq P(j)\left[ZL(j) - C(j)\right] + \left[M - \sum_{i\in I/j} P(i)C(i)\right].$$

The first condition is the cash-in-advance condition which states that the household can only spend as much to buy goods as it has in cash. The notation I/j means the set I less element j. The second constraint is its budget constraint, which says that the household's net period wealth is whatever it has left out of its money holdings and the proceeds of what it sells in the goods market. For now, we are allowing the price of the different goods that the household buys to be different and denoting them by $P(i)$.

This is a complicated multidimensional maximization problem. To address it, we form the Lagrangian, which is given by

$$\mathcal{L} = \max_{\{C(i)\}_{i\in I},L(j),W} \min_{\lambda,\mu} u(C) - v(L(j)) + V(W) \tag{4}$$

$$+ \lambda \left\{ M - \sum_{i\in I/j} P(i)C(i) \right\}$$

$$+ \mu \left\{ P(j)\left[ZL(j) - C(j)\right] + \left[M - \sum_{i\in I/j} P(i)C(i)\right] - W \right\}.$$

In this Lagrangian, the multipliers λ and μ are the "penalty prices" that we attach to violations of the constraint. In this maximization we are simultaneously trying to minimize the impact of these penalty prices on the overall objective and maximize the value of the objective in terms of the direct choice variables.

The impact of the penalties coming through the violations of the conditions can be minimized by setting them so that there is no violation. To see this, assume for the moment that $V(W) = 0$ and $\mu = 0$. So labor is 0 and the only choice is with respect to consumption. Note that if $\lambda = 0$, then it would be optimum to set consumption to infinity. But this would give the largest possible value of the overall objective, and it could be lowered by raising λ. Next, note that when λ is just large enough so that $M = \sum_{i \in I/j} P(i)C(i)$, the overall impact of $\lambda\{\cdot\}$ must be zero. Then, note that if we raise λ further, making the penalty price even higher, it will become optimal to lower consumption so that $M > \sum_{i \in I/j} P(i)C(i)$. But now we've gone too far, and we're raising the objective by not consuming everything.

This discussion so far has assumed that the constraint always binds. But this need not be the case. To understand when the cash-in-advance constraint doesn't bind, assume that we spend all our money. But now allow $V(W) > 0$, and in particular $V'(W) > 0$. If the payoff from wealth is big enough, it will no longer be optimal to spend all of M. If the payoff is small, then it will be.

In the review on optimization, I discuss Lagrangians with inequality constraints in some detail. The upshot of that discussion is that with an inequality constraint, we get a slight change in the first-order condition. Now, the multiplier is constrained to be nonnegative and can only take on a nonzero value if the constraint holds as an equality.

Note the value of the objective $\mathcal{L}$ is always just equal to our payoff. This is because either the constraints hold as equalities, in which case the value of the multipliers cannot affect $\mathcal{L}$, or they don't and the multipliers have to be equal to zero, and hence, the constraint portions of the objective again do not affect $\mathcal{L}$. One final thing to note is that because the marginal utility of wealth is always positive, the budget constraint in the asset market will always hold as an equality. Only the cash-in-advance constraint has the potential to not hold as an equality.

Remark 1. *There is some fancy math that says that the solution to the Lagrangian is the solution to our constrained optimization problem subject to a fancy caveat called the Kuhn-Tucker constraint qualification. That fancy caveat doesn't apply here, so we are good to go. There's some more fancy math that says that we can interchange the max and min operators in this problem, which means we can simply take the multipliers as predetermined constants when we choose the optimal actions. There is even more fancy math that says that this optimum, including both the choices and the multipliers, can be determined by satisfying the first-order conditions for this problem. The first-order conditions are meant to ensure that there are no simple first-order gains from adjusting one of the variables.*

The first-order conditions are obtained by differentiating the Lagrangian separately with respect to each choice variable (note that this includes the multipliers even though we are minimizing with respect to their choice) and setting each one of these first-order gains/losses terms to zero. This gives us a system of equations to pin down the choice variables. By construction there are the same number of conditions as there are choice variables. So, in general, this will completely characterize the solution.

The first-order conditions will include the consumption conditions for each type of consumption, or

$$u'(C)\left\{\frac{1}{\#I}\sum_i C(i)^\rho\right\}^{(1-\rho)/\rho} \frac{1}{\#I}C(i)^{\rho-1} = (\lambda + \mu)P(i)$$

for each $i \neq j$. For their own good j, the condition is

$$u'(C)\left\{\frac{1}{\#I}\sum_i C(i)^\rho\right\}^{(1-\rho)/\rho} \frac{1}{\#I}C(j)^{\rho-1} = \mu P(j).$$

Note that this implies that the household will consume more of its own good to the extent that the cash-in-advance constraint binds and $\lambda > 0$. The optimal condition for labor effort, or

$$v'(L(j)) = \mu P(j)Z. \tag{5}$$

The optimal choice of wealth, or

$$V'(W) = \mu.$$

Remark 2. *The treatment of consumption here illustrates a very general point. Goods that must be purchased by low-return assets like money are more costly to acquire to the extent that money is scarce.*

In the next two subsections we will remove the complexity arising from the different goods $i \in I$ because we will not need this feature until we try to construct a New Keynesian model.

1.1.1. CONSUMPTION
To keep things simple and symmetric, we will now assume that you have to use cash even to buy your own consumption good. So, the constraints become

$$M \geq \sum_{i \in I} P(i)C(i)$$

and

$$W \leq P(j)ZL(j) + \left[M - \sum_{i \in I} P(i)C(i) \right].$$

If the prices of the consumption good are the same $P(i) = \tilde{P}$ and $C(i) = C$, and note that the derivative of our inside aggregator wrt $C(i)$ is given by

$$\left\{ \frac{1}{\#I} \sum_i C(i)^\rho \right\}^{(1-\rho)/\rho} C(i)^{\rho-1} = \left\{ \frac{1}{\#I} \#I \right\}^{(1-\rho)/\rho} \{C^\rho\}^{(1-\rho)/\rho} C^{\rho-1}$$

$$= \{C^\rho\}^{(1-\rho)/\rho} C^{\rho-1} = C^0 = 1.$$

Then, note that if you buy dC in total by increasing our consumption of each of the goods by the same amount (i.e., by $dC/\#I$), and if all of the prices are the same, the change in $\mathcal{L}$ is

$$\sum_i u'(C)\frac{1}{\#I}dC = \sum_i (\lambda + \mu)\tilde{P}\frac{1}{\#I}dC \text{ or}$$

$$u'(C) = (\lambda + \mu)\#I * \tilde{P}$$

So, denote the price of a unit of the composite good (which means one of each individual good) by $P = \#I\tilde{P}$. As a result, this, the first-order condition (f.o.c.) becomes simply

$$u'(C) = (\lambda + \mu)P. \tag{6}$$

Remark 3. *To understand why we need to make this adjustment to the per unit price so that $P = \#I\tilde{P}$, consider the following thought experiment. Set all of the consumptions to C, i.e., $C(i) = C$. Then note that the amount that the individual will consume of the composite good is also C. But the amount that the household will spend on this composite good is $\#I\tilde{P}$ because the household needs to buy all of the I goods.*

With this simplified notation and set-up, we can more easily see the constraints the household faces with respect to its consumption choice. To see this note the shape of the consumption set graphed in Figure 2. Wanting to spend everything means that the budget constraint in the asset market must bind, but the cash-in-advance constraint limits how far the household can go in terms of its consumption choice.

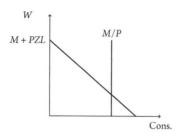

Figure 2. The Consumption Choice Set

If the cash-in-advance constraint doesn't bind, then $\lambda = 0$, and we get a very simple condition by using our f.o.c. for wealth to get

$$u'(C) = V'(W)P, \qquad (7)$$

which says that the marginal utility of consumption should be equal to the cost of consumption times the marginal value of future wealth.

If the cash-in-advance constraint does bind, then $\lambda > 0$,

$$C = \frac{M}{P}, \qquad (8)$$

and λ will be chosen so that

$$\lambda = \frac{u'(C)}{P} - V'(W).$$

Exercise 1. *Consider the following pure spending problem. The household has M units of money which it can spend today on consumption good C, or carry over to tomorrow and derive benefit γ times the number of money units it saves, S. Thus, its overall payoff as a function of its consumption choice C and savings choice S is*

$$u(C) + \beta\gamma S,$$

and it is subject to the cash-in-advance constraint

$$PC \leq M$$

and the budget constraint

$$S \leq M - PC.$$

1. *Form the Lagrangian for this choice problem. Try to show that the multiplier on the budget constraint must be equal to $\beta\gamma$ and that the sum of the two multipliers must be equal to $U'(M/P)/P$ if this is greater than $\beta\gamma$.*
2. *Discuss what happens to the multiplier on the cash-in-advance (c.i.a.) constraint as we increase M or decrease P.*
3. *What happens if the amount of money is so large that $U'(M/P)/P < \beta\gamma$?*

1.1.2. LABOR

Turn next to the optimal choice of labor. By again using the f.o.c. for wealth, we get that

$$v'(L(j)) = V'(W)P(j)Z, \tag{9}$$

which says that the optimal labor choice is to set the marginal disutility of effort equal to the nominal marginal production of labor, $P(j)Z$, times the marginal value of nominal wealth, $V'(W)$.

We want to rewrite this in terms of the composite price, and this becomes

$$v'(L(j)) = V'(W)PZ/\#I.$$

Then if we change Z to $Z * \#I$, we get

$$v'(L) = V'(W)PZ.$$

This gives us a nice simple condition to work with later.

1.1.3. COMPARATIVE STATICS CONSUMPTION

We can use our optimal consumption and labor conditions along with our budget constraint in the asset market and our cash-in-advance constraint to determine how our endogenous variables will response to changes in our exogenous variables. To do that, we want to linearize our conditions. These conditions are

$$u'(C) = V'(W)P + \lambda P$$
$$v'(L) = V'(W)PZ$$
$$W = M + PZL - PC$$
$$M \geq PC.$$

Because the c.i.a. condition is an inequality, there are two cases: case 1 when it does not bind and case 2 when it binds. Let's start with the case in which it does not bind. In that case, we can drop this condition and we are left with the first 3, which gives us three equations in three endogenous variables: C, L, and W. Start from initial values of $\bar{C}$, $\bar{L}$, and $\bar{W}$, which solve these first three equations at $\bar{P}$ and $\bar{Z}$. Then consider linearizing around this solution to get that

$$u'(\bar{C}) + u''(\bar{C})dC = V'(\bar{W})\bar{P} + V'(\bar{W})dP + V''(\bar{W})\bar{P}dW$$

which simplifies to

$$u''(\bar{C})dC = V'(\bar{W})dP + V''(\bar{W})\bar{P}dW$$

because we started from a solution. Note that all deviations are respect to the solution values (for example, dC is with respect to $\bar{C}$, etc.). Similar logic implies that

$$v''(\bar{L})dL = V'(\bar{W})\bar{P}dZ + V'(\bar{W})\bar{Z}dP + V''(\bar{W})\bar{P}\bar{Z}dW$$

$$dW = dM + \bar{P}\bar{Z}dL + \bar{P}\bar{L}dZ + \bar{Z}\bar{L}dP - \bar{P}dC - \bar{C}dP.$$

Plugging in for dW in the first two equations and simplifing gives us

$$\left[u''(\bar{C}) + V''(\bar{W})\bar{P}^2\right]dC - \left[V''(\bar{W})\bar{P}^2\bar{Z}\right]dL$$
$$= V'(\bar{W})dP + V''(\bar{W})\bar{P}\{dM + \bar{P}\bar{L}dZ + \bar{Z}\bar{L}dP - \bar{C}dP\} \qquad (10)$$

$$\left[v''(\bar{L}) - V''(\bar{W})\bar{P}^2\bar{Z}^2\right]dL + \left[V''(\bar{W})\bar{P}^2\bar{Z}\right]dC$$
$$= V'(\bar{W})\bar{P}dZ + V'(\bar{W})\bar{Z}dP + V''(\bar{W})\bar{P}\bar{Z}\{dM + \bar{P}\bar{L}dZ + \bar{Z}\bar{L}dP - \bar{C}dP\} \quad (11)$$

This looks a bit complicated but it's just two linear equations in two unknowns: dC and dL. The exogenous changes determine the right-hand-side (r.h.s.) values of each equation, and then given those, we solve for the endogenous change in consumption and labor.

Next, consider what happens when the cash-in-advance constraint binds. In this case, the consumption response is determined by this condition and we get that

$$\bar{P}dC = dM - \bar{C}dP. \qquad (12)$$

This condition replaces (10) and, along with (11), determines the optimal response. However, in this case, we can use (10) to solve directly for the change in consumption and then plug that into the labor condition (11).

2. THE ASSET MARKET

We now extend our simple model to incorporate an asset market at the end of the period. In the asset market households can exchange money for bonds and vice versa. They can also buy and sell government bonds.

Adding the choice between money and bonds means that we now have to distinguish between the two types of wealth that the household can carry out of the period.We denote its new bond and money positions by B' and M' to distinguish them from the household's initial levels. Denote by $V(B',M')$ the future payoff to the household if its bond position as it leaves the period is B' and its money position is M'. All bonds are pure discount bonds, which means that the payoff is \$1 for each unit of the bond and the cost is q per unit today. Note that $1/q$ is the gross interest rate offered by the bond and, hence, q will generally be taken to be less than 1.

The household faces a budget constraint in the bond market, which we can write as

$$PZL + [M - PC] + B \geq M' + qB'.$$

This new budget constraint replaces the wealth constraint in the household's problem. In addition, it is now choosing M' and B', not determining W. With these changes we can rewrite its Lagrangian as

$$
\mathcal{L} = \max_{\{C(i)\}_{i \in I}, L(j), M', B'} \min_{\lambda, \mu} u(C) - v(L(j)) + V(M', B') \tag{13}
$$
$$
+ \lambda \{M - PC\}
$$
$$
+ \mu \{PZL + [M - PC] + B - M' - qB'\}.
$$

We can redo the prior analysis replacing $V'(W)$, the marginal utility of wealth, with $V_1(M', B')$ the marginal utility of money. Almost all of the discussion with respect to (w.r.t.) consumption and labor will be essentially unchanged. The new aspect is choosing between money and bonds as a vessel of future wealth. Saying more will need to await a genuine dynamic model in which we can talk about how future money and future bonds are different. Here we can just begin the mechanics of the exercise.

The first-order condition for money M' is

$$-\mu + V_1(M', B') = 0.$$

Note that $V_1(\cdot)$ denotes the partial derivative of V w.r.t. the first argument of the function, which is money. Similarly, the first-order condition for bonds B' is

$$-\mu q + V_2(M', B') = 0,$$

where $V_2(\cdot)$ is the partial derivative w.r.t. the second argument of the function. These two conditions differ in important ways. First, bonds are cheaper per unit of future value to the extent that $q < 1$. Second, they contribute future value in different ways to the extent that money and bonds in the future are imperfect substitutes. To determine the answers to these sorts of questions, we need to move on to a genuine dynamic version of the model, which we do next.

## 3

The Cash-in-Advance Model — Second Step

We now extend our model by creating a genuine dynamic model. To do this, we will simply push out in time by one period the point at which we use a continuation payoff function, $V(M, B)$, to characterize outcomes. The model now becomes a bit more complicated, but it is still relatively tractable and we can get all of the insight we need. To keep things simple, we will continue to assume that there is only one good, but that the household must purchase it in order to consume the good (i.e., it cannot eat its own endowment).

We can think of our household as taking as given the price in the first and second periods, P_1 and P_2, and the productivity levels, Z_1 and Z_2. It also takes as given its initial money position M_1 and bond position B_1. Finally, it takes as given the payoff from money and bonds going into the third period $V(M_3, B_3)$. The household is choosing consumptions C_1 and C_2, labor L_1 and L_2, money holdings M_2 and M_3, and bond holdings B_2 and B_3.

We want to allow for at least one means by which the government can change the overall money supply. The simplest mechanism for doing so is through taxes and transfers of money in the asset market at the end of the period. Denote by T_t the net transfer that the government is making in cash to the household. When $T_t > 0$, the household is receiving cash, and when the reverse is true, it is making a cash payment to the government.

The household's problem can be written as

$$\max_{\{C_t, L_t, M_{t+1}, B_{t+1}\}_{t=1,2}} u(C_1) - v(L_1) + \beta\left[u(C_2) - v(L_2)\right] + \beta^2 V(M_3, B_3) \text{ subject to}$$

Monetary and Fiscal Policy through a DSGE Lens. Harold L. Cole, Oxford University Press (2020).
© Oxford University Press. DOI: 10.1093/oso/9780190076030.001.0001

$$M_t \geq P_t C_t \text{ and}$$

$$P_t Z_t L_t + [M_t - P_t C_t] + B_t + T_t \geq M_{t+1} + q_t B_{t+1} \text{ for } t = 1, 2.$$

The real difference between this version of the household's problem and the prior one has to do with the impact of choosing M_2 and B_2. For that reason, we focus on these choices. Before that, we need to set up the household's Lagrangian problem in order to derive its first-order conditions.

The household's Lagrangian is now given by

$$\mathcal{L} = \max_{\{C_t, L_t, M_{t+1}, B_{t+1}\}_{t=1,2}} \min_{\{\lambda_t, \mu_t\}_{t=1,2}} \tag{14}$$

$$u(C_1) - v(L_1) + \beta \left[u(C_2) - v(L_2) \right] + \beta^2 V(M_3, B_3) \tag{15}$$

$$+ \sum_{t=1,2} \lambda_t \{ M_t - P_t C_t \}$$

$$+ \sum_{t=1,2} \mu_t \{ P_t Z_t L_t + M_t - P_t C_t + B_t + T_t - M_{t+1} - q_t B_{t+1} \}.$$

In this problem we are now assuming the discounting of future utils by multiplying the next period's payoff by $\beta < 1$, and the payoff two periods ahead by β^2.

The first-order conditions for consumption and labor are still given by

$$\beta^{t-1} u'(C_t) = [\lambda_t + \mu_t] P_t \tag{16}$$

and

$$\beta^{t-1} v'(L_t) = \mu_t P_t Z_t. \tag{17}$$

To derive the first-order conditions for M_2 note that it shows up in the date $t = 1$ budget constraint as M_{t+1}, and it also shows up in the date $t = 2$ cash-in-advance and budget constraints as M_t. Thus, when we differentiate, we need to be careful to pick up all of these terms. (Note that if you're confused here, simply write out the explicit conditions, dropping the fancy summation notation $\sum_{t=1,2}$.) Doing the differentiation correctly leads to

$$-\mu_1 + \lambda_2 + \mu_2 = 0. \tag{18}$$

This says that the cost of increasing money holdings, M_2, is the shadow price of the first period budget constraint, μ_1, while the gain is the sum of the shadow price of the second period c.i.a constraint, λ_2, and the shadow price of the second-period budget constraint, μ_2. Here λ_2 is capturing the service yield of money in that it allows the household to not just transfer wealth but also buy some extra consumption in period 2. This condition now makes clear what stood behind the mystery term $V_1(M', B')$ in our static model of the previous chapter.

We next turn to the first-order condition for bonds and the choice of B_2. Once again this term shows up as B_{t+1} when $t = 1$ and B_t when $t = 2$. So here too we have to differentiate a bit carefully. When we do so, we get the following expression,

$$-\mu_1 q_1 + \mu_2 = 0. \tag{19}$$

This expression highlights the difference between buying bonds vs. holding money. With bonds we get a price break to the extent that $q_1 < 1$, but we don't get the future service yield, λ_2, just the future benefit of having more wealth, μ_2.

To get a bit more insight into the gain from having more money in period 2, use the f.o.c. for C_2

$$\beta u'(C_2) = (\lambda_2 + \mu_2)P_2.$$

Note that the cost of second period consumption is the combination of the shadow prices of the c.i.a. and budget (b.c.) constraints. Using this expression we can rewrite the first-order condition for money as

$$\mu_1 = \frac{\beta u'(C_2)}{P_2}.$$

From this condition we can see more sharply that the household is trading off the benefit of being able to buy consumption tomorrow vs. the lower return on savings offered by money (again to the extent that $q_1 < 1$).

What does our model say about the comparison between consumption and labor? In most models this is a standard intratemporal (within-period) condition, but not here. This is because income earned from labor cannot be used to fund consumption today, only tomorrow. Moreover, to fund consumption tomorrow these funds must be carried over in the form of money, a non-interest-bearing asset. Starting from the first-order condition for L_1, we use the f.o.c. for M_2 to replace μ_1, and then the f.o.c. for C_2 to finally get

$$\begin{aligned}
v'(L_1) &= \mu_1 P_1 Z_1 \\
&= [\mu_2 + \lambda_2] P_1 Z_1 \\
&= \left[\frac{\beta u'(C_2)}{P_2}\right] P_1 Z_1 \\
&= \frac{P_1}{P_2} Z_1 \beta u'(C_2).
\end{aligned}$$

This is the optimal labor-consumption condition in our model. It compares the disutility of labor today to the current marginal product of labor, adjusted for the purchasing power lost due to inflation, times the discounted marginal utility of consumption tomorrow. To the extent that money is a bad asset here,

$P_1/P_2 \ll 1/q$, and this will discourage people from working. This is one of the key inefficiency wedges that the presence of money has created in our model.

What about consumption today vs. consumption tomorrow? The f.o.c. for C_1 is given by

$$u'(C_1) = [\mu_1 + \lambda_1] P_1, \text{ and for } C_2$$
$$\beta u'(C_2) = [\mu_2 + \lambda_2] P_2.$$

How can we compare these two? First, note that if we reduce spending today we have more money as a result, and we have to transfer funds using money in order to increase spending tomorrow. Hence, the payoff per dollar spent is the number of consumption units we buy times the appropriate marginal utility of consumption, or $u'(C_1)/P_1$ and $\beta u'(C_2)/P_2$. Also, the f.o.c. for money says that $\mu_1 = \mu_2 + \lambda_2$. Making this substitution and rearranging we get that

$$\frac{u'(C_1)}{P_1} = [\mu_2 + \lambda_2 + \lambda_1], \text{ and for } C_2$$
$$\frac{\beta u'(C_2)}{P_2} = [\mu_2 + \lambda_2].$$

So, for these two r.h.s. expressions to be equal, we need $\lambda_1 = 0$ or the shadow price of the c.i.a. constraint to be 0. Otherwise, we strictly prefer to spend our money in the first period.

When will the shadow price of money be 0? Note that from our money and bond conditions

$$\mu_1 = \mu_2 + \lambda_2 \text{ and}$$
$$\mu_1 q_1 = \mu_2.$$

So, if $q_1 < 1$, these conditions say that $\lambda_2 > 0$. In other words, the household will adjust the composition of its savings between money and bonds to ensure that the c.i.a. constraint binds enough to offset the extra interest return that they get from holding bonds. Thereby the household raises the true value of money to offset the interest factor on bonds. This true value includes both the intertemporal savings return and the service return from relaxing the c.i.a. constraint.

Remark 4. Earlier we saw how a shortage of cash could distort consumption across goods that required money and those (which we produced at home) that did not. But why should there ever be a shortage of cash if households get to choose their cash balances? The answer this insight provides is that there will always be a shortage of cash whenever and to the extent that the gross nominal interest rate is positive. This is because holding cash is expensive, so a forward-looking household economizes on it, leaving it cash constrained in the future.

Exercise 1. *Here we want to think about being able to extend our analysis to many periods. We want to determine that the equations we have derived to characterize the households' two-period problem will carry over and in what form. To do that, consider the following three-period version of our model. The household's Lagrangian is now given by*

$$\mathcal{L} = \max_{\{C_t, L_t, M_{t+1}, B_{t+1}\}_{t=1,2,3}} \min_{\{\lambda_t, \mu_t\}_{t=1,2,3}}$$

$$\sum_{t=1,2,3} \beta^{t-1} [u(C_t) - v(L_t)] + \beta^3 V(M_4, B_4)$$

$$+ \sum_{t=1,2,3} \beta^{t-1} \lambda_t \{M_t - P_t C_t\}$$

$$+ \sum_{t=1,2,3} \beta^{t-1} \mu_t \{P_t Z_t L_t + M_t - P_t C_t + B_t + T_t - M_{t+1} - q_t B_{t+1}\}.$$

Note that I have made a slight change in variables by multiplying the multipliers by the discount rate raised to the $t-1$. This helps to clean up the static f.o.c.'s. Use this setup to show how the equations we derived for the two-period model will carry over to a three-period model and, by extension, to an infinite horizon model.

1. CLOSING THE MODEL

So far, we have focused on the household's problem. But we want to think about what our model says about the aggregate equilibrium variables, such as prices and output. The aggregate resource constraint implies that per capita output is equal to per capita consumption, so

$$Z_t L_t = Y_t = C_t.$$

This gives us the first of our key aggregate constraints.

The per capita money supply evolves over time here because of net transfers. Let $\bar{M}_t$ denote the per capita money supply at the beginning of period t. Because the money supply can change over time, we will often find it useful to think of monetary policy in terms of the growth rate of the money supply. If we denote the net growth rate of money in period t by τ_t, then

$$\bar{M}_{t+1} = (1 + \tau_t)\bar{M}_t, \text{ and}$$
$$T_t = \tau_t \bar{M}_t.$$

The money market clearing condition requires that the amount of money with which the household leaves the asset market must equal the supply, or

$$M_{t+1} = \bar{M}_{t+1}.$$

In closing the model, let's assume that c.i.a. constraint binds. Then, this implies that

$$C_t = \frac{\bar{M}_t}{P_t}, \text{ or } P_t = \frac{\bar{M}_t}{Z_t L_t}. \tag{20}$$

This is a simple velocity type f equation, familiar from very old-school macro models: $Mv = PY$ where v is the velocity of money. The standard assumption in this type of equation is that velocity is fixed, at least in the short run, and hence changes in the money supply have to be offset by changes in either prices or income, and vice versa. In relating to this condition, note that consumption is equal to output here, and money turns over once per period.

Next, we turn to our optimality conditions to finish closing the model. The f.o.c. for consumption and labor imply that

$$\beta^{t-1} u'(Z_t L_t) = (\lambda_t + \mu_t)\frac{\bar{M}_t}{Z_t L_t}$$

and

$$\beta^{t-1} v'(L_t) = \mu_t Z_t \frac{\bar{M}_t}{Z_t L_t},$$

where we have made use of the fact that $C_t = Z_t L_t$ from our resource constraint. The money and bond conditions imply that

$$\mu_t = \mu_{t+1} + \lambda_{t+1} \text{ and}$$
$$\mu_t q_t = \mu_{t+1}.$$

We can use the money condition along with our conditions for consumption and labor to get that

$$\beta^{t-1} v'(L_t) = [\mu_{t+1} + \lambda_{t+1}]\frac{\bar{M}_t}{L_t}$$
$$= \left[\beta^t u'(Z_{t+1}L_{t+1})\frac{Z_{t+1}L_{t+1}}{\bar{M}_{t+1}}\right]\frac{\bar{M}_t}{L_t}$$
$$= \frac{1}{(1+\tau_t)}\frac{Z_{t+1}L_{t+1}}{L_t}\beta^t u'(Z_{t+1}L_{t+1}). \tag{21}$$

This is our key dynamic equation. It is dynamic because it involves both L_t and L_{t+1}. However these are the only endogenous variables in the equation. So, solving this equation will essentially solve our model.

Finally, we can determine the bond price off of the optimality conditions for labor and bonds, just as we did in the steady-state analysis. Note that

$$\mu_t q_t = \mu_{t+1} \Rightarrow \frac{v'(L_t)L_t}{\bar{M}_t} q_t = \frac{\beta v'(L_{t+1})L_{t+1}}{\bar{M}_{t+1}}$$

or

$$q_t = \frac{\beta}{(1 + \tau_t)} \frac{v'(L_{t+1})L_{t+1}}{v'(L_t)L_t}. \tag{22}$$

The unusual aspect of this equation is that we are pinning down the interest rate through the intertemporal tradeoff of working more today vs. tomorrow rather than consuming more today vs. tomorrow. This is because labor income shows up in the asset market, and hence, we use the bond to shift it forward in time. We will discuss this condition in more detail in the section on steady-state analysis and again in the section on the stochastic equilibrium.

Long Run Analysis: We are going to use this model, and the many variants that follow, to analyze outcomes not only for two periods but also in the longer and even long run. Rather than go into the notation and mathematics that accompany doing this carefully, we are going to use a shortcut. Our shortcut is to assume that the dynamic equations that we develop for periods $t = 1$ and $t = 2$ hold for all time periods $t \geq 1$. We are then going to charge ahead and compute these longer-run and long-run outcomes. Our assumption turns out to be valid, but proving that takes us too close to the "sun" of a true graduate macro course.

1.1. Steady State 1

We are going to shut down as much of the time variation as we can and solve for a steady-state equilibrium of our model. So, we will assume for now that productivity is constant; i.e., $Z_t = Z$. In this steady state we will allow the money supply to grow, but at a constant rate τ. Because the money supply is growing, the price level cannot be constant. But we will conjecture and then verify that consumption, labor, and the real value of the money supply are all constant.

If $L_t = L$, then our key dynamic equation becomes

$$v'(L) = \frac{\beta}{(1 + \tau)} Z u'(ZL).$$

One can pretty much see from inspection that this equation is going to admit a unique solution in L. The left-hand side (l.h.s.) is increasing in L because we assumed that $v' > 0$. The right-hand side (r.h.s.) is decreasing in L because u' is decreasing in C ($u'' < 0$).

Before actually solving our model, we have to take a stand on the explicit function forms of our preferences. The standard assumption for consumption is that preferences are CRRA, or

$$u(C) = \begin{cases} \frac{C^{1-\alpha}-1}{1-\alpha} & \text{if } \alpha \neq 1 \\ \log(C) & \text{otherwise (o.w.)} \end{cases} .^{1}$$

In this case, the intertemporal elasticity of consumption is defined as

$$\frac{d\log(C_{t+1}/C_t)}{d\log(u'_{t+1}/u'_t)}.$$

This term is looking at the percentage change in the ratio of consumption that needs to occur per unit of the percentage change in the ratio of marginal utilities. This magnitude will govern how consumption today vs. tomorrow responds to interest rate changes. A given change in the interest rate will force a corresponding change in the ratio of the marginal utilities of consumption, and this, in turn, will change the ratio of consumption.[2] Using our utility function

$$U'(C) = C^{-\alpha}, \text{ so}$$
$$\frac{U'(C_{t+1})}{U'(C_t)} = \left(\frac{C_{t+1}}{C_t}\right)^{-\alpha},$$
$$\Rightarrow \log\left[\frac{U'(C_{t+1})}{U'(C_t)}\right] = -\alpha\log\left[\frac{C_{t+1}}{C_t}\right]$$
$$\Rightarrow d\log\left[\frac{C_{t+1}}{C_t}\right] = -\frac{1}{\alpha}d\log\left[\frac{U'(C_{t+1})}{U'(C_t)}\right].$$

1. One can show that $\log(C)$ is the limiting version of the power utility function we specified as $\alpha \to 1$.

2. A standard consumption savings problem with a real interest rate of r and income y leads to the following problem:

$$max_{c_1,c_2} u(c_1) + \beta u(c_2) \text{ s.t. } c_1 + c_2/(1+r) \leq y_1 + y_2/(1+r)$$

which, in turn, leads to the following first-order condition:

$$u'(c_1) = \beta(1+r)u'(c_2).$$

So the intemporal elasticity calculation emerges from this sort of problem.

So, the intertemporal elasticity of consumption is $-1/\alpha$. Common values for this are around 1. We will see why, once we allow Z to grow over time.

The standard assumption with respect to labor is to also assume a power utility form, or

$$v(L) = \frac{L^{1+\gamma}}{1+\gamma}. \tag{23}$$

The common way to evaluate how elastic labor is, is with respect to the Frisch elasticity of labor. This concept asks how labor will change if we change the wage while holding fixed the marginal value of wealth. From our f.o.c. for labor, we get that

$$v'(L) = V'(W)PZ,$$

where PZ is our stand-in for the nominal wage w. To compute this elasticity, note that we can rewrite our f.o.c. as

$$L^{\gamma} = V'(W)w.$$

Taking logs, holding fixed the marginal utility of wealth, and differentiating yields

$$\gamma d\log(L) = \log[V'(W)] + d\log(w).$$

The Frisch elasticity, which is an elasticity of substitution since we are effectively holding income constant, is given by

$$\left.\frac{d\log(L)}{d\log(w)}\right|_{V'(W)} = \frac{1}{\gamma}.$$

These's a lot of debate about this elasticity. Many micro studies estimate it to be quite low (0 to 0.5), while macro studies generally estimate a significantly higher value (2 to 4). Naturally, the macroeconomists are right on this one. But, just in case, we will play around with the value to see how this matters.

We close this section by examining the determination of the price of the bond, q. Using (22) and the fact that labor is constant in a steady state, we get the following expression for the steady-state bond price

$$q = \frac{\beta}{(1+\tau)}, \tag{24}$$

where τ will be both the steady-state net growth rate of money and the inflation rate. To understand what is going on here, note that

$$q = \frac{1}{1+i},$$

where i is the nominal interest rate. Hence, a lower bond price is associated with a higher nominal interest rate. Next, note that the steady-state bond price has two components: a real component, β, arising from preferences, and an inflation component $(1+\tau)^{-1}$. Using the fact that the real interest rate r is such that

$$\beta = \frac{1}{1+r},$$

and that the inflation rate $\pi = \tau$, it follows that we can rewrite our steady-state bond price condition in a familiar form. This is

$$(1+i) = (1+r)(1+\pi) \approx 1+r+\pi. \tag{25}$$

This last expression is Fisher's famous equation, which says that the nominal interest rate is the sum of the real rate and the inflation rate. This expression is essentially tautological since we define the real rate off this equation, but it turns out to be a very useful way of understanding bond prices and interest rates in our model.

Now that we have determined the bond price, we can discuss the only other parameter we need to specify, which is the discount rate β. The right value of this parameter depends on, among other things, our period length. Risk-free real interest rates are quite low, say 1-2%. This is commonly taken to imply that, at an annual frequency, $\beta = 0.98$, and at a quarterly frequency, $\beta = 0.98^{1/4} = 0.99$.

1.2. Solving for the Steady State

Here we discuss how to solve for the steady state using Matlab. We need to solve the following single equation in one unknown L and several preset parameters in order to compute the steady state

$$L^\gamma = \frac{\beta}{(1+\tau)} Z(ZL)^{-\alpha}.$$

However, this example is particularly easy since it has an analytic solution

$$\Rightarrow L^{\gamma+\alpha} = \beta \frac{Z^{1-\alpha}}{(1+\tau)},$$

$$\Rightarrow L = \left[\beta \frac{Z^{1-\alpha}}{(1+\tau)}\right]^{1/(\gamma+\alpha)}.$$

So, all we need to do is compute L. To do this we need to define an m-file, which is really a function. This function takes in our parameters, solves for L, and spits out the results. The code for the m-file should look something like the following.

We are constructing a function SS1. This is a script file that you save as SS1.m and run in the command window of Matlab by typing SS1. The function has an end statement and below that a subfunction called comp. The main function calls this subfunction to solve for the equilibrium level of labor effort. Subfunctions can be either tacked on to the main function in this way or saved as a separate function in the same folder as the main function.

```
function SS1
    % This function computes the labor level for a variety of different
    % parameter configurations and produces those results
    Z = 1; % ending statements with a semicolon means the result is not
    % displayed.
    gamma = 0.5;
    alpha = 2;
    beta = .98;
    Results = []; % initializing Results matrix
    for tau = 1:.05:2. % this is the beginning of the for loop.
    L = comp(Z,tau,gamma,alpha,beta); % function call for comp
    Results = [Results;Z tau gamma alpha beta L];
    end % loop end
    disp('Here are our results')
    Results
    % By setting a figure number you will not write over the plot
    % if the next figure is number 2. Here we also save
    % the figure as a pdf in the same folder.
    figure(1)
    plot(Results(:,2),Results(:,6),'-b','LineWidth',3)
    title('Labor vs. Money Growth Rates')
    xlabel('Money Growth Rate')
    ylabel('Labor')
    h = gcf;
    set(h,'PaperOrientation','landscape');
    print(gcf,'InfFig1','-dpdf','-fillpage')
    end % function end

    % This is our subroutine
    function solution = comp(Z,tau,gamma,alpha,beta)
```

% here tau is the net growth rate of money,
% Z is productivity, −1/alpha is the IES and 1/gamma is the Frisch
% the solution is to our simple CIA model with constant money growth
solution = (beta*Z^(1-alpha) / (1+tau))^(1/(gamma+alpha));
end

1.3. Multipliers in the Steady State

In the steady state that we are considering, labor and productivity are constant. If we impose these conditions along with market clearing and the c.i.a. constraint binding, we get that

$$\beta^{t-1}v'(L)\frac{L}{\bar{M}_1(1+\tau)^{t-1}} = \mu_t,$$

and

$$\beta^{t-1}u'(ZL)\frac{ZL}{\bar{M}_1(1+\tau)^{t-1}} = (\lambda_t + \mu_t).$$

The first equation implies that μ_t is shrinking at the rate $\beta^{t-1}/(1+\tau)^{t-1}$. Given this, the second equation implies that λ_t is shrinking at the same rate. This means that the *relative values* of the multipliers are staying constant, as are the ratios of the t and $t+1$ values, which is what drives the optimal choices. For future reference, note that if we adjust our multipliers as follows

$$\mu_t(1+\tau)^{t-1}/\beta^{t-1}$$

the result will be constant. This is an important insight that we will use later.

2. OPTIMAL POLICY

To talk about how good a policy is, we need something to measure it against. This is typically done relative to the socially efficient outcome. The socially efficient outcome can be found by solving a planner's problem where the planner seeks to maximize the payoff of the representative consumer. Since the planner is free to set prices, prices don't matter. For example, prices can always be set low enough so that the c.i.a. constraint cannot bind no matter what L_t is. This implies that we can work directly with the real allocation problem and that leads to the following form of the social planner's problem which is

$$\max_{L_1} u(Z_1 L_1) - v(L_1) + \beta V,$$

and V is the continuation payoff to the planner. In this problem we have directly imposed the resource constraint. Note also that there are no state variables since money and bond balances don't matter.

The f.o.c. for this problem is

$$u'(Z_1 L_1)Z_1 - v'(L_1) = 0.$$

If we compare this condition to the one that emerges from our model, (16) and (17), we can see that they will line up if and only if (iff) $\lambda_1 = 0$. That is, if the cash-in-advance constraint does not bind.

How can this be the case? If we look at the f.o.c.'s for money (18) and bonds (19), we can see that q must equal 1. This means that the net nominal interest rate is being set to zero. The notion that the net nominal interest rate should be zero is often called the *Friedman rule*, after Milton Friedman, who first proposed it.

Looking at our interest rate condition (22) we get that

$$(1 + \tau_t) = \beta \frac{v'(L_{t+1})Z_{t+1}L_{t+1}}{v'(L_t)Z_t L_t}.$$

To better understand what this implies, assume that $Z_t = Z$. Then our optimality condition will imply that $L_t = L_{t+1} = L$. In which case q_t is simply give by our steady state condition (24). So, for $q = 1$, it must be the case that

$$q = \frac{\beta}{(1 + \tau)} = 1, \text{ or}$$
$$(1 + \tau) = \beta.$$

This condition implies that $\tau < 0$. But if the money supply is shrinking, prices will also be falling and we will have *deflation*. In fact, with L constant, it follows that in the optimum $P_{t+1} = \beta P_t$. So the discount rate sets the optimal level of deflation and the optimal rate at which money must shrink.

3. QUANTITATIVE ANALYSIS

Now that we've constructed our model and learned how to solve it, we want to put it to use. Here we're going to work through some classic questions in monetary policy.

3.1. Quantitative Section 1

How big a cost is inflation? Or, put somewhat differently, how high does the inflation rate have to be before it becomes costly? We are going to compute the solution to our economy described above for various values of τ, and then examine their implications. But in order to say how costly something is, we need a unit of measurement. Utils are a bad unit of measurement, since they have no real scale. So we're going to go with the standard measure, which is the share of consumption equivalents, i.e., the fraction of lifetime consumption that we would have to add or take away to make you just as well off.

This turns out to be very easy to compute given a solution to our model. Denote by $L(\tau)$ the solution for a given value of inflation. Then lifetime utility is given by[3]

$$U(\tau) = \frac{1}{1-\beta}\left[\frac{(ZL(\tau))^{1-\alpha}-1}{1-\alpha} - \frac{L(\tau)^{1+\gamma}}{1+\gamma}\right].$$

If we fix some particular τ as our benchmark—call it τ_0—then our cost/benefit measure $\phi(\tau)$ from varying τ can be computed as the solution to

$$\frac{1}{1-\beta}\left[\frac{(\phi(\tau)ZL(\tau))^{1-\alpha}-1}{1-\alpha} - \frac{L(\tau)^{1+\gamma}}{1+\gamma}\right] = U(\tau_0)$$

which can be rewritten as

$$\frac{(\phi(\tau)ZL(\tau))^{1-\alpha}-1}{1-\alpha} = U(\tau_0)(1-\beta) + \frac{L(\tau)^{1+\gamma}}{1+\gamma},$$

which leads to

$$\phi(\tau)^{1-\alpha} = \frac{\left\{U(\tau_0)(1-\beta) + \frac{L(\tau)^{1+\gamma}}{1+\gamma}\right\}(1-\alpha)+1}{(ZL(\tau))^{1-\alpha}}. \tag{26}$$

Once we compute $\phi(\tau)$ using this last expression, the consumption equivalent variation is just given by $\phi(\tau) - 1$.

---

3. In deriving this expression, I have made use of the following result. If

$$Z = W + \beta W + \beta^2 W + \beta^3 W + \ldots$$

(where W is the per period payoff), then $Z - \beta Z = W$, and hence $Z = W/(1-\beta)$.

Exercise 2. *What are the gains from setting the money growth rate optimally, as opposed to setting it to achieve zero inflation? How does it depend on our elasticity parameter assumptions? Please report. Central bankers around the world would like to know the answers to these questions. Along with computing the consumption equivalent, please report on consumption, labor, and real balances.*[4]

3.2. Accounting for Growth

The prior model left out growth. This is a concern since it might change our answer fairly dramatically. The natural way to incorporate growth is to assume that $Z_{t+1} = (1 + g)Z_t$. If labor effort was independent of the level of Z, then this would imply that output would grow at the rate g. A standard value for g would be 0.02, which is the per capita growth rate of the United States over the past 100 years.

But will L be independent of Z? Return to our fundamental equation (21), now modified to take account of growth in Z and normalized $Z_0 = 1$:

$$v'(L_t) = \frac{\beta}{(1+\tau_t)} \frac{Z_{t+1} L_{t+1}}{L_t} u'(Z_{t+1} L_{t+1}).$$

$$= \frac{\beta}{(1+\tau_t)} \frac{(1+g)^{t+1} L_{t+1}}{L_t} u'((1+g)^{t+1} L_{t+1}).$$

Unless the growth terms cancel in the r.h.s. the solution will not be invariant to the level of Z. So L will be changing over time. In the data, L does seem to be drifting down, but it's a bit mixed. Men seem to be working a bit less and women (at least in terms of measured work in the market) quite a bit more. Overall, there has been a modest drop over the past 100 years, but it's small enough to be taken to be 0 for our purposes. So, we need these terms to cancel. But this then forces us to assume that $u(C) = \log(C)$.

When we specialize our utility function for consumption in this fashion our fundamental equation (21), which we used to determine the equilibrium level of labor, becomes

$$\beta^{t-1} v'(L_t) = \frac{1}{(1+\tau_t)} \frac{Z_{t+1} L_{t+1}}{L_t} \beta^t \frac{1}{Z_{t+1} L_{t+1}}. \tag{27}$$

---

4. The original treatment of this question along the lines we consider here was done in Cooley, Thomas F., and Gary D. Hansen. "The inflation tax in a real business cycle model." The American Economic Review (1989): 733–748.

and this leads to a very simple expression for the equilibrium level of labor

$$L^{1+\gamma} = \frac{\beta}{1+\tau}.$$

In the model without growth, the growth rate of the money supply was the growth rate of prices and hence of inflation. That is no longer true now. The price level is given by

$$P_t = \frac{M_1(1+\tau)^{t-1}}{Z_1(1+g)^{t-1}} = \frac{M_1}{Z_1}\left(\frac{1+\tau}{1+g}\right)^{t-1}$$

So, the inflation rate $1 + \pi = (1+\tau)/(1+g)$ depends on the growth rate gap between money and output. This is essentially a velocity equation type of result and is driven by the fact that money turns over once per period, assuming that the c.i.a. constraint binds.

Since the labor condition is

$$\beta^{t-1}v'(L_t) = \mu_t Z_t \frac{\bar{M}_t}{Z_t L_t},$$

it follows that the steady-state interest rate is still

$$q = \frac{\beta}{1+\tau}.$$

3.3. Consumption Equivalence with Growth

To see how adding growth changes our calculation of the consumption equivalent variation, let us focus on the consumption term in the payoff. This becomes

$$\sum_{t=1}^{\infty} \beta^{t-1} \log\left(ZL(\tau)(1+g)^{t-1}\right) = \frac{\log(ZL(\tau))}{1-\beta} + \sum_{t=1}^{\infty} \beta^{t-1}(t-1)\log(1+g)$$

Then, note that

$$\frac{d}{d\beta}\sum_{t=1}^{\infty}\beta^{t-1} = \sum_{t=1}^{\infty}\frac{d}{d\beta}\beta^{t-1} = \sum_{t=1}^{\infty}(t-1)\beta^{t-2},$$

while at the same time,

$$\frac{d}{d\beta}\sum_{t=1}^{\infty}\beta^{t-1} = \frac{d}{d\beta}\frac{1}{1-\beta} = \frac{1}{(1-\beta)^2}.$$

Hence, it follows that our consumption payoff is

$$= \frac{log(ZL(\tau))}{1-\beta} + log(1+g)\frac{\beta}{(1-\beta)^2}.$$

It follows that our lifetime utility is given by

$$U(\tau) = \frac{1}{1-\beta}\left[log(ZL(\tau)) - \frac{L(\tau)^{1+\gamma}}{1+\gamma}\right] + log(1+g)\frac{\beta}{(1-\beta)^2}. \qquad (28)$$

where the last term is a constant that is independent of the inflation rate, though it does depend on the growth rate. This expression implies that the impact of money growth and growth in productivity comes in through two completely separate terms. Moreover, it means that our prior results on the cost of the money growth rate deviating from the optimal rate are unaffected by adding in productivity growth.

Remark 5. *This derivation of the growth term in consumption was nice. But we could have just used the computer to approximate it by computing it for, say, 50 years. In Matlab, this would look something like:*

n = 50; % the number of years in our approximation
g = .02; % growth rate
beta = 1/1.02; % interest rate
N = [0:n]';
*A = beta. ^ N * N * log(1+g);*
term = sum(A). % this gives us our answer.

Note that the dot in front of the up arrow means this is done element by element. Also, to check that our approximation is long enough make sure that the final term in A is close to zero. If not increase n.

Exercise 3. *Robert Lucas famously argued that growth is key, and fluctuations, which imply static losses, are small potatoes. Let's examine the inflation vs. growth* *argument in our model. Take as our benchmark the steady state of an economy with 2% inflation and 2% output growth. What level of growth would compensate for 10% inflation? To do this, start from our growth-adjusted expression for the present discounted payoff, (28). Use it to derive the appropriate version of consumption adjustment $\phi(\tau)$ (which before was given by (26)). With this in hand, you can examine Lucas's claim.*

## 4

Some Interesting Extensions

We start this chapter by considering a variety of extensions to our model. The first extension will allow us to break out of the unit velocity straitjacket implied by our cash-in-advance (c.i.a.) constraint. We will then consider two different ways to allow for negative interest rates which share a common theme: making the holding of money costly. In the second approach, we derive an elastic demand for money, and we can use this model to do a calibration exercise to understand how such an exercise is done.

1. VARYING VELOCITY

The velocity of money has been increasing over time because of the increased sophistication in the payments system, more sophisticated cash management, and the introduction of means of payment other than cash—in particular, credit cards. Here we want to extend our model to allow for differences in the extent to which an alternative means of payment can be used. To do this, we will adjust one of the fundamental building blocks of our theory, the c.i.a. constraint. Assume now that the constraint is given by

$$M_t \geq \kappa P_t C_t,$$

where κ captures the extent to which cash is used in transactions. Note that a reduction in κ will relax the c.i.a. constraint. If we reexamine the aggregate implications of a binding c.i.a. constraint (20), we now get that

Monetary and Fiscal Policy through a DSGE Lens. Harold L. Cole, Oxford University Press (2020).
© Oxford University Press. DOI: 10.1093/oso/9780190076030.001.0001

$$P = \frac{M}{\kappa ZL}. \tag{29}$$

Since velocity is given by

$$v = \frac{PZL}{M} = \frac{M}{\kappa ZL}\frac{ZL}{M} = \frac{1}{\kappa}.$$

So decreases in κ will raise velocity.[1]

Here is our Lagrangian, adjusted for this change,

$$\mathcal{L} = \max_{\{C_t, L_t, M_{t+1}, B_{t+1}\}_{t=1,2}} \min_{\{\lambda_t, \mu_t\}_{t=1,2}} \tag{30}$$
$$u(C_1) - v(L_1) + \beta\left[u(C_2) - v(L_2)\right] + \beta^2 V(M_3, B_3)$$
$$+ \sum_{t=1,2} \lambda_t \{M_t - \kappa P_t C_t\}$$
$$+ \sum_{t=1,2} \mu_t \{P_t Z_t L_t + M_t - P_t C_t + B_t + T_t - M_{t+1} - q_t B_{t+1}\}.$$

Note that the only change is w.r.t. the c.i.a. constraint. The budget constraint in the asset market is exactly as before. If we look at our choice variables, the only one that is impacted by this change is consumption, which becomes

$$\beta^{t-1} u'(C_t) = [\mu_t + \kappa \lambda_t] P_t.$$

We still get the following first-order conditions (f.o.c.') for labor, money and bonds:

$$\beta^{t-1} v'(L_t) = \mu_t Z_t P_t$$
$$\mu_t = \mu_{t+1} + \lambda_{t+1},$$
$$\mu_t q_t = \mu_{t+1},$$

and our modified pricing equation (29).

Unfortunately, things don't reduce quite as neatly once we conjecture that L is constant and use the fact that M grows at a constant rate. To keep things simple assume that Z is constant and $\bar{M}_0 = 1$, and hence we can rewrite these conditions as

---

1. We have assumed that κ was constant because the model does not have a steady state if it is time-varying.

$$\beta^{t-1} u'(ZL) = [\mu_t + \kappa\lambda_t]\left(\frac{(1+\tau)^t}{\kappa ZL}\right)$$

$$\beta^{t-1} v'(L_t) = \mu_t Z\left(\frac{(1+\tau)^t}{\kappa ZL}\right),$$

$$\mu_t = \mu_{t+1} + \lambda_{t+1}.$$

If you stare at these equations for a while, you'll realize that things aren't stationary. In other words, μ_t and λ_t cannot be constants because of discounting and money growth. This is something that was also true in our initial simple model with velocity implicitly set to one. But there we were able to replace $\mu_{t+1} + \lambda_{t+1}$ with μ_t from the money f.o.c. in deriving condition (21). Here we need to do something else to render things stationary to solve for a steady state.

Therefore, we're going to exploit a clever trick, called a "change in variables," to rewrite our equations in terms of variables that are stationary. Looking at these equations, it seems that μ_t and λ_t probably must grow with $\beta^{t-1}/(1+\tau)^t$. So, we're going to construct new variables

$$\tilde{\mu}_t = \mu_t\left((1+\tau)\frac{1}{\beta}\right)^t \beta, \tag{31}$$

$$\tilde{\lambda}_t = \lambda_t\left((1+\tau)\frac{1}{\beta}\right)^t \beta. \tag{32}$$

Using a change in variables along these lines will turn out to be a much more robust method of analyzing our models.

Then, we're going to rewrite the equations in terms of these new variables and cancel anything out that we can to get

$$u'(ZL) = \left[\tilde{\mu}_t + \kappa\tilde{\lambda}_t\right]\left(\frac{1}{\kappa ZL}\right) \tag{33}$$

$$v'(L) = \tilde{\mu}_t Z\left(\frac{1}{\kappa ZL}\right), \tag{34}$$

$$\left(\frac{1+\tau}{\beta}\right)\tilde{\mu}_t = \tilde{\mu}_{t+1} + \tilde{\lambda}_{t+1}. \tag{35}$$

Now, this is a nice equation system and we can guess that there is a constant solution where $\tilde{\mu}_t = \tilde{\mu}$ and $\tilde{\lambda}_t = \tilde{\lambda}$.

The system (33-35) seems too complicated to solve analytically, even once we realize our new multipliers are constant. so we are going to use an equation solver to get our answer. This will expand our computational tool set in an important manner.

> Remark 6. *For reasons we will discuss below, nonlinear equation solvers are tricky and do not always work. Before doing that, I am going to lay out briefly a more brute force method that one could use for this system of equations because of their block structure. This method has the advantage of also revealing a lot of information about our equation system. First, consider a grid on labor of $\mathbf{L} = [L_0, L_1, ..., L_N]$ values where the highest level of labor is the efficient level and the lowest is so low that we don't think our answer will be below this value. Then use a for loop to sequentially compute the following:*
>
> 1. *Use (34) to solve for $\tilde{\mu}_i$ given L_i.*
> 2. *Use (33) to solve for $\tilde{\lambda}_i$ given $\tilde{\mu}_i$ and L_i.*
> 3. *Given this, construct the deviations*
>
> $$ERR(i) = \left(\frac{1+\tau}{\beta}\right)\tilde{\mu}_i - \tilde{\mu}_i - \tilde{\lambda}_i.$$
>
> 4. *plot $ERR(i)$ and see where the zeros are.*
>
> *These are our solutions. If the plot is nice, there is only one solution. Once we know where the solution is, we can make our grid much finer in this region. We can also do a better job of having a good initial guess value for our nonlinear equation solver, which is often the key to getting it to work.*

1.1. How Do Equation Solvers Work?

It is useful to know how the equation solver you are using works so that you can understand how things can go wrong. The most basic equation solver, which can only solve for one equation in one unknown, is called bisection. It is simple, quick, and bullet proof *if* your solution lies between the two bounds you specify. Another method is called the Newton method, and it is much more general because it can handle higher-dimensional problems. Almost all standard equation solvers are some variant of the Newton method. It is a bit more tricky and can be quite sensitive to the initial starting guess. More sophisticated methods try to reduce the problems with the Newton method using various forms of cleverness.

Bisection works as follows. You specify an upper bound a and lower bound b. The key is that the signs of $f(a)$ and $f(b)$ are opposite, so $f(a)f(b) < 0$. Then, the function works as follows:

1. Compute $f(a), f(b)$ and $f((a+b)/2)$.
2. If $\| f((a+b)/2) - 0 \| < tol$ (our tolerance for a solution), quit setting the solution $= (a+b)/2$. If not, continue
3. If the sign of $f((a+b)/2)$ is the same as a, then $a' = (a+b)/2$, and $b' = b$ o.w. $b' = (a+b)/2$, and $a' = a$.
4. Go back to step (1), treating a' and b' as our new starting values.

The **Newton Method** works as follows. You specify an initial guess x. Then,

1. Compute the numerical derivative of f at x, which is given by

$$f'(x) \cong \frac{f(x+\delta) - f(x)}{\delta}$$

   for small δ.
2. Solve the following linear equation for our new guess value x'

$$f(x) + f'(x)(x' - x) = 0.$$

3. If $\| f(x') - 0 \| < tol$, quit. Otherwise, go back to step 1 using x' as the initial starting guess.

The problem with the Newton method is that we need a function that can be nicely approximated by a linear function over the range of values that we're working with. Since all smooth functions are approximately linear for a small enough range of x values, if we get a close enough starting guess, we're good. If not, we're bad, and you might have to monkey around, trying new starting values, and so on.

Remark 7. *When we have more than one equation in one unknown, we end up using a higher-dimensional version of the first-order Taylor approximation in the Newton method. For example, imagine we have two equations in two unknowns as follows:*

$$F(x,y) = 0$$
$$G(x,y) = 0.$$

Then starting from a guess of $(\bar{x}, \bar{y})$, we would construct the new guess by first taking a Taylor expansion around our system at the guess value. Each equation would have a slope with respect to each variable, which we would determine by taking the partial derivative of the equation w.r.t. that variable and evaluating it at the guess value. This would lead to

$$F(\bar{x}, \bar{y}) + \frac{dF(\bar{x}, \bar{y})}{dx} dx + \frac{dF(\bar{x}, \bar{y})}{dy} dy = 0$$

$$G(\bar{x}, \bar{y}) + \frac{dG(\bar{x}, \bar{y})}{dx} dx + \frac{dG(\bar{x}, \bar{y})}{dy} dy = 0.$$

This is a system of two equations in two unknowns, dx and dy, which are the changes relative to our original guess. Our new guess values would then be given by

$$\tilde{x} = \bar{x} + dx$$
$$\tilde{y} = \bar{y} + dy.$$

With our new guess in hand, we would then restart the process unless this new guess turned out to be close enough to our desired solution.

1.2. Computing the Solution with Velocity

Now we can try to compute the solution to our modified economy. The key to note here is that we have to guess three variables $(L, \tilde{\mu}, \tilde{\lambda})$ to satisfy three equations. Here is some code to do this:

```
function solution = SS2
    % This version uses a function handle to pass variables into the function
being solved by fsolve.
    % This way we avoid the use of global variables.
    % here X0 is the initial guess, tau is the growth rate of money,
    % Z is productivity, -1/alpha is the IES and 1/gamma is the Frisch
    % the solution is to our simple CIA model with constant money growth
    Z=1;
    tau=1.1 ;
    gamma = .5;
    alpha =2;
    kappa=.5;
    beta =.98;
    X0 = [.5 .5 .5]';
    ERR = @(X) ERRB(X,Z,tau,gamma,alpha,kappa,beta);  % defining
function handle to pass in variables.
    ERR(X0) % Produces check value to see how far off guess is
    solution = fsolve(ERR,X0);
    disp('solution check')
```

```
ERR(solution)
end
% This is our subroutine
function error = ERRB(X,tau,gamma,alpha,kappa,beta);
% unraveling X
L=X(1);
mu = X(2);
lamda = X(3);
% constructing our errors
error = []; % initializing with null vector
error = [error; ...
(Z*L)^(-alpha) - (mu + kappa*lamda)*(kappa*Z*L)^(-1)];
error = [error; ...
L^gamma - mu*(kappa*L)^(-1)];
error = [error; ...
(1+tau)*mu/beta - mu - lamda];
end
```

Exercise 4. *How do changes in velocity affect the costs of inflation? Please report. In constructing your report, it would be helpful if you came up with plausible levels of velocity to plug in.*

2. NEGATIVE INTEREST RATES

Negative nominal interest rates mean that banks, and the central bank in particular, will charge a payment on deposits rather than paying you for your deposit. Since the Great Recession of 2008-2009 and the associated financial crises a number of major central banks have set persistently negative interest rates for their major policy rate in order to stimulate their economies. These negative rates are shown in Figure 1 for the Swedish, Swiss, and European Central (ECB) banks.[2] These low central bank rates resulted in negative rates on longer-term government bonds in the Euro-area during the height of the crisis in 2015.

Our model has implied that rates cannot be negative, since this would lead everyone to go negative on nominal debt and long on money. This raises the question: What is our model getting wrong? The most obvious thing our model

---

2. Data source is Organization for Economic Co-operation and Development, Immediate Rates: Less than 24 Hours: Call Money/Interbank Rate for Sweden, Switzerland and the Euro Area, retrieved from FRED, Federal Reserve Bank of St. Louis; https://fred.stlouisfed.org

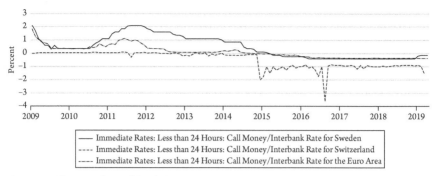

Figure 1. Negative Central Bank Rates

SOURCE: U.S. Bureau of Economic Analysis Retrieved from FRED, Federal Reserve Bank of St. Louis.

leaves out is that money has storage costs: it must be protected and you have to be careful not to lose it. Here we consider two ways of modeling these costs.

To model a simple direct cost, let's assume that you lose some fraction of the money you take out of the asset market before you get to the next period. This loss can be thought of as the security costs of storing the money. These security costs can take the form of the amount that insurance companies charge you to insure you against losing your money, and the loss then is the per capita share of the money that gets stolen. This way we don't have to worry about the fact that some people get robbed and some don't.

Let δ denote the fraction of your money that you lose. Then if M_{t+1} is the amount of money you show up with in the next period, you must have actually set aside $M_{t+1}/(1-\delta)$. In this case the household's problem becomes

$$\max_{\{C_t, L_t, M_{t+1}, B_{t+1}\}_{t=1,2}} u(C_1) - v(L_1) + \beta\left[u(C_2) - v(L_2)\right] + \beta^2 V(M_3, B_3) \text{ subject to}$$

$$M_t \geq P_t C_t \text{ and}$$
$$P_t Z_t L_t + [M_t - P_t C_t] + B_t + T_t \geq M_{t+1}/(1-\delta) + q_t B_{t+1} \text{ for } t = 1,2.$$

From this problem, one can see that the new f.o.c. for money is

$$-\mu_t/(1-\delta) + \mu_{t+1} + \lambda_{t+1} = 0.$$

The bond condition is still

$$-\mu_t q_t + \mu_{t+1} = 0.$$

Thus, $q_t > 1$ implies that $\mu_t < \mu_{t+1}$. This led to a contradiction before when implicitly $\delta = 0$ (since it implied that $\lambda_{t+1} < 0$, which cannot happen with an inequality constraint). But not now with $\delta > 0$. However, there is clearly a limit on things since $\mu_t/(1 - \delta) \geq \mu_{t+1}$ because $\lambda_{t+1} \geq 0$.

To close the model we would have to think about what happens with the money that gets stolen. If it disappears, we would need to adjust the money supply transition equation to be

$$\bar{M}_t(1 + \tau)(1 - \delta) = M_{t+1}. \qquad (36)$$

Working through the analysis of this model and deriving the steady-state conditions is now a bit trickier than before. The reason is that we can no longer use our f.o.c. for money to line up the date t marginal disutility of effort and the date $t + 1$ utility from consumption, as we did in (21). Instead, we are going to have to follow the line of analysis in the velocity model and make a change in variables with respect to our multipliers. The good news is that the same change in variables that we considered in (31-32) will work here too. Note that in this case, we can actually get a closed-form solution for labor.

> Exercise 5. *Close the model and construct the set of equations that characterize a steady state solution to our model. How does the real size of government transfers change with δ, holding fixed the overall growth rate of money?*

> Exercise 6. *Governments typically correct the growth rate of money for the estimated destruction of the currency. Consider two economies in which the inflation rate is the same, but $\delta = 0$ in the first economy, while $\delta > 0$ in the second. Compute the steady state of your two economies and discuss how having money loss changes the outcomes.*

> Exercise 7. *Assume that money disappears according to (36). How does losing money change the optimal rate of money growth and inflation? Do you think that your answer would change if instead the "lost" money ended up being randomly found? The amount found by each person would be the same as the amount they lost in equilibrium, BUT each person would treat the found money as being independent of their own actions. (Careful, this is a bit tricky.)*

3. ELASTIC MONEY DEMAND

For the final extension in this chapter, we are going to consider a version of our model that features costly money holdings. We will assume that these costs come in the form of labor costs associated with each unit of real balances the individual holds. As a result, this version of our model will both have endogenous velocity and allow for negative interest rates. We will use this version of our model to undertake our first calibration exercise and to revisit the costs of inflation.[3]

The labor cost function we will assume is then given by

$$Z_t H_t = \phi M_{t+1}/P_t,$$

where H_t is the number of extra labor units the individual must provide if his real balances are M_{t+1}/P_t and his productivity level is Z_t. The parameter ϕ governs the sensitivity of productive labor $(Z_t H_t)$ to real balances. The total number of units the individual must work is therefore given by $L_t + H_t$. Hence, his disutility from labor effort is $v(L_t + H_t)$.

The household's problem can be written as

$$\max_{\{C_t, L_t, H_t, M_{t+1}, B_{t+1}\}_{t=1,2}} u(C_1) - v(L_1 + H_1) + \beta\left[u(C_2) - v(L_2 + H_2)\right]$$

$$+ \beta^2 V(M_3, B_3) \text{ subject to}$$

$$M_t \geq P_t C_t,$$

$$Z_t H_t = \phi M_{t+1}/P_t,$$

$$P_t Z_t L_t + [M_t - P_t C_t] + B_t + T_t \geq M_{t+1} + q_t B_{t+1} \text{ for } t = 1, 2.$$

Since the constraint on H_t is an equality constraint, we are going to start by using it to substitute out for H_t in our preferences. This gives us

$$v\left(L_t + \frac{\phi M_{t+1}}{Z_t P_t}\right)$$

After this we can drop the constraint since it is already being enforced and H_t only appears implicitly. With this, the problem is fairly similar to what we had before.

The next step is to write down the Lagrangian for the individual's problem. This is given by

3. The classic elastic money demand model with a c.i.a. constraint is Lucas Jr, Robert E., and Nancy Stokey. "Money and interest in a cash-in-advance economy." NBER Working Paper No. 1618. (1985). They used a CES aggregator over goods that had to be purchased with money and those that could be purchased on credit.

$$\mathcal{L} = \max_{\{C_t,L_t,M_{t+1},B_{t+1}\}_{t=1,2}} \min_{\{\lambda_t,\mu_t\}_{t=1,2}}$$

$$\sum_{t=1,2} \beta^{t-1}\left[u(C_t) - v\left(L_t + \frac{\phi M_{t+1}}{Z_t P_t}\right)\right] + \beta^2 V(M_3, B_3)$$

$$+ \sum_{t=1,2} \lambda_t\{M_t - P_t C_t\}$$

$$+ \sum_{t=1,2} \mu_t\{P_t Z_t L_t + M_t - P_t C_t + B_t + T_t - M_{t+1} - q_t B_{t+1}\}.$$

We turn next to deriving the f.o.c.s. By inspection we can see that this change will only affect two of our f.o.c.s—those for labor and money. The f.o.c.s for consumption and bonds are unchanged. Starting with the other conditions, they take their, by now, familiar form

$$\beta^{t-1} u'(C_t) = [\mu_t + \lambda_t] P_t,$$

$$\mu_t q_t = \mu_{t+1},$$

The labor condition is new and given by

$$\beta^{t-1} v'\left(L_t + \frac{\phi M_{t+1}}{Z_t P_t}\right) = \mu_t Z_t P_t,$$

while that for money is given by

$$\beta^{t-1} v'\left(L_t + \frac{\phi M_{t+1}}{Z_t P_t}\right)\frac{\phi}{Z_t P_t} + \mu_t = \mu_{t+1} + \lambda_{t+1},$$

From the first of these new conditions we can see that our marginal disutility of labor reflects the fact that (implicitly) with $H_t > 0$, the marginal disutility of labor is now higher fixing L_t. Thus, costly money holding uses up labor and will discourage working to produce output. Turning now to our second new f.o.c. for M_{t+1}, it now includes a new labor cost term. The fact that we have an additional cost means that it is possible for $q_t > 1$ (implying negative interest rates) without this leading to a contradiction since we can safely have $\mu_t < \mu_{t+1}$ because of this cost. This aspect of our model works just like the "money loss model" we presented earlier.

These new conditions make things seem more confusing, but let's follow our standard path, update the consumption condition to $t+1$, and then use our model conditions to see what we get:

$$\beta^t \frac{u'(C_{t+1})}{P_{t+1}} = \mu_{t+1} + \lambda_{t+1}$$

$$= \beta^{t-1} v' \left(L_t + \frac{\phi M_{t+1}}{Z_t P_t} \right) \frac{\phi}{Z_t P_t} + \mu_t$$

$$= \beta^{t-1} v' \left(L_t + \frac{\phi M_{t+1}}{Z_t P_t} \right) \frac{\phi + 1}{Z_t P_t}.$$

The first step was to substitute for $\mu_{t+1} + \lambda_{t+1}$ using our money condition, and the second step was to substitute for μ_t using our labor condition.

What we get in the end is kind of neat. There is an extra labor term inside v' and there is an extra term outside in the form of $\phi + 1$ instead of 1. But otherwise it is "surprisingly" similar to what we got before. Okay, maybe not so surprising because we need it to be like this for everything to work out.

Maintaining our standard assumptions that productivity and money grow at constant rates

$$Z_t = (1+g)^t Z_0, \quad \bar{M}_{t+1} = (1+\tau)^t \bar{M}_0 \text{ and } T_t = \tau \bar{M}_t,$$

we can seek to close the model and derive the final set of conditions that we can use to solve for the equilibrium values. Assuming that the c.i.a. constraint binds, we get our standard equation for the price level P_t. Then, if we assume that there exists a steady state with a constant level of labor, substitute $\bar{M}_t$ for M_t using the money market clearing condition, and for C_t using the goods market clearing condition, we again get that $Z_t P_t = \bar{M}_t / L$.

Plugging this last result into our main equation above and assuming log preferences for consumption, we get that

$$\frac{\beta^t}{\bar{M}_{t+1}} = \beta^{t-1} v' \left(L + \frac{\phi \bar{M}_{t+1}}{\frac{\bar{M}_t}{L_t}} \right) \frac{\phi + 1}{\frac{\bar{M}_t}{L}}$$

One more step of cleaning things up and we get our final expression

$$\frac{\beta}{1+\tau} = v' \left(L [1 + \phi(1+\tau)] \right) L(\phi + 1). \tag{37}$$

In the end, the final equation we get that determines steady-state labor, (37), is a very tractable change to our standard condition. The labor cost term will raise the marginal disutility of labor, discouraging effort (this is analogous to an income term). At the same time, when fixing the marginal disutility, work effort is more costly, since transforming this into consumption requires more money holdings, which in turn require more effort (this is analogous to a substitution term). Note that with $\phi = 0$ we get back our original model, so this extension nests our standard model. However, increasing ϕ from zero will dial up this cost term.

3.1. Our First Calibration Exercise

Up until now, we have simply taken our model parameters from elsewhere or posited various values of, say, money growth. Here we want to consider how to pick model parameters so as to make our quantitative exercises a useful guide to policy analysis (or anything else for that matter). There is a variety of ways to pick model parameters. The most obvious (and aggressive) is to try to estimate the model given the data. This is often done by solving for the shocks that would allow the model to replicate the data for each potential value of our parameter, and then picking the parameter so that it yields *the most likely shock predictions*. This is called maximum likelihood estimation for that reason. This is much too hard for us,since our model is too primitive to think that it can account for the data; moreover, it isn't even stochastic at this point.

So, we are going to use a much simpler and more conservative method, called *calibration*, to line up with the data. Under calibration we compute one particular moment or feature of the data, such as the change in real money demand when the average rate of inflation goes from 5 to 10% and seek to have our model replicate this feature. To make this exercise meaningful, one should carefully select a feature of the data that one thinks the model is well designed to address and which is important for determining one's results. The model's implications for this feature should also be sensitive to the parameter(s) we are seeking to calibrate. The one new parameter in our model is the elasticity parameter ϕ. And it seems natural to try to calibrate it so that its implications for real money demand line up with some long-run features of the data.

Exercise 8. *Here we try to determine a plausible value of ϕ. Robert Lucas (2000) estimates that the elasticity of money is around 0.5. This suggests that a plausible range is probably 0.3 to 0.7. To calibrate your value of ϕ, change the money growth rate from, say, $\tau = 0.05$ to 0.10, and try to adjust ϕ so that the ratio of the percentage change in real balances relative to the percentage change in the net interest rate is roughly equal to your target. Then examine how changing inflation affects the variables in your model. In undertaking this analysis, assume our standard power function form for the disutility of labor and consider some plausible numbers for our Frisch elasticity. Note also that in calibrating our model, our preference parameters,* *which determine the degree of risk aversion in consumption, and the elasticity of labor, also play an important role in determining the interest elasticity of money. You may need to make certain choices with respect to these parameters to get your calibration to work.*

Exercise 9. *Given your calibration examine what happens to labor effort as a function of τ and what this implies for the cost of inflation.*

## 5

The Cash-in-Advance Model — Third Step

In this chapter we want to extend our dynamic analysis to allow for stochastic money and productivity growth. This is a big change, but we will try to make it as painless as possible. Unfortunately, additional complexity does not come for free. However, the methods we are going to use are those commonly used in constructing actual macro models, so we get to understand what makes them tick. Also, we will be able use the model in a fairly rich manner to gain insight.

We are going to start by assuming that both the monetary growth rate and the growth rate in productivity follow a fairly simple stochastic process called first-order Markov. Then, we're going to construct the equations that characterize an equilibrium. Next we are going to do a change of variables to make everything stationary. The final step will be to compute an equilibrium of our model and examine what it says about how the world works and how it depends on parameters and shocks.

1. SOME STATISTICS

1.1. Markov Process

A first-order Markov process is sufficiently flexible that it can cover almost any shock process we are interested in. According to this process, the probability distribution over the future realizations only depends on the current realization. To explain this, let the sequence $\{x_t\}_{t=0}^{\infty}$ be our sequence of random variables. In

Monetary and Fiscal Policy through a DSGE Lens. Harold L. Cole, Oxford University Press (2020).
© Oxford University Press. DOI: 10.1093/oso/9780190076030.001.0001

our case $x_t = (\tau_t, g_t)$. Denote by $x^t = (x_0, x_1, \ldots, x_t)$ the history through t. Then, our shock process is first-order Markov if

$$\Pr\{x_{t+1}|x^t\} = \Pr\{x_{t+1}|x_t\},$$

or in words, the probability of x_{t+1} taking on a particular value only depends on the current realization x_t and not the entire history x^t.

In what follows, we will always assume that we are working with Markov processes. This will allow us to capture the relevant history of the model in a concise state vector. The key here is that we do not need the history of the shocks to forecast the future, just the current level.

2. THE STOCHASTIC MODEL

The state at the beginning of each period will consist of the productivity level and money supply levels from the last period, and the new realization of the random variable $x_t = (\tau_t, g_t)$. So, denote the state by

$$s_t = (Z_{t-1}, \bar{M}_{t-1}, \tau_t, g_t).$$

Remark 8. *Keep in mind here that the productivity level at the beginning of the period is $Z_t = (1 + g_t)Z_{t-1}$, so the growth rate shock has an immediate effect. In contrast, the money supply level is M_{t-1} up until the asset market at the end of the period when the household receives its cash transfer of T_t. So the money growth rate has a delayed effect. This is a bit unfortunate, because we will want to denote the household's beginning-of-period money holdings by M_t and their money holdings when they leave the asset market at the end of the period by M_{t+1}.*

Figure 1 shows a piece of a typical event tree with two possible realizations of the state in each period. At each date, we can think of our current and past history as being the sequence of realizations of the state, which we denote by

$$s^t = \{s_1, s_2, \ldots, s_t\}.$$

We call this the history state, and it uniquely defines what has happened so far. Every history state s^t has a unique predecessor history state, which is given by simply removing the last element in the current history state. However, each history state can have many successor history states, where the number here simply depends on how many different realizations of s_{t+1} can occur. Define $s^{t-1}(s^t)$ as the prior history node implied by history s^t. Define $S^{t+1}(s^t)$ as the set

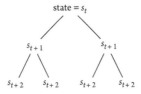

Figure 1. Event Tree

of successor history nodes given that the current history is s^t. We will also use the notation $s^{t+1} > s^t$ to indicate that the history state s^{t+1} is a successor to s^t.

The probability of a history state is the probability of seeing the sequence of states implied by the history state. A couple of things to note here. First, if we sum over all of the possible history states at a given date

$$\sum_{s^t} Pr\{s^t\} = 1,$$

because we have summed over all of the possible events at that date. Another thing to note is that

$$\sum_{s^{t+1} \in S^{t+1}(s^t)} Pr\{s^{t+1}\} = Pr\{s^t\},$$

because the total probability mass in this portion of the event tree is preserved. Note that the reverse is true as well: if we know the probabilities of the future history states, then summing over the successor nodes determines the probability of the current history states. Finally, the conditional probability of a history state s^{t+1} given that we are in history state s^t is 0 if s^{t+1} is not a successor to s^t, and if $s^{t+1} > s^t$ then it is given by

$$Pr\{s^{t+1}|s^t\} = \frac{Pr\{s^{t+1}\}}{Pr\{s^t\}}.$$

2.1. The Household's Problem

We will formulate the household's maximization problem as making decisions for two periods, taking as given their continuation payoff from period 2 onward given the state s_3 and their money and bond holdings as they leave the asset market at the end of period 2. Because their asset holdings (money and bonds) in period 2 will depend on their decisions in the prior period, their decisions will depend on the past history as well as the current state. To account for this, we need to expand our notation a bit more using history states. We will do so in a fairly general way that allows us to see what a model with many more periods would look like. To accomplish this, we will think of the household's choice variables as depending on the history state they are in.

The household's objective function can be expressed as

$$\sum_{t=1,2} \sum_{s^t} \beta^{t-1} \left[u(C_t(s^t)) - v(L_t(s^t))\right] \Pr\{s^t\}$$
$$+\beta^2 \sum_{s^2} \sum_{s^3 \succ s^2} \left\{V(M(s^2), B(s^2), s_3)\right\} \Pr\{s^3\}.$$

To understand this objective, note that in the first expression we are summing over the first two dates and the set of possible histories at each of these dates. For each of these outcomes we are computing the discounted payoff and multiplying it by the probability of that outcome, $\Pr\{s^t\}$. In the second expression, we are computing all of our possible continuation payoffs. To do this, we are summing over all of the histories in the second period, s^2, and for each of these history states, we are summing over all of the third period history states that can occur given that (or that follow from) state, $s^3 \succ s^2$.

Note that for a state to follow from another, it must agree for all of the elements of the prior history. In this second expression, we are weighting outcomes by the probability of the third period history state $\Pr\{s^3\}$ because, for each second period history we are summing over all of the possible successors and the sum of the probabilities of these successors is $\Pr\{s^2\}$. Moreover, the sum over all $\Pr\{s^t\}$ must equal one.

In what follows we will use an expectation operator to write this objective more simply, but keep in mind that this is what we mean. Given this, we can formulate the household's problem as choosing a sequence of functions $\{C_t(s^t), L_t(s^t), M_t(s^t), B_t(s^t)\}_{t=1}^2$ so as to

$$\max E\left\{\sum_{t=1,2} \beta^{t-1}\left[u(C_t(s^t)) - v(L_t(s^t))\right] + \beta^2 V(M(s^2), B(s^2), s_3)\right\}$$

subject to

$$M(s^{t-1}(s^t)) \geq P(s^t)C(s^t) \text{ and}$$
$$P(s^t)Z(s^t)L(s^t) + \left[M(s^{t-1}(s^t)) - P(s^t)C(s^t)\right] + B(s^{t-1}(s^t)) + T(s^t)$$
$$\geq M(s^t) + q(s^t)B(s^t) \text{ for all } t \leq 2 \text{ and } s^t \in S^t.$$

In words, the objective function is summing dates 1 and 2, and all possible states given a date. We evaluate the household's payoff at that state discounted back to time 1. The expectation is saying that we are weighting each object in this summation by the probability of that history state: $\Pr\{s^t\}$. The constraints are the same as before, except that we've jazzed them up to refer to history states. Note that $M(s^{t-1}(s^t))$ and $B(s^{t-1}(s^t))$ denote the amount of money and bonds the household acquired in the prior history state.

Once again we are using a continuation value function to deal with the future, $V(M(s^2), B(s^2), s^3)$, which here is everything beyond period 2. In this continuation value function we have included as arguments both the individual choices of his state variables, $M(s^2), B(s^2)$ and the aggregate state variable s_3. While the individual and aggregate state variables must line up in equilibrium, once again we must allow for them to be different and set equilibrium prices so that they are consistent.

The Lagrangian for this problem is kind of similar to what we had before:

$$\mathcal{L} = \max_{\{L(s^t),\, C(s^t),\, M(s^t),\, B(s^t)\}_{t=1}^2} \min_{\{\mu(s^t),\, \lambda(s^t)\}_{t=1}^2}$$

$$E\left\{ \begin{array}{l} \sum_{t=1,2} \beta^{t-1}\left[u(C_t(s^t)) - v(L_t(s^t))\right] \\ + \beta^2 V(M(s^2),\, B(s^2),\, s_3) \end{array} \right\}$$

$$+ \sum_{t=1,2} \sum_{s^t} \lambda(s^t)\{M(s^{t-1}(s^t)) - P(s^t)C(s^t)\}$$

$$+ \sum_{t=1,2} \sum_{s^t} \mu(s^t)\left\{ \begin{array}{l} P(s^t)Z(s^t)L(s^t) + \left[M(s^{t-1}(s^t)) - P(s^t)C(s^t)\right] \\ + B(s^{t-1}(s^t)) + T(s^t) - M(s^t) - q(s^t)B(s^t) \end{array} \right\}.$$

The f.o.c.'s will characterize a solution and they are derived just as before by differentiating. The f.o.c. for $C_t(s^t)$ is

$$\beta^{t-1}u'(C_t(s^t))\Pr(s^t) - [\lambda(s^t) + \mu(s^t)]P(s^t) = 0.$$

Modulo the fact that we're weighting the marginal utility by the probability, and the change in notation, it is essentially the same as before. The f.o.c. for $L(s^t)$ is

$$-\beta^{t-1}v'(L_t(s^t))\Pr(s^t) + \mu(s^t)P(s^t)Z(s^t) = 0.$$

Next up is money, but this one was always a bit tricky, since we had to worry about the fact that we pick money at date t and then use it at date $t + 1$. Doing that we get

$$-\mu(s^t) + \sum_{s^{t+1} \in S^{t+1}(s^t)} \left[\lambda(s^{t+1}) + \mu(s^{t+1})\right] = 0.$$

Note that we are summing over all of the histories that can follow from s^t in computing the benefit of relaxing the next period's c.i.a. constraints and budget constraints (b.c.'s). Similarily, for bonds $B(s^t)$ we get that

$$- \mu(s^t)q(s^t) + \sum_{s^{t+1} \in S^{t+1}(s^t)} \mu(s^{t+1}) = 0. \tag{38}$$

Exercise 10. *We are being a bit slippery here. Our objective only dates out to $t = 2$, with a continuation function thereafter. So, just to be sure we've got things right, extend the analysis to $t = 3$ and make sure that the f.o.c.'s continue along the lines we have written down.*

2.2. The Equilibrium

We want to construct a stationary equilibrium. We have already seen with deterministic growth that we need $u(C) = \log(C)$, so let's start by assuming this again. To construct the equilibrium, we are going to use the conjecture and verify method. In this method one conjectures that an equilibrium has certain properties, derives what it looks like based on these conjectures, and shows that the result satisfies the original conjectures. We're going to make our conjectures in a couple of steps.

Start with something we've conjectured before: that the c.i.a. holds with equality. Given this, and making use of the resource constraint, we get that

$$P(s^t) = \frac{\bar{M}(s^{t-1}(s^t))}{Z(s^t)L(s^t)}. \tag{39}$$

Next, conjecture that labor effort only depends on the current shock and not on the history state. Given this, we can write it as $L(s_t)$ (where we're being a bit sloppy and not saying $L(s_t(s^t))$). If L is just varying with s_t but not growing or shrinking over time, then the only other endogenous variable $P(s^t)$ must be picking up all of the slack. To verify this, plug the expressions for money and productivity in terms of our accumulated growth terms to get that

$$P(s^t) = \frac{\prod_{j=1}^{t-1}(1 + \tau_j(s^t))}{\prod_{j=1}^{t}(1 + g_j(s^t))} \frac{1}{L(s_t)}, \tag{40}$$

where we are assuming that $Z_0 = \bar{M}_0 = 1$. Note here that $\tau_j(s^t)$ denotes the money growth rate in the jth period in history state s^t. Note also that we only have the money growth rates accumulated through $t-1$ since the tth injection shows up in the asset market.

Now, we need to make a change-in-variables again with respect to our multipliers to render things stationary again. Let's start by looking again at our f.o.c. for consumption once we have substituted in for the price, or

$$\beta^{t-1}\frac{1}{Z(s^t)L(s_t)}\Pr(s^t) = [\lambda(s^t) + \mu(s^t)]\left[\frac{\prod_{j=1}^{t-1}(1+\tau_j(s^t))}{\prod_{j=1}^{t}(1+g_j(s^t))}\frac{1}{L(s_t)}\right]$$

$$\Rightarrow \beta^{t-1}\Pr(s^t) = [\lambda(s^t)+\mu(s^t)]\left[\prod_{j=1}^{t-1}(1+\tau_j(s^t))\right].$$

Great news! The $Z(s^t)L(s_t)$ term cancels from both sides and we're left with what we had before.

This suggests that essentially the same change in variables will work again. So define

$$\mu(s^t) = \frac{\beta^{t-1}\tilde{\mu}(s^t)\Pr(s^t)}{\prod_{j=1}^{t-1}(1+\tau_j(s^t))} = \frac{\beta^{t-1}\tilde{\mu}(s^t)\Pr(s^t)}{\bar{M}(s^{t-1}(s^t))}, \text{ and}$$

$$\lambda(s^t) = \frac{\beta^{t-1}\tilde{\lambda}(s^t)\Pr(s^t)}{\prod_{j=1}^{t-1}(1+\tau_j(s^t))} = \frac{\beta^{t-1}\tilde{\lambda}(s^t)\Pr(s^t)}{\bar{M}(s^{t-1}(s^t))}.$$

Using this change, rewrite our f.o.c.'s for consumption and labor as

$$1 = \left[\tilde{\lambda}(s^t) + \tilde{\mu}(s^t)\right], \tag{41}$$

$$v'(L(s_t)) = \tilde{\mu}(s^t)\left[\frac{1}{L(s_t)}\right]. \tag{42}$$

The f.o.c. conditions for money and bonds become

$$\tilde{\mu}(s^t)\Pr(s^t) = \sum_{s^{t+1}\in S^{t+1}(s^t)} \left[\tilde{\mu}_{t+1}(s^{t+1}) + \tilde{\lambda}_{t+1}(s^{t+1})\right]\frac{\beta}{(1+\tau_t(s^t))}\Pr(s^{t+1}),$$

$$\tilde{\mu}(s^t)q(s^t)\Pr(s^t) = \sum_{s^{t+1}\in S^{t+1}(s^t)} \tilde{\mu}(s^{t+1})\frac{\beta}{(1+\tau_t(s^t))}\Pr(s^{t+1}).$$

These two expressions still seem complicated, but note that $\Pr(s^{t+1})/\Pr(s^t) = \Pr(s_{t+1}|s_t)$; i.e., it is the conditional probability of s^{t+1} given that s^t has occurred. With this insight we can rewrite these expressions as

$$\tilde{\mu}(s^t) = \sum_{s^{t+1} \in S^{t+1}(s^t)} \left[\tilde{\mu}_{t+1}(s^{t+1}) + \tilde{\lambda}_{t+1}(s^{t+1}) \right] \frac{\beta}{(1 + \tau_t(s^t))} \Pr(s_{t+1}|s_t), \quad (43)$$

$$\tilde{\mu}(s^t)q(s^t) = \sum_{s^{t+1} \in S^{t+1}(s^t)} \tilde{\mu}(s^{t+1}) \frac{\beta}{(1 + \tau_t(s^t))} \Pr(s_{t+1}|s_t). \quad (44)$$

If you stare at the three key characterization equations (41–43) for a while, you will notice that the history before t doesn't come in anymore. This suggests that we can take $\tilde{\mu}(s^t) = \tilde{\mu}(s_t)$ and $\tilde{\lambda}_t(s^t) = \tilde{\lambda}_t(s_t)$ to be the case. (That is, these variables, along with L do not depend on stuff before t, just the current state at time t.) Let's explore this by rewriting our three equations under this assumption

$$1 = \left[\tilde{\lambda}(s_t) + \tilde{\mu}(s_t) \right], \quad (45)$$

$$v'(L(s_t)) = [\tilde{\mu}(s_t)] \left[\frac{1}{L(s_t)} \right]. \quad (46)$$

$$\tilde{\mu}(s_t) = \sum_{s^{t+1} \in S^{t+1}(s^t)} \left[\tilde{\mu}(s_{t+1}) + \tilde{\lambda}(s_{t+1}) \right] \frac{\beta}{(1 + \tau_t(s^t))} \Pr(s_{t+1}|s_t) \quad (47)$$

Note that the r.h.s. of equation (47) does not depend on the realized state in period $t + 1$, since we have summed over the probability-weighted possibilities to construct the expectation of these terms based on date t information, i.e., the state s_t.

Next note that we can use equation (45) to greatly simplify equation (47) so it becomes

$$\tilde{\mu}(s_t) = \sum_{s^{t+1} \in S^{t+1}(s^t)} \frac{\beta}{(1 + \tau_t(s^t))} \Pr(s_{t+1}|s_t) = \frac{\beta}{(1 + \tau_t(s^t))} \quad (48)$$

This result is a product of our log preference assumption but it's pretty neat. Then, we can use this result to reduce equation (46) to

$$v'(L(s_t))L(s_t) = \frac{\beta}{(1 + \tau_t(s^t))}. \quad (49)$$

So once again we have a very simple one equation in one unknown setup which we can use to determine the equilibrium of our model. Note that the r.h.s. is simply β divided by the realized gross growth rate of money.

Doing the same analysis as we did before, we get that

$$\left[v''(\bar{L})\bar{L} + v'(\bar{L}) \right] dL = -\frac{\beta}{(1+\bar{\tau})^2} d\bar{\tau},$$

or

$$\frac{dL}{d\bar{\tau}} = -\frac{\beta}{\left[v''(\bar{L})\bar{L} + v'(\bar{L}) \right](1+\bar{\tau})^2} < 0. \tag{50}$$

From this we see that money growth is driving down labor. This is happening because high money growth is raising the price level tomorrow directly, but not today. As a result, the return from working in order to consume is being reduced because the money one acquires today will buy less consumption tomorrow.

What about changes in the growth rate? Since they do not show up in (49), it follows that

$$\frac{dL}{d\bar{g}} = 0.$$

This is a product of our log preferences assumption, which leads to income and substitution effects canceling out.

Finally, turn to our interest rate determination equation (44), and note that if we use (48) to substitute for $\tilde{\mu}(s_t)$ and also for $\tilde{\mu}(s_{t+1})$ we get that

$$\frac{\beta}{(1+\tau_t(s^t))} q(s^t) = \sum_{s^{t+1} \in S^{t+1}(s^t)} \frac{\beta}{(1+\tau_{t+1}(s^{t+1}))} \frac{\beta}{(1+\tau_t(s^t))} \Pr(s_{t+1}|s_t)$$

$$\implies q(s^t) = \sum_{s^{t+1} \in S^{t+1}(s^t)} \frac{\beta}{(1+\tau_{t+1}(s^{t+1}))} \Pr(s_{t+1}|s_t). \tag{51}$$

This equation is the stochastic analog of the condition we derived earlier (22). It says that the discount rate is simply the real discount rate times the expected component of inflation coming from the expected increase in the money supply.

## 6

The Statistical Model

In this chapter we will start by going over some additional material on statistics. This will concern some additional material on first-order autoregressive (AR-1) stochastic process. Then, we will see how to solve and simulate our model economy. Finally, we will discuss Monte Carlo simulation methods to compute the properties of some of the statistic moments of model that we might be interested in.

1. SOME MORE STATISTICS

The Markov process we are going to work with involves shocks to the growth rates of money and productivity. We will think that the actual growth rate can be driven by a persistent and a new element. To capture this, we can represent x_t as follows

$$x_t = Ax_{t-1} + B + C\varepsilon_t,$$

where $\varepsilon_t \sim N(0,1)$. Here, ε_t is a standard normal random variable and C will determine its actual variance by scaling up or down relative to one. B is determining the mean of the process, while A determines the persistence of the shocks. To keep things bounded we will always want to assume that $A < 1$.

> Remark 9. *Any linear combination of independent normally distributed random variables is also normally distributed. This is one reason we like the normal distribution for linear models.*

Monetary and Fiscal Policy through a DSGE Lens. Harold L. Cole, Oxford University Press (2020).
© Oxford University Press. DOI: 10.1093/oso/9780190076030.001.0001

To see how things work, note first that

$$\mathbb{E}\{x_t\} = A\mathbb{E}\{x_{t-1}\} + B.$$

Since this is an unconditional expectation, it follows that $E\{x_t\} = \mathbb{E}\{x_{t-1}\}$, and hence

$$\mathbb{E}\{x_t\} = \frac{B}{1-A},$$

so this is the long-run or ergodic mean of the series. (Clearly we need $A < 1$.) Next, note that we can recursively substitute to get that

$$x_t = B + C\varepsilon_t + A\{B + C\varepsilon_{t-1}\} + A^2\{B + C\varepsilon_{t-2}\} + \dots$$
$$= \frac{B}{1-A} + C\sum_{j=0}^{\infty} A^j \varepsilon_{t-j}.$$

Thus the rate at which the impact of a shock dies out is completely controlled by A. This relationship tells us that the variance of deviations around trend is given by

$$\left[C\sum_{j=0}^{\infty} A^j \right]^2.$$

What happens if we start at the unconditional mean, $B/(1-A)$, and build up? Note that

$$x_0 = \frac{B}{1-A}, \quad x_1 = A \times \frac{B}{1-A} + B + C\varepsilon_1 = \frac{B}{1-A} + C\varepsilon_1$$
$$x_2 = A \times \left[\frac{B}{1-A} + C\varepsilon_1 \right] + B + C\varepsilon_2 = \frac{B}{1-A} + AC\varepsilon_1 + C\varepsilon_2$$
$$x_3 = \frac{B}{1-A} + A^2 C\varepsilon_1 + AC\varepsilon_2 + C\varepsilon_3.$$

From this you can see how our random variable naturally divides into the permanent mean component and the stochastic component. We can use this insight to simply tack on the mean to a zero-mean stochastic component.

In addition, the time series relationship between x_t and its past values, like x_{t-1}, are determined by A as well. To see this note that

$$cov(x_t, x_{t-1}) = \mathbb{E}\{[x_t - \mathbb{E}\{x_t\}][x_{t-1} - \mathbb{E}\{x_{t-1}\}]\}$$
$$= C^2 \sum_{j=1}^{\infty} A^{j+j-1}.$$

So there will be positive covariance if $A > 0$, negative if $A < 0$, and independence if $A = 0$.

Clearly then, we can select the values of our stochastic process parameters, A, B, and C, to hit three natural statistical moments of the time series we are trying to match. These three natural moments would include the mean, the variance, and the lagged covariance.

In our setup, x_t will be a vector

$$x_t = \begin{bmatrix} \tau_t \\ g_t \end{bmatrix}.$$

So, B will also be a vector, while A and C will be 2×2 matrices. A would normally control not only how fast the impact of the shock dies out but also the spillover of one shock to the other. The same is true for C, which would control not only the variance of the shocks, but also their covariance. However, to keep things simple, we are going to assume that they are both diagonal matrices, so there is no spillover, and our shocks are independent of each other. In this case

$$x_t = \begin{bmatrix} \rho_\tau & 0 \\ 0 & \rho_g \end{bmatrix} x_{t-1} + \begin{bmatrix} B_\tau \\ B_g \end{bmatrix} + \begin{bmatrix} \sigma_\tau & 0 \\ 0 & \sigma_g \end{bmatrix} \begin{bmatrix} \varepsilon_{\tau,t} \\ \varepsilon_{g,t} \end{bmatrix},$$

and each of the innovations, $\varepsilon_{\tau,t}$ and $\varepsilon_{g,t}$, will be standard normals. Note that to keep things stationary, we will need to assume that $|\rho_\tau| < 1$ and $|\rho_g| < 1$.

Because these two variables are in fact completely independent, we can think of the two processes separately. Additionally, we can really think of them as the mean parts $\bar{\tau}$ and $\bar{g}$, and the deviation from the mean parts

$$\tilde{\tau}_t = \rho_\tau \tilde{\tau}_{t-1} + \sigma_\tau \varepsilon_{\tau,t},$$
$$\tilde{g} = \rho_g \tilde{g}_{t-1} + \sigma_g \varepsilon_{g,t}.$$

Then

$$\tau_t = \tilde{\tau}_t + \bar{\tau}, \text{ and } g_t = \tilde{g}_t + \bar{g},$$
$$\bar{\tau} = B_\tau/(1 - \rho_\tau), \text{ and } \bar{g} = B_g/(1 - \rho_g).$$

We can then use our statistical model to fill in the details of our transition probabilities. Start from our state vector $s_t = (Z_{t-1}, \bar{M}_{t-1}, \tau_t, g_t)$. The only state s_{t+1} that can follow from this state must have $Z_t = Z_{t-1}(1 + g_t)$ and $\bar{M}_t = (1 + \tau_t)\bar{M}_{t-1}$. However, there is a wide range of possible values for τ_{t+1} and g_{t+1} that could follow. But for a given τ_{t+1} to follow from τ_t, it must be the case that the realized shock satisfies

$$\tau_{t+1} = \rho_\tau \tau_t + B_\tau + \sigma_\tau \varepsilon_{\tau,t+1}.$$

Hence, there is a unique shock associated with this realization. Denote the probability of that shock as

$$\Pr(\varepsilon_{\tau,t+1}) = \Pr\left(\frac{\tau_{t+1} - \rho_\tau \tau_t - B_\tau}{\sigma_\tau}\right).$$

In a similar vein, if g_{t+1} is the realized growth rate, then the associated shock must satisfy

$$g_{t+1} = \rho_g g_t + B_g + \sigma_g \varepsilon_{g,t+1}$$

and hence the probability of that realization is

$$\Pr\left(\varepsilon_{g,t+1}\right) = \Pr\left(\frac{g_{t+1} - \rho_g g_t - B_g}{\sigma_g}\right).$$

Thus, the conditional probability of going from $s_t = \left(Z_{t-1}, \bar{M}_{t-1}, \tau_t, g_t\right)$ to

$$s_{t+1} = \left(Z_{t-1}(1+g_t), (1+\tau_t)\bar{M}_{t-1}, \tau_{t+1}, g_{t+1}\right)$$

is given by

$$\Pr(s_{t+1}|s_t) = \Pr\left(\frac{\tau_{t+1} - \rho_\tau \tau_t - B_\tau}{\sigma_\tau}\right) \Pr\left(\frac{g_{t+1} - \rho_g g_t - B_g}{\sigma_g}\right).$$

(Notice that we have constructed s_{t+1} so that we can think of $s^{t+1} = (s^t, s_{t+1})$ as a successor to s^t.) We will make use of this construction when we develop our characterization of the bond price $q(s^t)$ in the next section.

2. DEVELOPING THE STATISTICAL MODEL

We break the further analysis of the model into three parts. In the first part, we are going to construct a reduced model in three variables that are transformations of our original variables. These transformations make them stationary. We can solve this fairly easily as it turns out. In part two, we need to map our results back into the original model. This too turns out to be fairly straightforward. Finally, in part three we show how to write out our computer code to simulate our model and see what it implies for the data.

2.1. Part 1: The Reduced Model

Our economy can be boiled down to three key equations. The first is our labor supply condition (49); once we impose our labor preference assumption that the disutility of labor takes on a power function form as in (23), we get that

$$L(s_t)^{1+\gamma} = \frac{\beta}{(1 + \tau_t(s^t))},$$

$$\Rightarrow L(s_t) = \left[\frac{\beta}{(1 + \tau_t(s^t))} \right]^{\frac{1}{1+\gamma}}. \qquad (52)$$

The second is the price level equation (39), which we have rewritten in terms of the productivity-adjusted ratio of the price to the initial level of the money supply in order to express things in terms of a stationary object:

$$p(s_t) \equiv \frac{Z(s^t)P(s^t)}{\bar{M}(s^{t-1}(s^t))} = \frac{1}{L(s_t)} = \left[\frac{\beta}{(1 + \tau_t(s^t))} \right]^{\frac{-1}{1+\gamma}}, \qquad (53)$$

so the normalized price level is simply the inverse of labor. The third equation is our interest rate condition (51):

$$q(s_t) = \sum_{s^{t+1} \in S^{t+1}(s^t)} \left[\frac{\beta}{(1 + \tau_{t+1}(s^{t+1}))} \right] \Pr(s_{t+1}|s_t). \qquad (54)$$

This equation is a bit more complicated, since it involves evaluating an integral.

> Remark 10. *Note that labor is the key endogenous variable in all of these equations. Moreover, solving for labor means solving one equation in one unknown. This sort of setup is called block recursive, since we can solve it in blocks. Moreover, once we know labor, we know everything about p and q. In addition, our preference assumptions have allowed us to solve analytically for labor as a function of the shocks. Note also that productivity has dropped out with our change in variables. So the only shock we have to worry about is money growth. This makes things fairly simple.*

In light of this remark, we can drop productivity growth for now, and just solve for everything in terms of labor to pin down our key variables. Later we'll see how to map these results into the actual variables. We have analytic expressions for L_t, p_t, and q_t, but q_t involves an expectation of our shocks rather than their level. This means that we need to come up with a simple way to approximate this integral.

Approximating an integral can be done in clever and efficient ways, but we are not going to bother. Instead, we need only draw enough ε_{t+1} shocks using a random number generator to get a representative distribution and then use them in the approximation. Assume that we have a vector of standard normal shocks $\varepsilon = \{\varepsilon_1, ..., \varepsilon_N\}$. Then we can approximate our integral and the value of q by setting

$$q(s_t) \simeq \frac{1}{N} \sum_{i=1}^{N} \left[\frac{\beta}{(1 + \bar{\tau} + \rho_\tau \tilde{\tau}_t + \sigma_\tau \varepsilon_i)} \right]. \tag{55}$$

We only need to draw these shocks once and henceforth can treat them as a fixed vector in the functional relationship we have created.

2.2. The Code

1. To compute an equilibrium of our model, we first choose our shock process parameters, $\left[\bar{\tau}, \bar{g}, \rho_\tau, \rho_g, \sigma_\tau, \sigma_g \right]$ and our elasticity of labor parameter γ.

2. Then, we need to draw our shocks using a random number generator and construct the realized sequence of $\tilde{\tau}_t$ and $\tilde{g}_t$. ep=randn(1,T) will generate a random string of length T of randomly distributed random numbers. We need to draw two such strings—one for τ and one for g. Then we can construct these random variables using a loop:

   ```
   tau(1)=0; g(1)=0;
   for i = 2 : T,
   tau(i)=rhotau*tau(i-1)+sigmatau*eptau(i);
   g(i)=rhog*g(i-1)+sigmag*epg(i);
   end
   tau=tau+taubar;
   g=g+gbar;
   ```

3. Caution: we need to make sure that $1 + tau > 0$ and $1 + g > 0$. Because the normal admits extreme outcomes, we might want to adjust by truncating. This can be done by setting:

   ```
   tau=max(tau,-.9);
   g=max(g,-.9);
   ```

4. Then we can construct our labor level
   ```
   L=((1+tau).^(-1/(1+gamma)))*beta^(1/(1+gamma));
   ```

5. Then we can use loops to construct our key variables such as the growth rate of output, and the growth rate of prices. Note that we already have the growth rate of money and productivity.

6. We can construct q also by looping and using a single large draw of our random normals. We could even just reuse our initial shock draw for, say, $\varepsilon_{\tau,t}$.

7. In constructing a reasonable prediction for our economy, we probably want to throw out the initial observations since they are heavily influenced by our starting values.

2.2.1. Nonstationary Random Variables

We've focused on the stationary random variables implied by our model. We can construct the nonstationary one too. Let's turn to the actual money supply. It depends on the accumulated growth rates of money. We can construct it recursively using the fact that

$$M_{t+1} = M_t(1 + \tau_t)$$

where we take $M_0 = 1$. We can do the same thing for productivity, Z_t. Consumption is given by

$$C_t = Z_t L_t.$$

The price level is given by

$$P_t = \frac{M_t}{Z_t L_t}.$$

Exercise 11. *Write a computer code to simulate our model and generate its predicted outcomes. This is a big assignment, so understand that it will take some work.*

Exercise 12. *We want to look at what our model implies for the properties of money, prices, output, and inflation. Let's start by developing some short-run facts. Try to answer the following questions about the implications of your model by computing the following objects from the simulated data:*

1. *What is the correlation between money growth and inflation?*
2. *What is the correlation between money growth and output growth?*
3. *What is the correlation between inflation and output growth?*

Exercise 13. *Now, let's try to develop some long-run facts. To do that we will time-average the growth rates of our model. For example, for output Y_t, compute*

$$\hat{y}_t = \frac{1}{J} \sum_{j=0}^{J} \log\left(\frac{Y_{t-j}}{Y_{t-j-1}}\right)$$

$$= \frac{1}{J} \left[\log(Y_t) - \log(Y_{t-J-1})\right] \text{ for all } t \geq J.$$

This way of constructing long-run growth rates is called rolling windows. Once you have coded this, redo questions (1–3) in the above exercise using the time averaged growth rates. A good number for J is probably 10 years, which here is 10 periods.

3. OUR MODEL GOES TO MONTE CARLO

When we compute a statistic in the data or a comparable statistic in the model-simulated data, how seriously should we take it? With respect to the data, this value is fixed until we get more data. But when we do, is the estimated value likely to be much different? How much should we anticipate that it will change and thereby decide how seriously to take the current value? With respect to the model-simulated data, we can create more simulated data and try again. Clearly the results will vary when we change the parameters, but they can also vary across individual computations given the parameters from the randomness of different draws. We could prevent the model simulated randomness by having a very long sequence of draws. But then the statistic we would be calculating would not match up well with the world we live in, where data are inherently pretty finite. So when we compute a statistic based on an amount of data similar to what we have in the real world, how sensitive is this statistic to individual random shocks we drew? These are the kind of questions one has in mind when evaluating our estimated statistics.

To organize our thinking, let us consider a very well-known example from statistics. If we have a sample of size n of normal random variables with mean μ and standard deviation σ, then the sample mean has expected value

$$\mathbb{E}\bar{X} = \mathbb{E}n^{-1}\sum_{t=1}^{n} X_t = \mu$$

and variance

$$\mathbb{E}(\bar{X} - \mu)^2 = \mathbb{E}\left[n^{-1}\sum_{t=1}^{n} X_t - \mu\right]^2 = \mathbb{E}\left[n^{-2}\sum_{t=1}^{n}(X_t - \mu)^2\right] = \frac{\sigma^2}{n}.$$

This gives us an analytic expression for how accurate our sample mean is, given our sample size and the variance of the random variable. From it, we can see clearly how we need to increase the sample size to maintain a desired degree of accuracy when the variance of the random variable increases. We can also compute a two standard deviation confidence interval and say that the likelihood that the new estimate is inside this band is 95%. We want to derive something similar from our model for the accuracy of the statistics we are computing.

One standard way of doing this is through Monte Carlo simulation, where we draw different sequences of the shocks indexed by i, $\{\epsilon_t^i\}$, and then build up the implied outcomes for each sequence. Finally one computes the sample statistic for each sequence i, which we can denote by m_i, and then examines the distribution of this sample statistic. This distribution gives us a lot of information about the accuracy of our estimate and is suggestive as to the accuracy of the data estimate as well. One way to think about accuracy is the standard deviation of m_i just as in our example with the sample mean of the normally distributed random variable. However, a more fundamental way to examine m_i is to plot the histogram. From this plot we can determine a 95% confidence interval for our model-based statistic.

Exercise 14. *Construct a sample of 100 estimates of the growth rate correlations from the exercise and plot your results, assuming you have 30 years of annual data and are constructing 10-year-long rolling windows. Examine how the sample distribution changes as you make the shocks more or less persistent. Try to explain why the shape of the distribution is changing with persistence.*

## 7

Some History

There are two concerns about the interaction among money, prices, and output. The first is what happens over the long term, and the second is what happens over the short term. An example of a long-term question would be: *How will prices and output be different over the next 10 years if the growth rate of money is 5% as opposed to 10%?* An example of a short-term question would be: *What will happen over the next year if we decrease the rate of growth of money from 10% to 5%?*

In the first question, there are no issues of expectations adjustment, since presumably everyone will learn over this period what the growth rate of money is. Similarly, there are no adjustment costs or delays. However, in the short term we have to worry about all of these things and they can affect the answer one expects to get.

An article by McCandless and Weber lays out three long-run facts about the relationship among money growth, prices, and output.[1] They used a broad set of countries and many periods because they were concerned about how the specific details of the central bank's policy function might impact their answer. For example, during certain periods in certain countries the central bank targets the money supply, the inflation rate, or the exchange rate. Also, it may operate by choosing the growth rate of the monetary base, the overnight interest rate on interbank lending, or the exchange rate. The hope is that by having many different observations of the long-run relationship, we will find the facts that are

1. McCandless, George T., and Warren E. Weber. "Some monetary facts." Federal Reserve Bank of Minneapolis Quarterly Review 19.3 (1995): 2–11.

Monetary and Fiscal Policy through a DSGE Lens. Harold L. Cole, Oxford University Press (2020).
© Oxford University Press. DOI: 10.1093/oso/9780190076030.001.0001

independent of the central bank's policies beyond its choice of the growth rate of money.

The three main facts are:

1. The correlation between the growth rate of money and inflation is very close to 1.
2. There is no correlation between the growth rate of money and the growth rate of output in the overall sample.
3. There is no correlation between inflation and output.

To organize our thinking about these facts, we use the old velocity equation:

$$PY = vM,$$

where P is the price level, Y is real output, M is the money supply, and v is the income velocity of money. The idea here is that v denotes the number of times that money must on average turn over if we are financing nominal expenditures PY with money M. Note that in actuality, money may turn over more or less than this, depending on the pattern of transactions and whether money is the sole medium of exchange (as opposed to credit cards).

Fact 1 does not say that the growth rate of money is equal to the rate of inflation, just that the *correlation* is near 1. Part of the reason for this is that velocity is changing over time with technology. Examples include ATMs and the increased use of credit cards. Another is that real output is also changing. If we take logs and differentiate this equation, we get that

$$p + y = d\log(v) + m,$$

where we use lowercase to indicate growth rates. From this expression, we can see that if v and Y are growing at independent rates across countries, then this simple quantity equation predicts that the correlation of the percentage change or growth rate in p and m is 1. If $d\log(v)$ or y is slightly affected by m, or if m is being chosen in response to these variables, this could lead to a different answer.

The classical dichotomy was that money affected nominal variables while real variables were affected by real factors. Facts 2 and 3 suggest that this assumption is largely correct over long time periods.

## 8

Measurement Error and Our Data

Data are measured with error. This fact is often ignored, but it greatly complicates how we should think about any data we use. This is especially true for small samples, or for short-run inference, or if the measurement error is large. Here we want to think about what that would imply for our model-simulated data as a means to understanding real-world data a bit better.

Let's return to our original model. I'm going to use a linearized form:

$$\begin{bmatrix} \tilde{L}_t \\ \tilde{p}_t \\ \tilde{q}_t \end{bmatrix} = \begin{bmatrix} D_1 \\ D_2 \\ D_3 \end{bmatrix} \tilde{\tau}_t.$$

Remember that all the "~" variables are deviations from their steady-state values. For reasons that will become clear in a moment, we will assume that

$$\tilde{\tau}_t = \exp(\sigma_\tau \varepsilon_{\tau t}),$$

where $\varepsilon_{\tau,t}$ is a standard normal. As a result, $\exp(\sigma_\tau \varepsilon_t)$ is log-normal. We assume that instead of seeing labor, we see this variable with some error, or

$$\hat{L}_t = \tilde{L}_t \exp(\sigma_L \varepsilon_{Lt}),$$

where $\exp(\sigma_L \varepsilon_{Lt})$ is the measurement error and ε_{Lt} is also a standard normal. This implies that our overall equation for labor is given by

Monetary and Fiscal Policy through a DSGE Lens. Harold L. Cole, Oxford University Press (2020).
© Oxford University Press. DOI: 10.1093/oso/9780190076030.001.0001

$$\hat{L}_t = D_1 \exp(\sigma_\tau \varepsilon_{\tau t} + \sigma_L \varepsilon_{Lt}).$$

Taking logs, this yields

$$\log(\hat{L}_t) = \log(D_1) + \sigma_\tau \varepsilon_{\tau t} + \sigma_L \varepsilon_{Lt}.$$

The first term is just a constant, the second term is the shock that moves the true value of labor, and the third term is measurement error.

We now want to think about how likely different ways of generating a given observation are. To do this, take as given the observation $\hat{l}_t = \log(\hat{L}_t) - \log(D_1)$. Then, note that in order to generate the observation we need

$$\sigma_\tau \varepsilon_{\tau t} + \sigma_L \varepsilon_{Lt} = \hat{l}_t.$$

We can use this to determine one shock in terms of another, or

$$\varepsilon_{Lt} = \frac{\hat{l}_t - \sigma_\tau \varepsilon_{\tau t}}{\sigma_L}.$$

Using this function, we can think of $\varepsilon_{Lt}(\varepsilon_{\tau t})$. And we can determine the conditional likelihood of generating this observation using a particular pair of shocks as the probability of that pair divided by the probability of all of the pairs that can generate that outcome, or

$$\frac{F(\varepsilon_{Lt}(\varepsilon_{\tau t}))F(\varepsilon_{\tau t})}{\int_{-\infty}^{\infty} F(\varepsilon_{Lt}(\varepsilon_{\tau t}))F(\varepsilon_{\tau t}) d\varepsilon_{\tau t}},$$

where $F(\cdot)$ is the probability density function (p.d.f.) of a standard normal. The maximum likelihood values of the shocks are the ones for which this probability is the highest. Note here that the maximum can be thought of in terms of simply maximizing $F(\varepsilon_{Lt}(\varepsilon_{\tau t}))F(\varepsilon_{\tau t})$, since the term in the denominator is simply a normalizing constant.

Given this, our most likely set of shocks is the solution to

$$\max_{\varepsilon_{\tau t}} F\left(\frac{\hat{l}_t - \sigma_\tau \varepsilon_{\tau t}}{\sigma_L}\right) F(\varepsilon_{\tau t}).$$

The f.o.c. for this problem is

$$F\left(\frac{\hat{l}_t - \sigma_\tau \varepsilon_{\tau t}}{\sigma_L}\right) F'(\varepsilon_{\tau t}) = F(\varepsilon_{\tau t})F'\left(\frac{\hat{l}_t - \sigma_\tau \varepsilon_{\tau t}}{\sigma_L}\right) \frac{\sigma_\tau}{\sigma_L} = 0. \tag{56}$$

To get some insight into what this condition implies, let's consider a special case in which $\sigma_\tau = \sigma_L = \sigma$. With this simplification our condition becomes

$$F\left(\frac{\hat{l}_t - \sigma\varepsilon_{\tau t}}{\sigma}\right) F'(\varepsilon_{\tau t}) = F(\varepsilon_{\tau t}) F'\left(\frac{\hat{l}_t - \sigma\varepsilon_{\tau t}}{\sigma}\right).$$

A solution is to divide up things equally and set

$$\varepsilon_{\tau t} = \varepsilon_{Lt} = \frac{\hat{l}_t}{2\sigma}.$$

Now we return to our general model and try to make progress using the explicitly functional form of the normal p.d.f. The formula for the standard normal p.d.f. is

$$F(\varepsilon) = \frac{e^{-\frac{1}{2}\varepsilon^2}}{\sqrt{2\pi}},$$

and hence its derivative is

$$F'(\varepsilon) = -\varepsilon\frac{e^{-\frac{1}{2}\varepsilon^2}}{\sqrt{2\pi}}.$$

So,

$$\frac{F'(\varepsilon)}{F(\varepsilon)} = -\varepsilon.$$

Our f.o.c. can therefore be written as

$$F\left(\frac{\hat{l}_t - \sigma_\tau\varepsilon_{\tau t}}{\sigma_L}\right) F'(\varepsilon_{\tau t}) = F(\varepsilon_{\tau t}) F'\left(\frac{\hat{l}_t - \sigma_\tau\varepsilon_{\tau t}}{\sigma_L}\right) \frac{\sigma_\tau}{\sigma_L}$$

$$\frac{F'(\varepsilon_{\tau t})}{F(\varepsilon_{\tau t})} \frac{1}{\sigma_\tau} = \frac{F'\left(\frac{\hat{l}_t - \sigma_\tau\varepsilon_{\tau t}}{\sigma_L}\right)}{F\left(\frac{\hat{l}_t - \sigma_\tau\varepsilon_{\tau t}}{\sigma_L}\right)} \frac{1}{\sigma_L}$$

or

$$\frac{\varepsilon_{\tau t}}{\sigma_\tau} = \frac{\left[\frac{\hat{l}_t - \sigma_\tau\varepsilon_{\tau t}}{\sigma_L}\right]}{\sigma_L} = \frac{\varepsilon_{L,t}}{\sigma_L}.$$

For a normal random variable, $1/\sigma$ is called the precision, and our result is that our two shocks, scaled by their precision, are equal. Then, it follows that

$$\hat{l}_t = \sigma_\tau \varepsilon_{\tau t} + \sigma_L \varepsilon_{Lt}$$

$$= \left[\sigma_\tau \left(\frac{\sigma_\tau}{\sigma_L} \right) + \sigma_L \right] \varepsilon_{Lt}.$$

This shows that we will attribute the movement in $\hat{l}_t$ to the shocks in proportion to their relative standard deviations (s.d.'s). Since these shocks are then scaled by their s.d.'s, the shock with the higher s.d. will end up accounting for a much higher share of the movement in $\hat{l}_t$.

Example 1. *Let's consider the case in which* $\sigma_\tau = 2\sigma$ *and* $\sigma_L = \sigma$. *This implies that*

$$\varepsilon_{\tau,t} = 2 \left(\frac{\hat{l}_t - 2\sigma \varepsilon_{\tau t}}{\sigma} \right), \ or$$

$$\varepsilon_{\tau,t} = 2\varepsilon_{Lt}.$$

Next, just solve

$$\hat{l}_t = 2\sigma \varepsilon_{\tau t} + \sigma \varepsilon_{Lt} = 5\sigma \varepsilon_{Lt}.$$

which yields

$$\varepsilon_{Lt} = \frac{1}{5\sigma} \hat{l}_t.$$

This in turn implies that

$$\varepsilon_{\tau t} = \frac{2}{5\sigma} \hat{l}_t.$$

Now let's think about overall output and our inference with respect to productivity. To do this, assume that we know last period's productivity, Z_{t-1}, and that current productivity is given by

$$Z_t = (1 + g_t)Z_{t-1}.$$

This leads to our output equation

$$Y_t = Z_t L_t = Z_{t-1}(1 + g_t)L_t.$$

So,

$$\log(Y_t) = \log(Z_{t-1}) + \log(1 + g_t) + \log(L_t).$$

Assume that $\log(1 + g_t)$ is normally distributed and its realization is given by $\sigma_g \varepsilon_{gt}$ where ε_{gt} is a standard normal.

Let's assume that we do not see Y_t directly but with error, so

$$\hat{Y}_t = Y_t \exp(\sigma_Y \varepsilon_{Yt}).$$

Given this, we can rewrite our equation as

$$\log(Y_t) - \log(Z_{t-1}) = \log(L_t) + \sigma_g \varepsilon_{gt} + \sigma_Y \varepsilon_{Yt}.$$

For the purposes of insight, let's rethink our measurement error for labor and assume it is proportionate to the level, or

$$\hat{L}_t = L_t \exp(\sigma_L \varepsilon_{Lt}).$$

This leads us to

$$\log(Y_t) - \log(Z_{t-1}) - \log(\hat{L}_t) = \sigma_g \varepsilon_{gt} + \sigma_Y \varepsilon_{Yt} - \sigma_L \varepsilon_{Lt},$$

or

$$\sigma_g \varepsilon_{gt} = \log(Y_t) - \log(Z_{t-1}) - \log(\hat{L}_t) + \sigma_L \varepsilon_{Lt} - \sigma_Y \varepsilon_{Yt}.$$

Remark 11. *The inference of a variable such as productivity is going to be affected by the measurement error in all of the variables we use in that inference. Hence, it will be measured with poorer precision.*

Exercise 15. *Using our basic model, we want to reexamine the model's implication in the presence of measurement error. To do this, compute the short- and long-run correlations between money growth and inflation, money growth and output growth, and inflation and output growth. But this time, we will add measurement error to our observations. Given our standard parametric form for the disutility of labor, equilibrium labor is given by*

$$L_t = \left[\frac{\beta}{1 + \tau_t} \right]^{\frac{1}{1+\gamma}}.$$

From this, we can construct the levels of output and the price level conditional on Z_t and $\bar{M}_{t-1}$. Assume that all three of our key variables are measured with error

$$\hat{L}_t = L_t \exp(\sigma \varepsilon_{Lt}),$$
$$\hat{Y}_t = Y_t \exp(\sigma \varepsilon_{Yt}),$$
$$\hat{P}_t = P_t \exp(\sigma \varepsilon_{pt}).$$

(Note that we are setting all of the measurement error s.d. equal for simplicity and ease of inference.) Assume that we do not get to see productivity directly but can only infer it given $\hat{Y}_t$ and $\hat{L}_t$.

A. *Simulate this model and see what measurement error does to our inferences. To do this, draw the money and productivity shocks according to reasonable shock processes for one realization of a sample of length T, and determine the fundamental realizations. Then, draw a bunch of measurement shock sequences and look at the various realizations of the measured variables (i.e., plot them). Do at least two experiments with high and low values of the measurement error s.d.*

B. *Compute the long- and short-run correlations in each of your measurement error adjusted realizations. Report the distribution of outcomes. What do you conclude about the sensitivity of your short- vs. long-run correlations to measurement error?*

## 9

Money Supply Rules and Interest Rate Rules

We have assumed that central bank policy can be thought of as a stochastic policy for setting the growth rate of money. It should come as no surprise that this is a fairly poor description of how central banks actually operate. In fact central banks follow a variety of different procedures for determining monetary policy. These include different goals, such as trying to target the price level, the inflation rate, some particular interest rate, the growth rate of output, the level of the unemployment rate, or even the exchange rate. Typically, the interest rate target has involved something like the market for bank reserves, which is something the central bank can readily adjust through open market purchases. central bank rules or targets have been thought to include a variety of current economic indicators, such as the gap between the level of output and what was thought to be its appropriate level (commonly called the output gap).

For example, in the United States, the Federal Reserve has in recent history gone through four fairly distinct regimes for setting monetary policy:

1. From the mid-1960s to 1979, the Federal Reserve pursued an inflation-targeting regime with the explicit aim of producing a high level of inflation in order to increase/smooth employment and earn seigniorage in order to reduce the need to raise taxes to finance an unpopular war in Asia. During this period the inflation target gradually rose.
2. From October of 1979 to October of 1982, Paul Volcker was appointed chairman of the Federal Reserve and he pursued a regime of monetary

Monetary and Fiscal Policy through a DSGE Lens. Harold L. Cole, Oxford University Press (2020).
© Oxford University Press. DOI: 10.1093/oso/9780190076030.001.0001

targeting with price stability as the main focus and employment stability playing a distinctly limited role.

3. From October of 1982 to the end of 2008 the Federal Reserve used interest rate targeting with both price stability and employment stability being considered.

4. From December of 2008 to roughly December of 2015, the Federal Reserve responded to the Great Recession and its associated financial difficulties by pursuing something very close to a zero interest rate policy.

In this chapter, I want to discuss different operating rules for our monetary authority. Currently, our model generates fluctuations in labor only through money supply shocks. I want to enrich the model to include an additional source of labor variation in order to think about how the central bank might want to conduct monetary policy so as to smooth out these additional fluctuations. In so doing, the central bank would be using its ability to manipulate the equilibrium labor supply through the money growth rate to offset these other shocks. This makes clear why we need these other shocks.

The other shocks I am going to consider are shocks to the disutility of labor, which I denote by Υ_t. With this change, the flow utility becomes

$$u(C_t) - (1 + \Upsilon_t)v(L_t).$$

The interpretation is that there is a stochastic factor that makes the disutility of labor effort higher or lower, and that this factor can lead to changes in the equilibrium level of labor and, hence, output. One might argue that having labor fluctuate in response to this sort of shock would be efficient. That would be correct. However, we are going to assume that the government in the form of the central bank does not share this view that the cost of labor has been fluctuating and hence evaluates conditions using our old flow payoff $u(C_t) - v(L_t)$. As a result, it takes a dim view of these periodic instances of "hyperactivity" or "lethargy" and seeks to moderate or prevent them.[1]

---

1. The first example of a model with this sort of taste shock to move around labor in what we will eventually develop into a real business cycle model (that I know of) is Stockman, Alan C., and Linda L. Tesar. Tastes and technology in a two-country model of the business cycle: Explaining international comovements. No. w3566. National Bureau of Economic Research, 1990. I am particularly happy to cite this paper because Alan was my Ph.D. advisor and he really helped me in "back in the day."

1. AUGMENTED MODEL

We are returning to our standard model without any price-setting friction. Now, though, we need to include the preference shock Υ_t in our state s_t and correspondingly in our history state s^t. With this change, the Lagrangian for the household's problem is very similar, with the only change being to their preferences

$$\mathcal{L} = \max_{\{L(s^t),\,C(s^t),\,M(s^t),\,B(s^t)\}_{t=1}^{2}} \min_{\{\mu(s^t),\,\lambda(s^t)\}_{t=1}^{2}}$$

$$E\left\{\sum_{t=1,2}\beta^{t-1}\left[u(C_t(s^t)) - (1+\Upsilon_t(s^t))v(L_t(s^t))\right] + \beta^2 V(M(s^2),\,B(s^2),\,s_3)\right\}$$

$$+ \sum_{t=1,2}\sum_{s^t}\lambda(s^t)\{M(s^{t-1}(s^t)) - P(s^t)C(s^t)\}$$

$$+ \sum_{t=1,2}\sum_{s^t}\mu(s^t)\left\{\begin{array}{l}P(s^t)Z(s^t)L(s^t) + [M(s^{t-1}(s^t)) - P(s^t)C(s^t)]\\ +B(s^{t-1}(s^t)) + T(s^t) - M(s^t) - q(s^t)B(s^t)\end{array}\right\}.$$

The first-order conditions are unchanged, except for the labor condition and are given by

$$\beta^{t-1}u'(C(s^t))\Pr(s^t) - [\lambda(s^t) + \mu(s^t)]P(s^t) = 0.$$

$$-\beta^{t-1}(1+\Upsilon_t(s^t))v'(L(s^t))\Pr(s^t) + \mu(s^t)P(s^t)Z(s^t) = 0.$$

$$-\mu(s^t) + \sum_{s^{t+1}\in S^{t+1}(s^t)}[\lambda(s^{t+1}) + \mu(s^{t+1})] = 0.$$

$$-\mu(s^t)q(s^t) + \sum_{s^{t+1}\in S^{t+1}(s^t)}\mu(s^{t+1}) = 0.$$

We can make the same change in variables as before and use that to simplify our expressions, again just as before, in order to get

$$1 = [\tilde{\lambda}(s_t) + \tilde{\mu}(s_t)],$$

$$(1+\Upsilon_t)(v'(L(s_t)) = [\tilde{\mu}(s_t)]\left[\frac{1}{L(s_t)}\right], \tag{57}$$

$$\tilde{\mu}(s_t) = \frac{\beta}{(1+\tau_t(s^t))},$$

$$\tilde{\mu}(s^t)q(s^t) = \sum_{s^{t+1}\in S^{t+1}(s^t)}\tilde{\mu}(s^{t+1})\frac{\beta}{(1+\tau_t(s^t))}\Pr(s_{t+1}|s_t). \tag{58}$$

As before, we can simplify our q condition to get that

$$q(s^t) = \sum_{s^{t+1} \in S^{t+1}(s^t)} \frac{\beta}{(1 + \tau_{t+1}(s^{t+1}))} \Pr(s_{t+1}|s_t).$$

Everything is exactly the same as in our standard statistical model, except for the additional term in the labor condition (57). This then leads to a slightly modified version of our standard result with respect to the equilibrium level of the labor supply

$$(1 + \Upsilon_t)v'(L(s_t))L(s_t) = \frac{\beta}{(1 + \tau_t(s^t))}. \tag{59}$$

We will assume that on average Υ_t is equal to zero. We will assume that the central bank has some information about Υ_t, either because it follows an AR1 process, such as

$$\Upsilon_t = \rho_\Upsilon \Upsilon_{t-1} + \sigma_\Upsilon \upsilon_t,$$

or simply because it has other information it has gathered through following the markets and conducting surveys. We will denote its belief as to Υ_t by $\tilde{\Upsilon}_t$. We will assume that the central bank has a target level of labor $\bar{L}$ and money growth $\bar{\tau}$, which is a solution to

$$v'(\bar{L})\bar{L} = \frac{\beta}{(1 + \bar{\tau})}. \tag{60}$$

We will assume that the 's forecast is unbiased, so $\mathbb{E}\{\Upsilon_t\} = \tilde{\Upsilon}_t$, but that the variance of the forecast error, $\Upsilon_t - \tilde{\Upsilon}_t$, is not zero.

2. MONEY SUPPLY RULES

Here we will consider how the might follow a money supply rule based on its information to smooth out movements in labor relative to its target level. The solution is pretty obvious: simply choose the money growth rate so that it is a solution to

$$(1 + \tilde{\Upsilon}_t)v'(\bar{L})\bar{L} = \frac{\beta}{(1 + \tau(\tilde{\Upsilon}_t))}. \tag{61}$$

This money rule, $\tau(\tilde{\Upsilon}_t)$, will differ from the desired level of money growth $\bar{\tau}$ to the extent that the expected value of shock $\tilde{\Upsilon}_t$ differs from 0. It will be successful in smoothing out labor to the extent that the 's forecast of Υ_t is accurate. It will appear to be backward looking to the extent that the forecast is based on prior economic events involving data like such as output or labor, because the shock itself has a persistent component.

3. INFLATION TARGETING

Since the price-level equation is unchanged relative to our standard model, the inflation rate between t and $t+1$ is given by

$$1 + \pi_{t+1} = \frac{P_{t+1}}{P_t} = \frac{M_{t+1}C_t}{M_tC_{t+1}} = \frac{(1+\tau_t)L(\Upsilon_t,\tau_t)}{(1+g_{t+1})L(\Upsilon_{t+1},\tau_{t+1})} \qquad (62)$$

For the to target the inflation rate, it must forecast the future growth rate, g_{t+1}, of both the current and the future disutility of labor shocks, Υ_t and Υ_{t+1} respectively. Given these forecasts, which we denote with a "hat", and its inflation target $\bar{\pi}$, the central bank then chooses its money growth rate as the solution to

$$1 + \bar{\pi} = \frac{(1+\tau_t)L(\hat{\Upsilon}_t,\tau_t)}{(1+\hat{g}_{t+1})L(\hat{\Upsilon}_{t+1},\hat{\tau}_{t+1})} \qquad (63)$$

Note here that the future forecast of its own policy $\hat{\tau}_{t+1}$ shows up here too. This suggests that the central bank would be well served not to allow its money growth rate to swing too wildly since future swings will feedback on the current growth rate. Thus, targeting the inflation rate is sort of a smoothed forward-looking money supply target. Naturally, since all of the forecasts will have a backward-looking aspect, the rule itself must have some history dependence. However, the extent of the history dependence will depend even more explicitly on the persistence of the shocks.

4. INTEREST RATE RULES

The most direct impact of the interest rate, i.e. q_t, comes through the growth rate of the shadow price of nominal wealth since

$$\mu(s^t) = \frac{\sum_{s^{t+1}\in S^{t+1}(s^t)}\mu(s^{t+1})}{q(s^t)} = \mathbb{E}\left\{\frac{\mu_{t+1}}{q_t}\right\}. \qquad (64)$$

Increases in the expected growth rate of this multiplier depresses the current price of the debt and hence raises the implicit interest rate. But this is very specific to our current model and includes, among other things, the lack of endogenous state variables such as capital. So, ignoring this aspect, consider substituting into to the above expression to get that

$$\mu_t = \mathbb{E}\left\{\frac{\mu_{t+2}}{q_t \times q_{t+1}}\right\} = \mathbb{E}\left\{\frac{\mu_{t+T+1}}{\prod_{i=0}^{T} q_{t+i}}\right\}. \qquad (65)$$

Note that in equation (65) the future interest factors, i.e. q_{t+j}, have the same impact as the current one, q_t, on μ_t. Note also that a change in q_{t+j} will affect not only μ_t but also $[\mu_{t+1}, ..., \mu_{t+j}]$ and that it will do so by the same percentage (i.e., a 10% change will have a 10% impact).

The fact that future changes in the interest rate target have large *cumulative* effects encourages the central bank to be even more forward looking and set a long sequence of interest rate targets to achieve its policy goals. This sort of long-sequence of policy targets is called *forward guidance*.

Remark 12. *The second most famous example of an interest rate rule (after the Friedman rule) is the Taylor rule, named after John Taylor, who suggested that the central bank should (and largely did in practice) follow a rule for setting the interest rate in which the interest rate should respond to the deviation of the inflation rate from target and the deviation of output from "potential output".[2] The rule took the following form:*

$$i_t = \pi_t + r_t^* + 0.5(\pi_t - \pi_t^*) + 0.5(y_t - \bar{y}_t).$$

2. Taylor, John B. (1993). "Discretion versus Policy Rules in Practice" (PDF). Carnegie-Rochester Conference Series on Public Policy. 39: 195–214.

## 10

Price-Setting and Information Frictions

A wide variety of evidence is thought to suggest that monetary shocks both increase the inflation rate, which our model predicts, and, at least in the short run, increase the level of employment and output. This evidence is summarized in the "Phillips curve" and other such relationships. These relationships imply at least a short-run tradeoff between inflation and unemployment, because inflation is thought to be bad, while lowering unemployment is thought to be good. In fact, Mankiw (2001) cites the existence of this tradeoff as one of the ten fundamental laws of economics.[1] In this chapter we will modify our model to generate such an outcome. We will do this along the lines of the New Keynesian literature by imposing a price-setting friction.[2]

To understand what we are doing here, it is useful to realize that, in many ways, a model is a means of coherently telling a certain story. The story we want to tell is one in which prices are set in advance and then money shocks lead to increases in nominal demand, and, hence output. The question for us is: what sort of model

---

1. Mankiw, N. Gregory. "The inexorable and mysterious tradeoff between inflation and unemployment." The Economic Journal 111.471 (2001): 45–61.

2. Important papers in this tradition include: Fischer, Stanley. "Long-term contracts, rational expectations, and the optimal money supply rule." Journal of Political Economy 85.1 (1977): 191–205. Taylor, John B. "Staggered wage setting in a macro model." The American Economic Review 69.2 (1979): 108–113. Mankiw, N. Gregory. "Small menu costs and large business cycles: A macroeconomic model of monopoly." The Quarterly Journal of Economics 100.2 (1985): 529–537. Blanchard, Olivier Jean, and Nobuhiro Kiyotaki. "Monopolistic competition and the effects of aggregate demand." The American Economic Review (1987): 647–666.

Monetary and Fiscal Policy through a DSGE Lens. Harold L. Cole, Oxford University Press (2020). © Oxford University Press. DOI: 10.1093/oso/9780190076030.001.0001

do we have to buy into to get this outcome? We will see in what follows that we need to make several fundamental changes to our current model to get there. Then we can ask questions such as: (i) which model does a better job of accounting for the data? (ii) How plausible does each model seem? Or even (iii) are there some interesting other implications of the different models?

1. PRICE SETTING

The New Keynesian story has producers setting prices. But you cannot set a price in a competitive market because demand is either 0, infinite, or indeterminate (for an individual producer as she can sell as much as she wants at the competitive price). So, to have price setting we need some notion of the quantity response to a price. This is done by having each producer produce a unique good in which he or she has a monopoly. Producer's monopoly power is limited by the extent to which setting a high price will lead to a reduction in demand as buyers shift to other lower-priced goods.

To put this into our model, we will go back to the setup in which we had different goods. Now, though, we will think of each of our original goods which we indexed by $i \in I$, as being produced by an individual producer. This producer chooses the price at which she wants to sell his good. We will alter the timing of the model as follows. In the beginning of the period, the household that produces good i chooses the price at which to sell its good $P(i)$. Then, when the seller goes off to market, (s)he will work to produce the good according to the level of demand.

Timing within Each Period
1. Household i starts a period with M units of money and picks $P_t(i)$.
2. The seller and buyer split up and go to their respective markets.
3. The buyer spends M and the seller works L_t to meet demand.
4. The seller and buyer come back together in the asset market
5. They jointly consume the consumption good.
6. The period ends.

This timing does several things. First, it allows for current money injections to affect the level of nominal demand. Second, if we assume that the household does not know the level τ_t at the time it chooses $P_t(i)$, then it can turn out that money shocks lead to surprise demand shocks. This can in turn increase labor effort and output.

1.1. Deriving the Demand Function

Each household now faces a demand for its good that depends on the price. My goal here is to construct a price index $\bar{P}$ and a demand function $D(P(i)/\bar{P})$ that we can use to determine the optimal choice of $P(i)$.

Proposition 1. *Our demand function for good i can be written as*

$$C(i) = \left[\#I \frac{\bar{P}}{P(i)} \right]^{\frac{1}{1-\rho}} C.$$

Proof. The proof is in several steps. First, we set out the problem of an individual who is maximizing the value of his composite consumption given prices and an amount of money to spend. Since the payoff to this problem is C, the maximal amount of composite consumption, it follows that the derivative of this payoff w.r.t. M, the amount of money, gives one relationship involving dC/dM and the multiplier on the expenditure constraint. We can then use the budget constraint stated in terms of our composite price index to derive another relationship involving the price index. We then derive the f.o.c.'s and use them to construct demand functions as a function of the multiplier. Next, we substitute these into the budget constraint and replace the multiplier λ with the price index, and solve for the price index. Finally, we use the solution to our price index in the consumption demand functions to get the final form of our demand function.

To derive that demand function, start from our preferences over the different goods:

$$C = \left\{ \frac{1}{\#I} \sum_{i \in I} C(i)^\rho \right\}^{1/\rho}$$

Assume that households want to maximize their consumption aggregate C given a certain amount of money to spend M. Assume also that they buy all of the goods with this money, including the one they produce. Then their maximization problem is given by

$$\max_{C(i)} \left\{ \frac{1}{\#I} \sum_{i \in I} C(i)^\rho \right\}^{1/\rho} \quad \text{s.t.} \sum_i P(i)C(i) \leq M.$$

One quick thing to note here is that the objective is curved in individual consumption but linear if all consumptions are scaled up equally. This is also true of the constraint. Hence, the level of consumptions will be pinned down by M and the relative amounts by the prices. Forming the Lagrangian we get that

$$\mathcal{L} = \max_{C(i)} \min_{\lambda} \left\{ \frac{1}{\#I} \sum_{i \in I} C(i)^\rho \right\}^{1/\rho} + \lambda \left\{ M - \sum_i P(i)C(i) \right\}.$$

My price index $\bar{P}$ should price C, and hence it should be the case that

$$\bar{P}C = M.$$

So $\bar{P}$ is the nominal price of the consumption aggregate in terms of money or M. At the same time,

$$\frac{d\mathcal{L}}{dM} = \lambda,$$

and hence λ is the shadow value of more M in terms of more C. But, from our budget constraint with $\bar{P}$, it follows that

$$dC = \frac{1}{\bar{P}}dM.$$

So the two are each inverses of each other. This implies that $\lambda^{-1} = \bar{P}$ which we will use later. Differentiating leads to the following f.o.c. for some arbitrary good k

$$\frac{1}{\#I}\left\{\frac{1}{\#I}\sum_{i\in I}C(i)^\rho\right\}^{\frac{1-\rho}{\rho}}C(k)^{\rho-1} - \lambda P(k) = 0.$$

So, we get that

$$\frac{1}{\#I}C(k)^{\rho-1} = \lambda P(k)C^{\rho-1}.$$

For everything to add up, it must be the case that

$$\sum_i P(i)C(i) = \sum_i P(i)\left[(\#I)\lambda P(i)\right]^{1/(\rho-1)}C = \bar{P}C = M.$$

So making use of our inverse result to substitute out for λ, we get that

$$\sum_i P(i)\left[(\#I)\bar{P}^{-1}P(i)\right]^{1/(\rho-1)} = \bar{P},$$

$$\bar{P}^{1+\frac{1}{\rho-1}} = \left[(\#I)\right]^{1/(\rho-1)}\sum_i P(i)^{\frac{\rho}{\rho-1}}$$

$$\bar{P} = \left\{\left[(\#I)\right]^{1/(\rho-1)}\sum_i P(i)^{\frac{\rho}{\rho-1}}\right\}^{\frac{\rho-1}{\rho}}.$$

Finally, inserting $\bar{P}^{-1}$ for λ in our first-order condition, we get that

$$\frac{1}{\#I}C(i)^{\rho-1} = \frac{P(i)}{\bar{P}}C^{\rho-1},$$

so

$$C(i) = \left[\#I\frac{P(i)}{\bar{P}}\right]^{\frac{1}{\rho-1}}C.$$
$$= D\left(\frac{P(i)}{\bar{P}}\right)$$

For future reference, note that

$$\frac{d}{dP(i)}D\left(\frac{P(i)}{\bar{P}}\right) = D\left(\frac{P(i)}{\bar{P}}\right)\frac{1}{\rho-1}P(i)^{-1}. \qquad (66)$$

$\square$

Remark 13. *When we go to our model, we should really think of $D(\cdot)$ as a function of the entire state vector, or $D\left(\frac{P(i)}{\bar{P}}, s_t\right)$. However, in the interest of brevity, I shall typically take this as implicit.*

1.2. Optimal Price Setting

We can now add this price-setting feature to our original two-period version of the household's problem.

$$\max_{\{C_t, P_t(i), M_{t+1}, B_{t+1}\}_{t=1,2}} u(C_1) - v\left(D\left(\frac{P_1(i)}{\bar{P}_1}\right)/Z_1\right) + \beta\left[u(C_2) - v\left(D\left(\frac{P_2(i)}{\bar{P}_2}\right)/Z_2\right)\right]$$

$$+ \beta^2 V(M_3, B_3) \text{ subject to}$$

$$M_t \geq \bar{P}_t C_t \text{ and}$$

$$P_t(i)D\left(\frac{P_t(i)}{\bar{P}_t}\right) + [M_t - \bar{P}_t C_t] + B_t + T_t \geq M_{t+1} + q_t B_{t+1} \text{ for } t = 1, 2.$$

Note that we are imposing the condition that the household must work enough to satisfy demand for its product given the price it sets and the overall price index $\bar{P}$. This pins down the household's labor. We have directly inserted this value of labor effort into its objective and their budget constraint.

The first-order condition for pricing is then given by

$$0 = -v'\left(D\left(\frac{P_t(i)}{\bar{P}_t}\right)/Z_t\right)\frac{1}{Z_t}\frac{d}{dP_t(i)}D\left(\frac{P_t(i)}{\bar{P}_t}\right)$$
$$+\mu_t\left[D\left(\frac{P_t(i)}{\bar{P}_t}\right) + P_t(i)\frac{d}{dP_t(i)}D\left(\frac{P_t(i)}{\bar{P}_t}\right)\right]$$

$$0 = -v'\left(D\left(\frac{P_t(i)}{\bar{P}_t}\right)/Z_t\right)\frac{1}{Z_t}D\left(\frac{P_t(i)}{\bar{P}_t}\right)\frac{1}{\rho-1}P_t(i)^{-1}$$
$$+\mu_t\left[D\left(\frac{P_t(i)}{\bar{P}_t}\right) + D\left(\frac{P_t(i)}{\bar{P}_t}\right)\frac{1}{\rho-1}\right]$$

$$0 = -v'\left(D\left(\frac{P_t(i)}{\bar{P}_t}\right)/Z_t\right)\frac{1}{Z_t}P_t(i)^{-1} + \mu_t\rho.$$

So, finally, we get

$$v'\left(D\left(\frac{P_t(i)}{\bar{P}_t}\right)/Z_t\right)\frac{1}{\rho} = Z_t P_t(i)\mu_t. \tag{67}$$

If we compare this equation to the one we initially derived (5), we see that the only real difference, once we realize that $D\left(\frac{P_t(i)}{\bar{P}_t}\right)/Z_t = L_t$, is the presence of a mark-up term, $1/\rho > 1$. This scales up the cost factor coming from the disutility of labor, thereby raising the price. In essence, the household is now taking account of the fact that it faces a demand elasticity that is finite, and as a result, it is earning some monopoly profits.

1.3. Reconstructing the Fundamental Equation

In equilibrium every household will have the same pricing rule, so $P_t(i) = P_t(i') = \bar{P}_t$. So, we can drop the different prices and just return to our original price P_t, just as we did when we acted as if there was only one good. In addition, $D\left(\frac{P_t(i)}{\bar{P}_t}\right)/Z_t = L_t$, so we can just substitute labor back into our condition. Once we do this, the good news is that our system of equations has been only slightly modified. Everywhere we had v', we now have v'/ρ.

As a result, we can boil things down to a system of three equations, just as we did in the basic stochastic model to get our modified labor supply condition:

$$\frac{1}{\rho}v'(L(s_t))L(s_t) = \frac{\beta}{(1+\tau_t(s^t))}.$$

The second is the price-level equation rewritten in terms of the productivity-adjusted ratio of price to the initial level of the money supply in order to express things in terms of a stationary object:

$$p(s_t) \equiv \frac{Z(s^t)P(s^t)}{\bar{M}(s^{t-1}(s^t))} = \frac{1}{L(s_t)}.$$

This equation is unchanged. The third equation is our interest rate condition:

$$q(s^t) = \frac{\beta}{(1+\tau_t(s^t))} \frac{\sum_{s^{t+1} \in S^{t+1}(s^t)} [v'(L(s_{t+1}))L(s_{t+1})] \Pr(s_{t+1}|s_t)}{v'(L(s_t))L(s_t)}.$$

Because the $1/\rho$ terms cancel out, this condition is also unchanged.

The steady-state level of labor effort will now be given by the solution to

$$\frac{1}{\rho} v'(\bar{L}))\bar{L} = \frac{\beta}{(1+\bar{\tau})}.$$

Since $v'(\bar{L})\bar{L}$ is increasing in $\bar{L}$, and since $1/\rho > 1$, it follows that the steady-state labor supply will be lower with price setting.

What about the impact of changes in the growth rate of money? We can repeat our comparative statics exercise to get that

$$\frac{1}{\rho} [v''(\bar{L})\bar{L} + v'(\bar{L})] dL = -\frac{\beta}{(1+\bar{\tau})^2} d\bar{\tau},$$

so

$$\frac{dL}{d\bar{\tau}} = -\frac{\rho\beta}{[v''(\bar{L})\bar{L} + v'(\bar{L})](1+\bar{\tau})^2} < 0.$$

But this is very nearly what we had before in equation (50). In particular, the response of labor to a change in the inflation rate is *negative*. As we saw before, this will map right into our stochastic model and imply a negative response of labor to monetary shocks. Therefore, clearly our current model is missing something important.

2. ADDING A TIMING CHANGE + AN INFORMATION FRICTION

The problem we have so far is that there really aren't any nominal shocks in period t. The reason is twofold. First, the monetary injection was assumed to be known at the beginning of the period, so no surprise for our price-setting decision. Second, the money injection occurred in the asset market, so its direct effect was to raise spending and prices in period $t+1$. We need to change both of these features of our model to get the desired outcome from it.

2.1. New Timing

We will now assume that the buyer receives a money transfer T_t right as he enters the goods market and after the household has set the price of its good. This is our timing change. For now, we treat T_t and all of the future as known. With this change, the household's problem becomes

$$\max_{\{C_t,P_t(i),M_{t+1},B_{t+1}\}_{t=1,2}} u(C_1) - v\left(D\left(\frac{P_1(i)}{\bar{P}_1}\right)/Z_1\right) + \beta\left[u(C_2) - v\left(D\left(\frac{P_2(i)}{\bar{P}_2}\right)/Z_2\right)\right]$$

$$+\beta^2 V(M_3, B_3) \text{ subject to}$$

$$M_t + T_t \geq \bar{P}_t C_t \text{ and}$$

$$P_t(i)D\left(\frac{P_t(i)}{\bar{P}_t}\right) + [M_t + T_t - \bar{P}_t C_t] + B_t \geq M_{t+1} + q_t B_{t+1} \text{ for } t = 1, 2.$$

The only change is to the cash-in-advance constraint, which now includes T_t as being available to spend.

If we form the Lagrangian and differentiate w.r.t. our choice variables, we will get essentially the same first-order conditions as before as a result. The f.o.c. for our consumption aggregate C_t is still

$$\beta^{t-1}u'(C_t) - [\lambda_t + \mu_t]\bar{P}_t = 0.$$

The f.o.c. for $P_t(i)$ is still

$$\beta^{t-1}v'\left(D\left(\frac{P_t(i)}{\bar{P}_t}\right)/Z_t\right)\frac{1}{\rho} = Z_t P_t(i)\mu_t.$$

Money is still

$$-\mu_t + [\lambda_{t+1} + \mu_{t+1}] = 0.$$

And bonds are still

$$-\mu_t q_t + \mu_{t+1} = 0.$$

So far, very little has changed.

Next, we note that just as before, all households are behaving the same, so all prices in period t will be the same. Hence, $P_t(i) = P_t$, and this will be our price of the consumption aggregate too. Assuming that the c.i.a. constraint always binds implies that the price level will now be given by

$$\bar{P}_t = \frac{\bar{M}_t(1 + \tau_t)}{Z_t L_t}. \tag{68}$$

Now the current price level will respond directly to the monetary injection. Here is the first real change.

If we take into account that $D\left(\frac{P_t(i)}{\bar{P}_t}\right)/Z_t = L_t$ and make this change to the labor first-order condition, we get that

$$\beta^{t-1} v'(L_t) \frac{1}{\rho} = Z_t P_t(i) \mu_t.$$

If we use our f.o.c.'s for money and consumption, this equation becomes

$$\beta^{t-1} v'(L_t) \frac{1}{\rho} = Z_t P_t(i) [\mu_{t+1} + \lambda_{t+1}]$$

$$= \left[\frac{\beta^t u'(C_{t+1})}{\bar{P}_{t+1}} \right] \bar{P}_t Z_t$$

$$= \frac{\bar{P}_t}{\bar{P}_{t+1}} Z_t \beta^t u'(C_{t+1}),$$

which is just as before (given that everyone sets the same price $\bar{P}$).

However, when we substitute in for prices using our new condition we get

$$v'(L_t) \frac{1}{\rho} = \frac{\frac{\bar{M}_t(1 + \tau_t)}{Z_t L_t}}{\frac{\bar{M}_t(1 + \tau_t)(1 + \tau_{t+1})}{Z_{t+1} L_{t+1}}} Z_t \beta u'(C_{t+1})$$

$$= \frac{1}{1 + \tau_{t+1}} \frac{Z_{t+1} L_{t+1}}{L_t} \beta u'(C_{t+1}). \tag{69}$$

This is very similar to our earlier equation (21), only now it is the monetary injection *tomorrow* that influences things, not the one today. The reason is that the time t injection now scales up P_t and P_{t+1} by an equal amount and hence has no effect on the return you earn from holding money between today and tomorrow.

Remark 14. *In the steady state this timing change does not matter. We will still get*

$$v'(\bar{L})\frac{1}{\rho} = \frac{1}{1+\bar{\tau}}\bar{Z}\beta u'(\bar{Z}\bar{L}),$$

so only the mark-up factor matters there. Given this, the price level is given by

$$\bar{P}_t = \frac{\bar{M}_{t+1}}{\bar{Z}\bar{L}} = \frac{\bar{M}_1(1+\bar{\tau})^t}{\bar{Z}\bar{L}} \tag{70}$$

when money grows at the constant rate of $(1+\bar{\tau})$ and $Z_t = \bar{Z}$ always. Note the subtle change here. Prices depend not on the beginning-of-period level of the money supply, but the level after the money injection in this period has occurred, which in our notation is $\bar{M}_{t+1}$.

2.2. Information Change

Assume now that the household does not know the current monetary injection. The level of demand will now depend explicitly on the realized money supply shock, and to emphasize this, we will write

$$D\left(\frac{P_t(i)}{\bar{P}_t}, \tau_t\right).$$

If the forecasted money supply injection is $\bar{\tau}_t$, then the forecasted level of demand and hence consumption is given by

$$D(1, \bar{\tau}_t) = \bar{C}_t = \frac{M_t(1+\bar{\tau}_t)}{\bar{P}_t},$$

where the last equality follows from the c.i.a. constraint holding as an equality at the forecasted level of the money supply. However, the realized level of nominal spending and hence consumption will be scaled up by the realized money supply shock, so the *actual* level of consumption will be given by

$$C_t = \frac{M_t(1+\tau_t)}{\bar{P}_t} = \frac{M_t(1+\tau_t)}{M_t(1+\bar{\tau}_t)/\bar{C}_t} = \frac{(1+\tau_t)}{(1+\bar{\tau}_t)}\bar{C}_t.$$

So consumption today will be higher than forecasted if $\tau_t > \bar{\tau}_t$ and lower if the reverse is true. But since consumption is produced with labor, this implies that

$$Z_t L_t = \frac{(1+\tau_t)}{(1+\bar{\tau}_t)} \bar{C}, \text{ while } Z_t \bar{L}_t = \bar{C}_t.$$

Hence, the level of labor input is given by

$$L_t = \frac{(1+\tau_t)}{(1+\bar{\tau}_t)} \bar{L}_t, \tag{71}$$

and labor will be higher in response to an inflation surprise. This is now getting us what we wanted.

Remark 15. *Equation (71) is particularly useful, since it allows us to think in terms of a labor effort target $\bar{L}$, and the impact of the deviation in money growth relative to its mean on actual labor, given that output responds to demand and not prices here.*

3. PUTTING THE PIECES TOGETHER

Here we want to put everything together. To keep things simple, we are assuming that productivity is constant, that the utility over consumption is *log*, and that the disutility of labor takes a power function form as in (23). Now when the household chooses its price (or equivalently its target labor-effort level) it understands that this will only contribute to determining the distribution of outcomes and not the actual outcome.

The maximization problem is given by

$$\max_{\{C_t, P_t(i), M_{t+1}, B_{t+1}\}_{t=1,2}}$$

$$\mathbb{E}\left\{ \begin{array}{c} u(C_1) - v\left(D\left(\frac{P_1(i)}{\bar{P}_1}, \tau_1\right)/Z_1\right) + \beta\left[u(C_2) - v\left(D\left(\frac{P_2(i)}{\bar{P}_2}, \tau_2\right)/Z_2\right)\right] \\ + \beta^2 V(M_3, B_3) \end{array} \right\}$$

subject to

$$M_t + T_t \geq \bar{P}_t C_t \text{ and}$$

$$P_t(i)D\left(\frac{P_t(i)}{\bar{P}_t}, \tau_t\right) + [M_t + T_t - \bar{P}_t C_t] + B_t \geq M_{t+1} + q_t B_{t+1} \text{ for } t = 1, 2.$$

We have to be careful here about the timing of choices. The price is chosen at the beginning of the period, before the realization of τ_t is known, but all other choices are made knowing the money supply growth rate. Because of this, the f.o.c. for the optimal price choice is given by

$$
0 = \mathbb{E}_t \left\{ \begin{array}{l} -\beta^{t-1} v' \left(D\left(\frac{P_t(i)}{\bar{P}_t}, \tau_t\right)/Z_t \right) \frac{1}{Z_t} \frac{d}{dP_t(i)} D\left(\frac{P_t(i)}{\bar{P}_t}, \tau_t\right) \\ +\mu_t \left[D\left(\frac{P_t(i)}{\bar{P}_t}, \tau_t\right) + P_t(i) \frac{d}{dP_t(i)} D\left(\frac{P_t(i)}{\bar{P}_t}, \tau_t\right) \right] \end{array} \right\},
$$

where the expectation is with respect to the current growth rate of money, τ_t, and all of the future shocks.[3] If we make use of our result for the derivative of the demand function, this becomes

$$
\begin{aligned}
0 &= \mathbb{E}_t \left\{ \begin{array}{l} -\beta^{t-1} v' \left(D\left(\frac{P_t(i)}{\bar{P}_t}, \tau_t\right)/Z_t \right) \frac{1}{Z_t} D\left(\frac{P(i)}{\bar{P}}, \tau_t\right) \frac{1}{\rho-1} P_t(i)^{-1} \\ +\mu_t \left[D\left(\frac{P_t(i)}{\bar{P}_t}, \tau_t\right) + P_t(i) D\left(\frac{P(i)}{\bar{P}}, \tau_t\right) \frac{1}{\rho-1} P_t(i)^{-1} \right] \end{array} \right\} \\
&= \mathbb{E}_t \left\{ \begin{array}{l} -\beta^{t-1} v' \left(D\left(\frac{P_t(i)}{\bar{P}_t}, \tau_t\right)/Z_t \right) \frac{1}{Z_t} D\left(\frac{P(i)}{\bar{P}}, \tau_t\right) \\ +\mu_t D\left(\frac{P_t(i)}{\bar{P}_t}, \tau_t\right) \rho P_t(i) \end{array} \right\}.
\end{aligned}
$$

This expression equates the marginal gain from increasing the price of good $P_t(i)$ and therefore from working less in expected terms, with the expected loss in terms of wealth in the asset market. The demand function $D(\cdot)$ here should be thought of as a function of the relative price and the money growth rate. Hence, demand is stochastic. Moreover, the marginal value of wealth μ_t will also change depending on the exogenous shocks, and hence, it also is stochastic.

Then, again making use of the fact that $P_t(i) = \bar{P}_t$ since all prices are the same in equilibrium, and that $D\left(\frac{P_t(i)}{\bar{P}_t}, \tau_t\right) = Z_t L_t$, we get that

$$
0 = \mathbb{E}_t \left\{ -\beta^{t-1} v'(L_t) L_t + \mu_t \rho Z_t L_t \bar{P}_t \right\}.
$$

Formally, the f.o.c. for money also reflects future uncertainty, and hence

$$
\mu_t = \mathbb{E} \{ \mu_{t+1} + \lambda_{t+1} \}
$$

---

3. Formally, we are taking the history of past growth rates of money and productivity, along with the current realization of productivity, as given since they are known at the time of the decision. We are taking the expectation with respect to the unknowns, which here include both the current realization of the money growth rate τ_t and the future realizations of money growth and productivity.

because we don't know the future shadow prices. The f.o.c. for bonds also reflects this future uncertainty

$$q_t \mu_t = \mathbb{E}\{\mu_{t+1}\} \tag{72}$$

However, because consumption is taken once all uncertainty within the period has been resolved, we still get that

$$\beta^{t-1} u'(C_t) = [\mu_t + \lambda_t] \bar{P}_t.$$

This plus our log assumption about $u(\cdot)$ yields

$$0 = \mathbb{E}_t \left\{ -\beta^{t-1} v'(L_t) L_t + \beta^t \frac{1}{Z_{t+1} L_{t+1} \bar{P}_{t+1}} \rho Z_t L_t \bar{P}_t \right\}.$$

If we assume that the c.i.a. condition always binds, then

$$\bar{P}_t = \frac{M_t(1 + \tau_t)}{Z_t L_t},$$

and we get that

$$0 = \mathbb{E}_t \left\{ -v'(L_t) L_t + \beta \frac{M_t(1 + \tau_t)}{M_{t+1}(1 + \tau_{t+1})} \rho \right\},$$

which simplifies to

$$0 = \mathbb{E}_t \left\{ -v'(L_t) L_t + \beta \frac{1}{(1 + \tau_{t+1})} \rho \right\}$$

Then, imposing our preference assumption for $v(\cdot)$ we get that

$$\mathbb{E}_t\{L_t^{1+\gamma}\} = \mathbb{E}_t \left\{ \frac{\beta \rho}{(1 + \tau_{t+1})} \right\}.$$

But remember, the household only gets to select its target level $\bar{L}_t$, and L_t is determined by (71). Putting this in we get that

$$\mathbb{E}_t \left\{ \left(\frac{(1 + \tau_t)}{(1 + \mathbb{E}\{\tau_t\})} \right)^{1+\gamma} \bar{L}_t^{1+\gamma} \right\} = \mathbb{E}_t \left\{ \frac{\beta \rho}{(1 + \tau_{t+1})} \right\},$$

or

$$\frac{\mathbb{E}_t\{(1 + \tau_t)^{1+\gamma}\}}{(1 + \mathbb{E}\{\tau_t\})^{1+\gamma}} \bar{L}_t^{1+\gamma} = \rho \beta \mathbb{E}_t \left\{ \frac{1}{(1 + \tau_{t+1})} \right\}. \tag{73}$$

To work further with this expression, keep in mind that since the deviation of net money growth from its mean $\bar{\tau}$ is given by

$$\tilde{\tau}_t = \rho_\tau \tilde{\tau}_{t-1} + \sigma_\tau \varepsilon_{\tau t},$$

it follows that

$$\tilde{\tau}_{t+1} = (\rho_\tau)^2 \tilde{\tau}_{t-1} + \rho_\tau \sigma_\tau \varepsilon_{\tau t} + \sigma_\tau \varepsilon_{\tau t+1}.$$

Thus, this expression can be further simplified to

$$\frac{\mathbb{E}_t \left\{ (1 + \bar{\tau} + \rho_\tau \tilde{\tau}_{t-1} + \sigma_\tau \varepsilon_{\tau t})^{1+\gamma} \right\}}{(1 + \bar{\tau} + \rho_\tau \tilde{\tau}_{t-1})^{1+\gamma}} \bar{L}_t^{1+\gamma}$$

$$= \rho \beta \mathbb{E}_t \left\{ \frac{1}{(1 + \bar{\tau} + (\rho_\tau)^2 \tilde{\tau}_{t-1} + \rho_\tau \sigma_\tau \varepsilon_{\tau t} + \sigma_\tau \varepsilon_{\tau t+1})} \right\}.$$

This expression has three interpretable pieces. The first is the distortion to labor arising from monopoly power, or ρ. The second is the future distortion arising from the growth rate of money between the period t and $t+1$ consumption markets, which is the numerator in the r.h.s. expression. This term has a known component, $1 + \bar{\tau} + (\rho_\tau)^2 \tilde{\tau}_{t-1}$, and a stochastic component, $\rho_\tau \sigma_\tau \varepsilon_{\tau t} + \sigma_\tau \varepsilon_{\tau t+1}$. The third piece is the effect of the period t growth rate of money on the realized level of labor effort in t. Here, the known component, $1 + \bar{\tau} + \rho_\tau \tilde{\tau}_{t-1}$, enters in symmetrically to the numerator and denominator. So the major novel component is the stochastic risk element arising from today's money shock, $\sigma_\tau \varepsilon_{\tau t}$.

This expression is fairly difficult to deal with given our current level of sophistication. Hence, we are going to adopt a simplification. Before doing so, we discuss the nature of this simplification.

Remark 16. *We often get model conditions that imply that the endogenous variable x is being set given an exogenous parameter θ, which is known, and another, ε, which is unknown. This leads to an equilibrium condition of the form*

$$\mathbb{E}\{F(x, \theta, \varepsilon) | \theta\} = 0.$$

In words, the equilibrium value $x(\theta)$ is being determined for each known value of θ, taking as given the distribution of ε, but not the realization. A standard approach to characterizing what is going to happen is to linearize F to make this condition easier to solve. To do so, consider solving for $\bar{x}(\theta)$ where

$$F(\bar{x}(\theta), \theta, \mathbb{E}\{\varepsilon\}) = 0.$$

This will give us a solution for each value of θ, where we are treating the expected value of ε, $\mathbb{E}\{\varepsilon\}$, as if it was known with certainty. Next, note that

$$F(x,\theta,\varepsilon) \simeq F(\bar{x}(\theta),\theta,\mathbb{E}\{\varepsilon\}) + F_x(\bar{x}(\theta),\theta,\mathbb{E}\{\varepsilon\})(x - \bar{x}(\theta))$$
$$+ F_\varepsilon(\bar{x}(\theta),\theta,\mathbb{E}\{\varepsilon\})(\varepsilon - \mathbb{E}\{\varepsilon\}).$$

In words, we are approximating our function at each value of θ around the point $(\bar{x}(\theta),\theta,\mathbb{E}\{\varepsilon\})$. Then, consider replacing the true value of F with the approximation in our original condition. This yields

$$\mathbb{E}\left\{ \begin{array}{c} F(\bar{x}(\theta),\theta,\mathbb{E}\{\varepsilon\}) \\ +F_x(\bar{x}(\theta),\theta,\mathbb{E}\{\varepsilon\})(x - \bar{x}(\theta)) \\ +F_\varepsilon(\bar{x}(\theta),\theta,\mathbb{E}\{\varepsilon\})(\varepsilon - \mathbb{E}\{\varepsilon\}) \end{array} \middle| \theta \right\} = 0.$$

But note that $F(\bar{x}(\theta),\theta,E\{\varepsilon\}) = 0$, so this term drops out. Then, note that

$$F_x(\bar{x}(\theta),\theta,\mathbb{E}\{\varepsilon\})(x - \bar{x}(\theta))$$

and

$$F_\varepsilon(\bar{x}(\theta),\theta,\mathbb{E}\{\varepsilon\})$$

do not depend on ε, just its expectation. Finally, note that we can pass the expectations operator through to get that

$$F_x(\bar{x}(\theta),\theta,\mathbb{E}\{\varepsilon\})(x - \bar{x}(\theta)) + F_\varepsilon(\bar{x}(\theta),\theta,\mathbb{E}\{\varepsilon\})\mathbb{E}\{(\varepsilon - \mathbb{E}\{\varepsilon\})|\theta\} = 0.$$

*But $\mathbb{E}\{(\varepsilon - \mathbb{E}\{\varepsilon\})|\theta\} = 0$, so we get that the solution is to set $x(\theta) = \bar{x}(\theta)$ for all θ. That is, we end up acting as if we believed that the expected value of ε was going to arise for sure. This is called **certainty equivalence** and comes about in any model where we rely on linear approximations.*

Assumption 1. *We are going to assume that all of the agents in our model act with certainty equivalence and hence treat expectations as if they were sure to arise in making their decisions. This assumption is only valid with a linear approximation, since the nonlinear aspects will bring in the variation of ε. We will ignore this henceforth.*

Given this assumption/simplification our expression can be boiled down to

$$\bar{L}_t^{1+\gamma} = \frac{\rho\beta}{(1 + \bar{\tau} + (\rho_\tau)^2 \tilde{\tau}_{t-1})}, \tag{74}$$

where

$$L_t = \left[1 + \frac{\sigma_\tau \varepsilon_{\tau t}}{1 + \bar{\tau} + \rho_\tau \tilde{\tau}_{t-1}} \right] \bar{L}_t. \tag{75}$$

The determination of the target labor effort level $\bar{L}_t$ reflects the distorting effects of inflation between t and $t + 1$, while the realized labor effort level, L_t, reflects the impact of the nominal demand surprise induced by the monetary inject at time t.

To get a feel for what this model implies for the realized levels of labor we will see given a money supply process, let's simplify things a bit and consider independent and identically distributed (i.i.d.) money growth rate shocks where

$$1 + \tau_t = 1 + \bar{\tau} + \sigma_\tau \varepsilon_{\tau,t}.$$

I set $\bar{\tau} = 0.1$, $\sigma_\tau = .03$, and I used a standard normal random number generator and drew some shocks in order to create figure 1. The target level of labor is roughly 0.89, which is the mean of realized values in the plot. As we can see, realized labor is essentially linear in the realized money growth rate, which is something that was implied by (71). Increasing $\bar{\tau}$ will lower this scatterplot because it will lower the target level of labor. Increasing the variance of the money growth rate shocks will spread things out along the plot line. We turn next to further exploring what our New Keynesian model says that we should see in the data.

Definition 1. *An* **impulse response function** *is constructed by assuming that $\tilde{\tau}_0 = 0$, and hence that $\tilde{\tau}_1 = \sigma_z \varepsilon$ for some normalized value of the initial value of the shock. Thereafter, all future shocks are taken to be zero and hence*

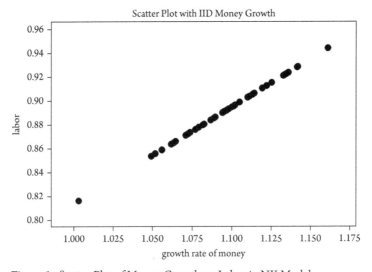

Figure 1. Scatter Plot of Money Growth vs. Labor in NK Model

$\tilde{\tau}_t = (\rho_\tau)^{t-1} \sigma_z \varepsilon_1$. *Plugging this sequence of deviations* $\{\tilde{\tau}_t\}_{t=1}^{T}$ *into our model allows us to trace out the implications of the initial shock for the predictions of the model. If we do this for labor, for example, this would be called the impulse response function of labor for a money shock.*

Impulse response functions are a nice way to understand the dynamic implications of a model. In the first period one gets the initial impact of the shock shutting down all other stochastic sources of time variation. Then the implications of that initial shock are traced out.

Exercise 16. *How does the impulse response to a monetary shock depend on the money supply process? To answer this question: for various values of the ρ_t and σ_τ trace out what happens if there is a one-unit innovation (i.e., $\varepsilon_1 = 1$) and no other shocks thereafter. Note that ρ_τ can be both negative and positive, but $\sigma_\varepsilon > 0$.*

We can also use our model to examine the implications for what we should see in the time series. To do this, we need to specify the stochastic processes for τ_t and g_t (i.e., $\bar{\tau}$, $\bar{g}$, ρ_τ, ρ_g, σ_τ, σ_g), along with our preference parameters γ and β.

Exercise 17. *Program up the model and then draw some innovation sequences $\{\varepsilon_{\tau t}\}$ and $\{\varepsilon_{gt}\}$, and simulate the model to see what it implies for the relationship between money, labor and prices. Then, you will need to carry out the simulation and analyze what you learned from them. How do the implications of our model stack up against some of the prior empirical results we reviewed. In particular, discuss the correlation between τ_t and L_t or Y_t.*

Exercise 18. *We want to construct the Phillips curves implied by our model and see how our Phillips curve changes as we change the mean growth rate of money, $\bar{\tau}$. To do this, we need to draw a sequence of money shocks $\varepsilon_{\tau t}$ and growth shocks ε_{gt}. Because P and L move exactly inverse to each other, plotting π against L does not work. So, plot τ against L. Do this for a mean growth rate of money of 2%, 6%, and 10%. Discuss how your Phillips curve—i.e., your scatter plot—changes. This exercise will help you understand the history in the next chapter.*

In doing this last exercise you may want to take advantage of the scatter plot feature in Matlab (called "scatter").

You can also use this basic model to think about what would happen during a period in which the public thought that the money supply process was one thing, while the actual process was another. This might be important if the government changed the process without telling people and it took a while for the public to catch on. Note that the parameters in the determination of $\bar{L}_t$ are the ones the public believes to be true. However, the ones in the determination of L_t are a combination of the two. To make that explicit, note that

$$L_t = \left[\frac{1 + \bar{\tau}^* + \rho_\tau^* \tilde{\tau}_{t-1} + \sigma_\tau^* \varepsilon_{\tau t}}{1 + \bar{\tau} + \rho_\tau \tilde{\tau}_{t-1}} \right] \bar{L}_t,$$

where $\bar{\tau}$ and ρ_τ reflect the public's beliefs while $(\bar{\tau}^*, \rho_\tau^*, \sigma_\tau^*)$ reflect the actual money supply process.

The Federal Reserve has sought to become more transparent over time. By this I mean that it ties to more clearly signal what it is going to be doing and why in the coming weeks and months. See this link for an extended discussion of this increased transparency and what it means: https://www.minneapolisfed.org/news-and-events/presidents-speeches/ toward-a-more-transparent-fomc

One way to think about modeling this change is to think that the Fed is actually telling households what the upcoming monetary shock is likely to be. In this regard, we can think of the shock ε_t as consisting of a preannounced component, ε_t^P, and an unannounced surprise component, ε_t^U. In this interpretation, the realized shock would be given by

$$\varepsilon_t = \alpha * \varepsilon_t^P + (1 - \alpha) * \varepsilon_t^U,$$

while α would govern the importance of the preannounced and the unannounced components given that both shocks are standard normals.

Exercise 19. *Show how the inclusion of preannounced and unannounced components to the monetary shock would change the impact of monetary policy. If the Fed was going to change α over time, in which direction would it want to change it and when, i.e., during crises or normal times?*

Remark 17. *If you experiment a bit, you will learn something very interesting about what you should expect to see in the data from our model's perspective. Start with assuming that the money shock is i.i.d. in which case we get that*

$$\bar{L}_t^{1+\gamma} = \frac{\rho \beta}{(1 + \bar{\tau})},$$

so target labor is a constant and realized labor is given by

$$L_t = \left[1 + \frac{\sigma_\tau \varepsilon_{\tau t}}{1 + \bar{\tau}} \right] \bar{L}_t.$$

Hence both money shocks and higher than average money growth move together, and money shocks raise output. However, if you make the growth rate of money fairly persistent, then τ_t will move around a lot because of the accumulated past money shocks and this can reverse the sign of the correlation between the money growth rate and labor. In fact, as $\rho_\tau \to 1$, the money growth rate becomes a random walk, and hence, the current shock becomes largely irrelevant. When that happens, the correlation between τ_t and L_t can become negative. Kind of wild!

4. STICKY PRICES OR STICKY WAGES?

In our current formulation we have assumed that it is prices that are preset. However, much of current New Keynesian analysis emphasizes wage stickiness. This is appealing in part because wages are often explicitly negotiated on an annual or multiyear basis. To see how our analysis might accommodate this change, consider the following variant of our model.

Each household works in one particular industry, labeled industry k. However, it receives a predetermined wage $W(k)$. At the same time each household owns an industry j, where it sells output and hires labor again at a predetermined wage $W(j)$. To keep things simple, assume that the wage is set prior to the realization of τ_t according to some protocol that we don't need to specify. The household is optimally choosing the price on the product line it owns, line j, after the realization of τ_t.

Since I wish to just consider the price-setting decision and how that will affect output, we need only consider a two-period version of our model.

$$\max_{\{C_t, P_t(k), M_{t+1}, B_{t+1}\}_{t=1,2}} u(C_1) - v\left(D\left(\frac{P_1(k)}{\bar{P}_1}\right)/Z_1\right) + \beta V(M_2, B_2)$$

subject to

$$M_1 + T_1 \geq \bar{P}_1 C_1 \text{ and}$$

$$D\left(\frac{P_1(j)}{\bar{P}_1}\right)[P_1(j) - W_1(j)/Z_1] + D\left(\frac{P_1(k)}{\bar{P}_1}\right)W_1(k)/Z_1$$

$$+ [M_1 - \bar{P}_1 C_1] + B_1 + T_1 \geq M_2 + q_1 B_2.$$

The optimal choice of the price is the solution to a very simple optimality condition since this term only shows up in the budget constraint. It is given by

$$D'\left(\frac{P_1(j)}{\bar{P}_1}\right)\frac{[P_1(j) - W_1(j)/Z_1]}{\bar{P}_1} + D\left(\frac{P_1(j)}{\bar{P}_1}\right) = 0.$$

If we once again make use of our marginal demand result (66), we get that

$$D\left(\frac{P_1(j)}{\bar{P}_1}\right)\frac{1}{\rho-1}P_1(j)^{-1}\left[P_1(j)-W_1(j)/Z_1\right]+D\left(\frac{P_1(j)}{\bar{P}_1}\right)=0,$$

or

$$P_1(j)=\frac{1}{\rho}W_1(j)/Z_1.$$

This is a simple markup rule over marginal cost, which implies that prices will only change if the wage does. Hence, wage stickiness here translates into price stickiness.

Additionally, if wages were set in a manner similar to competitive prices, we would get something like

$$W_t=\omega\mathbb{E}\{Z_t\bar{P}_t\}$$

for some factor ω (which to be consistent would need to be $\omega=\rho$). In this case, our model with sticky wages would work essentially the same as our model with sticky prices.[4]

---

4. The classic paper on sticky wages is Taylor, John B. "Aggregate dynamics and staggered contracts." Journal of Political Economy 88.1 (1980): 1–23.

## 11

Inflation, Output, and the Phillips Curve

Robert King has a very nice discussion of the intellectual and empirical history of the perceived tradeoff between inflation and unemployment, and how that influenced both research and policy in the United States during the post-WWII period through the 1990s. I draw on that to construct the following summary.[1]

In the late 1950s A.W. Phillips examined the empirical relationship between the change in wages and the unemployment level. The relationship he computed was somewhat complicated but was meant to capture the relationship between wage inflation and unemployment over several business cycles. Empirically, he found that there was a negative relationship. In 1960, P. Samuelson and R. Solow examined the relationship in the United States between average hourly earnings and the annual average unemployment rate over a period that King hypothesizes was 1890–1950s. After arguing that special factors affected the 1930s and the WWII period, they argued that the bulk of their observations suggested a negative relationship, much like Phillips had found. These findings led researchers to try to develop Keynesian models that could capture this relationship through dynamic demand factors. However, Samuelson and Solow also raised concerns about the long-run stability of this tradeoff as expectations gradually adjusted.

The Kennedy-Johnson administration sought to implement these new insights in order to keep unemployment low and output closer to its "potential level," which was defined as the output level associated with full employment. Full

---

1. King, Robert G. "The Phillips curve and US macroeconomic policy: snapshots, 1958–1996." Economic Quarterly-Federal Reserve Bank of Richmond 94.4 (2008): 311.

Monetary and Fiscal Policy through a DSGE Lens. Harold L. Cole, Oxford University Press (2020).

employment was taken to be the level consistent with normal structural or frictional unemployment and was thought to be around 4%. This period featured a fall in unemployment and a rise in inflation. The rise in inflation was initially attributed to a wage-price spiral that emerged from having output above "potential" and was thought to be self-enforcing and hence difficult to arrest. However, the rise in long-run inflation eventually led to a major rethinking of the empirical relationship behind the Phillips curve. The fundamental question was whether or not there was a stable long-run Phillips curve.

In the late 1960s, both M. Friedman and E. Phelps argued that the long-run Phillips curve was vertical. Thus, they both concluded that one could not permanently decrease unemployment using inflation. Friedman argued that there was a natural rate of unemployment determined by the real economy. He argued that workers evaluate their employment opportunities and how much labor to ultimately supply based on their estimate of the purchasing power of the wages they were being offered. He concluded that inflation could only temporarily influence this level until workers' expectations about inflation caught up with the change in the path of prices. Phelps (1967) set out the basic form of the price-adjustment equations that was to become widely accepted

$$P_t - P_{t-1} = \pi_t = -\beta(u_t - u^*) + \pi_t^e,$$

where u^* was Friedman's natural rate of unemployment and π^e was expected inflation. Under this relationship, if inflation is exactly as expected, then unemployment is equal to the natural rate. $u_t < u^*$ only if $\pi_t > \pi_t^e$; and there was surprise inflation.[2]

Phelps added to this relationship 1 for the determination of inflation expectations based on adaptive expectations, or

$$\pi_t^e = \theta \pi_{t-1} + (1 - \theta)\pi_{t-1}^e.$$

Substituting in for lagged expectations yields

$$\pi_t^e = \theta \pi_{t-1} + (1 - \theta)[\theta \pi_{t-2} + (1 - \theta)\pi_{t-2}^e].$$

Continuing to substitute yields

$$\pi_t^e = \theta \sum_{j=1}^{\infty}(1 - \theta)^{j-1}\pi_{t-j}.$$

2. See Phelps, Edmund S. "Phillips curves, expectations of inflation and optimal unemployment over time." Economica (1967): 254–281. See also Milton Friedman. "The role of monetary policy." American Economic Review 58.1 (1968): 1–17.

Thus, under Phelps' rule inflation was a weighted average of past inflation rates, with more weight being given to more recent observations. If inflation was constant at some level $\bar{\pi}$, then

$$\pi_t^e = \theta \sum_{j=1}^{\infty} (1-\theta)^{j-1} \bar{\pi} = \frac{\theta}{1-(1-\theta)} \bar{\pi} = \bar{\pi},$$

and expectations would eventually catch up to this fact. Note however that the period of adjustment could be quite long if θ isn't very close to 1. On the other hand, with θ close to one, inflationary expectations would be bouncing around pretty violently if inflation was just an i.i.d. draw from a high and a low rate.

This accelerationist model implied that only surprises affected unemployment and that when actual and expected inflation coincided, the Phillips curve was vertical.

There were a series of attempts to estimate a relationship such as

$$P_t - P_{t-1} = \pi_t = -\beta(u_t - u^*) + \alpha \pi_t^e$$

with various assumptions about the formation of expectations. These estimates suggested that $\alpha < 1$, and hence a long-run stable tradeoff was possible. However, it was eventually noted (i.e., by R. Lucas and T. Sargent), that if inflation itself was persistent (because it moved slowly in response to the underlying shocks) then this persistence could be reflected in expectations and through them in α. Hence, α was likely to be an estimate of the persistence of inflation and not the impact coefficient for expectations in Phelps' relationship.[3]

The rational expectations school of thought, led by Lucas, went on to argue that the formation of expectations was going to reflect the actual stochastic processes driving the variables being forecast. This view implied that changes in these processes brought on by, say, policy would eventually be reflected in expectations. This reasoning implied that expectations formation equations were not structural and hence would not remain invariant across different policy regimes. Lucas (1972) constructed a general equilibrium model that featured rational expectations and a short-run expectational Phillips curve, consistent with the rational expectations view as the gradual increase in the estimates of α over the period from 1966 to 1980.[4] During this period the average inflation rate was also rising.

3. See Sargent, Thomas J. "A note on the 'accelerationist' controversy." Journal of Money, Credit and Banking 3.3 (1971): 721–725.

4. Lucas Jr, Robert E. "Expectations and the neutrality of money." Journal of Economic Theory 4.2 (1972): 103–124.

One response to the rational expectations critique was to move away from the simple fixed Phillips curve to a model in which wage and price dynamics were driven by the "tightness" of the labor market. Modiglinani et al. suggested that unemployment below a certain level was likely to lead to price increases, and the reverse above. This led them to propose the NAIRU model in which

$$\pi_t = \pi_{t-1} - \beta(u_t - u^n),$$

where u^n was named the nonaccelerating inflation rate of unemployment. Unemployment above this rate would lead π to decrease and below this rate to increase.[5]

One can think of the NAIRU model as combining an implicit model of learning with the natural rate model. From Phelps' model we get that

$$\pi_t - \pi_t^e = -\beta(u_t - u^*).$$

If we assume that $\theta = 1$, and hence expected inflation is

$$\pi_{t+1}^e = \pi_t,$$

then the relationship in period $t + 1$ is given by

$$\pi_{t+1} - \pi_t = -\beta(u_{t+1} - u^*),$$

which gives us the NAIRU relationship.

By the end of the 1970s, the combination of high inflation and high unemployment had led to the general abandonment of the long-run Phillips curve. However, it was still widely believed that there was a short-run tradeoff between inflation and unemployment, and that this tradeoff would make lowering the high inflation rates of the late 1970s very costly, implying a prlonged period of high unemployment. The rational expectations school criticized this view, arguing that changes in policy could, if credible, lead to fairly rapid changes in beliefs. Sargent examined the ends of four major hyperinflations and showed that inflation had been rapidly lowered (coupled with monetary and fiscal reforms) without a dramatic and sustained fall in employment, as implied by the Phillips curve trade-off.[6]

5. Modigliani, Franco, and Lucas Papademos. "Targets for monetary policy in the coming year." Brookings Papers on Economic Activity 1975.1 (1975): 141–165.

6. Sargent, Thomas J. "The ends of four big inflations." Inflation: Causes and effects. University of Chicago Press, 1982. 41–98.

Paul Volcker became chairman of the Federal Reserve in 1979 and instituted a tight money regime designed to lower inflation. The unemployment rate rose during the period in which the inflation rate was being lowered. However, G. Mankiw estimated that the tradeoff faced between inflation and unemployment—the so-called sacrifice ratio—was 1.5% (this is the temporary increase in the unemployment rate associated with a 1% decline in inflation). This was roughly half the level that had been anticipated by the prior analysis based on an estimate of the Phillips curve tradeoff. The difference has been ascribed in part to the credibility of Volcker, a well known inflation hawk.

Another intellectual response that has arisen to this history is the neo-Keynesian school, which emphasizes temporary price rigidities within a largely rational expectations framework. Mankiw (1985) emphasized small menu costs and how this could lead to thresholds that put an upper and lower bound on how far the firm would allow its price to vary from the optimal price, and O. Blanchard and N. Kiyotaki (1987) developed a price-setting model in which firms had to set their prices in advance.[7]

7. Mankiw, N. Gregory. "Small menu costs and large business cycles: A macroeconomic model of monopoly." The Quarterly Journal of Economics 100.2 (1985): 529–537. Also, Blanchard, Olivier Jean, and Nobuhiro Kiyotaki. "Monopolistic competition and the effects of aggregate demand." The American Economic Review (1987): 647–666.

## 12

The Great Depression through the Lens of Our Model

The Great Depression was probably the major economic event of the 20th century. It had profound consequences for a range of countries, including the United States. It was instrumental in creating macroeconomics as a special field. It also shaped the view that the market economy was fairly unstable. This then led to the notion that an important role of government was to help correct this instability. Here we want to examine the extent to which our New Keynesian model can help us understand this crucial period.

To set the stage for examining the Great Depression, note that World War I came to a close around the end of 1918. There was a period of some economic turmoil before the long boom of the "Roaring '20s". During this period there was widespread electrification throughout much of the U.S. and the automobile came to be widely adopted. In the first panel of Figure 1 I have plotted industrial production in the United States between 1921 and 1939.[1] In that figure, you can see the big boom in industrial output that occurred during the 1920s. You can also see how that period of prosperity ended with the huge downturn at the beginning of the Great Depression.

Industrial production, which is a measure of output for which we have data at a monthly frequency during the 1920s and 1930s, peaks in July of 1929 at 8.2, before falling sharply during the rest of the year to end at 7.2 in December of 1929.

---

1. Source is Board of Governors of the Federal Reserve System (US), Industrial Production Index [INDPRO], retrieved from FRED, Federal Reserve Bank of St. Louis.

Monetary and Fiscal Policy through a DSGE Lens. Harold L. Cole, Oxford University Press (2020).
© Oxford University Press. DOI: 10.1093/oso/9780190076030.001.0001

Figure 1. The Roaring, 20s and the Great Depression in the U.S.
SOURCE: Board of Governors of the Fed. Res. System (U.S.)
Retrieved from FRED, Federal Reserve Bank of St. Louis.

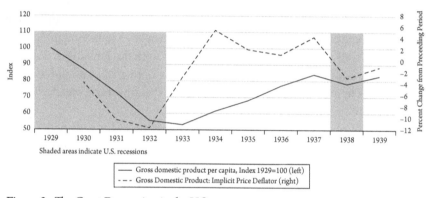

Figure 2. The Great Depression in the U.S.
SOURCE: U.S. Bureau of Economic Analysis
Retrieved from FRED, Federal Reserve Bank of St. Louis.

Industrial productivity continues to fall sharply in the years that follow, before bottoming out at 3.9 in August of 1932. It finally rebounds sharply starting after March of 1933.

We turn next to examining in more detail what happened in the 1930s. Our model suggests a tight connection with money and productivity growth and output. The exact analog of money in the data is always a little tricky since our money is held purely for transaction purposes and not as a means of saving. For that reason, we focus on output per capita and the price level in the next figure. Figure 2 plots the level of an index of output per capita and the percentage change in the GDP deflator.[2] Both of these series are available annually and

2. Source is the U.S. Bureau of Economic Analysis, Gross domestic product per capita [A939RC0A052NBEA] and Implicit Price Deflator [GDPDEF], retrieved from FRED, Federal Reserve Bank of St. Louis.

only beginning in 1929. (This is for official sources. Economic historians have constructed earlier estimates.)

From Figure 2 we can see that overall output falls sharply between the start of the Depression in 1929 to its trough in 1933, before recovering sharply afterward. Note, however, that output is not back to its 1929 level by the end of the decade. This is particularly negative, since we are not even taking out the standard 2% growth that we normally see on average.

Also in Figure 2 we can see the sharp drop in prices that occurred during this period. This is the great deflation that has forever afterward made deflation a bad word in policymakers' minds. The sharp fall in prices between 1929 and 1933 is particularly striking since the simultaneous fall in output should have raised prices (at least according to both our model and conventional economic theory). The fall in prices was not driven by deliberate policy actions. Instead, the waves of banking panics that took place during this period led to large withdrawals of money from the banking system. This in turn led to a large reduction in the base money to overall money multiplier. This, coupled with the limitations imposed on monetary policy by the desire to maintain the peg to gold as part of the gold standard that prevailed during the initial phase of the downturn, meant that the money supply collapsed as a result.

In 1933, Franklin Roosevelt became president. One of his early actions was to take the United States off the gold standard. This was done to end the long deflation and to increase the money supply in order to raise prices. In the figure we can see the gradual rise in the price level associated with this policy. However, note how modest this increase in the price level is, especially when compared to the sharp deflation that preceded it. Another factor to keep in mind here is that this modest inflation was widely anticipated after the United States left the gold standard.[3]

This rendition of the facts about the Great Depression suggests that our basic New Keynesian model may be able to account for some of the major economic

Table 1. SOME DATA ON THE GREAT DEPRESSION

Series	1929	1930	1931	1932	1933	1934	1935	1936	1937	1938
Output	100.0	87.4	78.1	65.2	61.9	64.6	68.1	74.9	76.0	70.6
Money Stock		46.60	45.73	42.69	36.05	32.22	34.36	39.07	43.48	45.68	45.51
Output per Hour	100.0	95.3	95.2	89.4	84.8	90.3	94.8	93.7	95.1	94.6
Total Private Hours	100.0	91.5	82.8	72.4	70.8	68.7	71.4	75.8	79.5	71.7
Price Level	100.0	96.8	87.9	78.2	76.5	83.0	84.6	85.0	89.1	87.0

3. The *New York Times* headline of April 20, 1933 announcing President Roosevelt's action read: "Gold Standard Dropped for the Present to Lift Prices and Aid Our Trade Position: Plans for Controlled Inflation Drafted." See New York Times Archive for a picture of this headline.

events that occurred. To examine this possibility, some key data from the Great Depression are presented in Table 1. All of the data are from an article I wrote with Lee Ohanian in *The Great Depressions of the Twentieth Century* which was edited by Timothy Kehoe and Edward Prescott. The data in that volume are all online at https://www.greatdepressionsbook.com/.[4]

The first series in the table is output. This series is per adult, which means that output is divided by the size of the adult population. Hence, we do not need to worry about the impact of population changes over time. Also, it has been detrended, which here means that a 1.98% rate of growth, the average growth we typically see in the U.S., has been taken out of output. Finally, the series was normalized to 100 in 1929. These adjustments are made to all of the series for comparability. In Table 1, we can see how output falls sharply between 1929 and 1933. We can also see that although it begins to rebound in 1934, it never really gets very close to its original level. This is part of the reason why this period is called the Great Depression.

The next series in Table 1 is Friedman and Schwartz's measure of the money stock. This series is not detrended or normalized. We can see that it declines sharply between 1929 and 1933, before recovering almost to its original level by 1938.

Since we do not have capital, output per hour seems like a natural measure of the productivity variable Z in our model. From the table we can see that productivity falls a great deal between 1929 and 1933, before rebounding thereafter. Normal growth in productivity has been taken out of this series. So, the fact that output per hour is back fairly close to 100 by 1937 indicates that the bulk of the productivity decline was over by this point. This contrasts sharply with the behavior in output.

The next series in the table is total private hours worked. This is normalized by the adult population. This variable seems like the natural analog to labor or L in our model. One of the striking aspects of the hours series is the sharp decline between 1929 and 1933. Another aspect to note is that private hours actually continue to decline in 1934, and only really begin to rebound in 1935. Additionally, note that the overall recovery in hours is extremely weak and that at the end of the decade hours are down 30%. This continues into 1939 when hours are down 25%.

The final series in our table is the price level. This is a tricky series for our model to match up to. First, we are not allowing for any sort of elasticity in money demand and that is clearly a major missing link. Second, we make no distinction

---

4. See Cole, Harold L., and Lee E. Ohanian. "A second look at the US Great Depression from a neoclassical perspective." *Great Depressions of the Twentieth Century*. Minneapolis: Federal Reserve Bank of Minneapolis (2007): 21–58.

between output and consumption in our model, since the two are equal. Later, when we add capital, we will want to think that investment goods do not require cash. This suggests that this too is a major issue for our model. Despite all this, we can hope that our model is roughly correct in its predictions with respect to prices.

1. WHAT DOES OUR MODEL SAY?

We want to examine the implications of our New Keynesian model for this period. Recall the key equations of that model. There is the target labor condition,

$$\bar{L}_t^{1+\gamma} = \frac{\rho\beta}{(1 + \bar{\tau} + (\rho_\tau)^2 \tilde{\tau}_{t-1})},$$

and the realized level of labor condition

$$L_t = \left[1 + \frac{\sigma_\tau \varepsilon_{\tau t}}{1 + \bar{\tau} + \rho_\tau \tilde{\tau}_{t-1}}\right] \bar{L}_t.$$

Given this, the level of output is simply $Y_t = Z_t L_t$ and the price level is $P_t = M_t(1 + \tau_t)/Z_t L_t$.

One simplifying feature of our model is that productivity does not affect labor. So, Z_t is just something that affects output once we have determined labor. In thinking about the data, we can set Z_t to simply be the output per hour series that we see in Table 1.

Turn next to money. Given an assumption about $\bar{\tau}$, ρ_τ, and σ_τ, we can use the money supply series to infer the sequence of shocks $\{\varepsilon_{\tau t}\}$. Given this sequence of shocks and the money supply process we assumed, we can determine $\bar{L}_t$ and L_t.

$$L_t = \left[\frac{\rho\beta}{(1 + \bar{\tau} + (\rho_\tau)^2 \tilde{\tau}_{t-1})}\right]^{1/(1+\gamma)} \left[1 + \frac{\sigma_\tau \varepsilon_{\tau t}}{1 + \bar{\tau} + \rho_\tau \tilde{\tau}_{t-1}}\right]$$

Given this, we can determine output and prices.

Exercise 20. *Write a computer code to compute the outcomes predicted by our New Keynesian model. Discuss the successes and failures of that model. Be careful to recognize that this is a pretty simplistic version of such a model. Therefore, you want to analyze things in pretty broad strokes.*

The results that we get will be sensitive to the persistence of the money supply growth rate we assume. If, we thought that growth rates were i.d.d. and that the expected growth rate was roughly 0, then it would seem like there was a surprise fall in prices of about 3% in 1930, another surprise fall of about 9% in 1931 and 1932, and a final surprise fall of 2% in 1933. If on the other hand, we thought that the growth rate of money was highly persistent so the anticipated growth rate tomorrow was equal to today's rate, then we get a very different picture: a surprise fall of 3% in 1930, followed by a surprise fall of 6% in 1931, no surprise in 1932, a positive surprise of 7% in 1933.

These issues are further magnified by what we take the period length to be for price setting. In the above discussion, I took it to be one year. Once could imagine it being shorter, especially in response to the large changes in prices we saw, or longer, which would make the implied output fall larger. But, of course, the measured price level fell so prices cannot be too rigid. One factor that might help our model is to think in terms of rigid or sticky wages, which do seemed to have fallen slower than prices in many sectors, rather than rigid or sticky prices.

2. PONDERING OUR RESULTS

Our model provides one answer as to the contribution of the combination of deflation and the fall in productivity to the fall in output between 1929 and 1933. However, one can see almost immediately that our model will struggle to account for the very poor recovery after 1933. In particular, the modest levels of inflation we see from that point on, coupled with the strong rebound in productivity, leads our model to predict an almost complete recovery in output and labor. But this is far from what we see in the data graphed in Figure 3.[5]

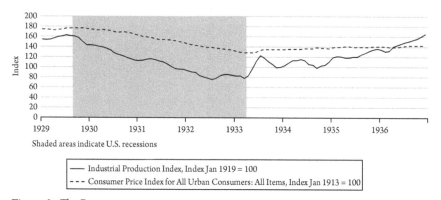

Shaded areas indicate U.S. recessions

> —— Industrial Production Index, Index Jan 1919 = 100
> - - - Consumer Price Index for All Urban Consumers: All Items, Index Jan 1913 = 100

Figure 3. The Recovery
SOURCE: BLS, Board of Governors
Retrieved from FRED, Federal Reserve Bank of St. Louis.

5. Source is Board of Governors of the Federal Reserve System (US), Industrial Production Index [INDPRO], and U.S. Bureau of Labor Statistics, Consumer Price Index for All Urban Consumers: All Items [CPIAUCNS], retrieved from FRED, Federal Reserve Bank of St. Louis.

This may seem surprising, since Keynesians have often argued that both the downturn and the recovery can be understood through nominal frictions. They would argue that the rebound in output after 1933 is due to FDR's restoring confidence in the banking system and generating a positive inflation rate once he took the United States off the gold standard.

To sort out this second claim it is useful to examine the timing of prices and output right around the peak and trough of the Great Depression. Unfortunately, we do not have a good high-frequency measure of overall output. The best we have is industrial production, and it has serious coverage limitations. We do have a fairly good high-frequency measure of final goods: the consumer price index.

In looking at both the downturn and the recovery, it's interesting to note that industrial production turns down before prices, as measured by the CPI, do. It also turns up several months before prices, as measured by the CPI, do.[6]

Another troubling aspect of the recovery from a simple New Keynesian perspective is that private hours continue to decline between 1933 and 1934. Manufacturing hours do rise slightly from 56.1% of their 1929 level in 1933 to 58.4% in 1934. Total employment-adult-population also recovers very slightly, from 78.6% of its 1929 level in 1933 to 83.7% of its level in 1934. However, the employment numbers are probably affected by the fact that work sharing was a prominent feature of FDR's policies. All in all, the evidence of the role of a nominal demand stimulus is surprisingly weak. This evidence becomes even weaker if one takes account of the fact that the inflation ushered in by FDR's leaving the gold standard was widely anticipated.

It is worth noting that there is historical data for the United States from around this time period, which suggests a modest reaction in output to deflation, probably more in line with the predictions of our model. After World War I, the United States experienced a sharp deflation as the country returned to the gold standard, which had been abandoned during the war. Measures of the price level suggest that prices fell 20% between 1919 and 1921. During this same period, measures of output suggest that detrended output per capita fell 6% in 1920 and only recovered by 2% in 1921.[7] The two-year fall in prices works out to be roughly

---

6. One standard response to this is to point to the wholesale price index which does turn up with industrial production. However, it is important to note that this index includes prices of goods at all stages of production. Commodity prices fell very sharply during the downturn, more sharply than the prices of final goods in many cases. Hence any recovery in production would be likely to led to a rise in their relative price. But this could happen prior to any rise in final goods prices. Moreover, the logic of Keynesianism is that a rise in final good demand from more money raises final output, dragging up output lower down the production chain.

7. See Cole, Harold L., and Lee E. Ohanian. "A second look at the US Great Depression from a neoclassical perspective." *Great Depressions of the Twentieth Century*. Minneapolis: Federal Reserve Bank of Minneapolis (2007): 21–58.

10% per year. This suggests a 10% fall in output in the first year, which is not too far from what we saw. If we then assume that the fall in the second year was at least partially anticipated, it is easy to rationalize the partial recovery in output in the data.

One can also point to a number of other policies implemented by FDR that may have had an important role in stimulating the recovery. This includes restoring confidence in the banking system through an initial bank holiday accompanied by a rigorous examination of the balance sheets of the surviving banks, along with the Glass-Steagall Act which separated banks into commercial banks and the more speculative investment banks. FDR also made the stock market more transparent by creating the Securities and Exchange Commission (SEC) and helped stabilize the housing market by creating Fannie Mae.

The weakness in the recovery, especially with respect to labor input is puzzling. In joint work with Lee Ohanian, I have argued that an important component in understanding the weak recovery from the trough of the Great Depression was many of the elements of the New Deal itself. These include a range of efforts to make both labor and goods market much less competitive. The policies deliberately raise the wages of workers by an amazing degree while offering firms a timeout from antitrust enforcement.[8]

8. Cole, Harold L., and Lee E. Ohanian. "New Deal policies and the persistence of the Great Depression: A general equilibrium analysis." Journal of Political Economy 112.4 (2004): 779–816.

## 13

Liquidity Effects and Interest Rates

The standard method by which central banks take policy actions is through open market operations. In these operations they either buy (or sell) government bonds. This involves paying for the bonds with reserves (or getting paid in reserves). This in turn increases (decreases) reserves held by the banking system. As a result, both reserves and the outstanding supply of government debt are affected. Changes in the level of reserves affect the "price" of these reserves, which is the interest rate charged on them in the interbank lending market. This interest rate is called the federal funds rate. For this reason, actual policy is often measured in terms of their impact on the federal funds rate.

The conventional wisdom about this sort of open market operation is that an open market operation that increases reserves is thought to increase the liquidity of these markets, and thereby to lower rates, particularly the fed funds rate. The decrease in rates is thought to encourage economic activity, particularly investment. As we can see from Figure 1, the central bank has varied the fed funds rate in the United States a great deal, and it is currently at a very low level by historical standards.[1]

What do monetary policy shocks, which for us are actual money supply shocks, do in our models? Our basic model implies that an increase in the money supply raises rates because of concerns about future inflation. In our New Keynesian model, with our changes in timing, and our information and price-setting assumptions, they raise output initially by increasing labor effort in period t, the period

1. Source is Board of Governors of the Federal Reserve System (US), Effective Federal Funds Rate [FEDFUNDS], retrieved from FRED.

Monetary and Fiscal Policy through a DSGE Lens. Harold L. Cole, Oxford University Press (2020).
© Oxford University Press. DOI: 10.1093/oso/9780190076030.001.0001

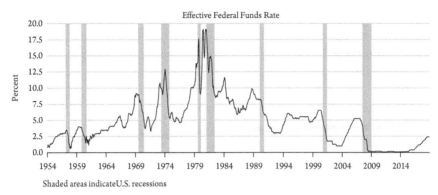

Figure 1. Effective Federal Funds Rate
SOURCE: Board of Governors of the Fed. Res. System (U.S.)
Retrieved from FRED, Federal Reserve Bank of St. Louis.

of the shock. They also increase inflation, measured as P_{t+1}/P_t, and as a result depress the bond price q_t. (If these shocks are persistent, then that persistence slightly depresses future labor effort and output, and can have a slight impact on bond prices too.)

What does the literature say about the impact of policy shocks? This is a tricky question since the impact will, as we have already seen, depend on the extent to which the central bank's action is a surprise. In practice, the actions of the central bank reflect its assessment of conditions and the future trajectory of the economy. Hence, disentangling the anticipated response and the surprise components of policy actions is key to answering this question. In "Monetary Policy Shocks: What Have We Learned and to What End?" Christiano, Eichenbaum and Evans survey and assess the literature on this topic. When they seek to estimate the central bank's policy rule and use that estimated rule to derive policy shocks, here is what they report:[2]

> The main consequences of a contractionary FF [Fed Funds] policy shock can be summarized as follows. First, there is a persistent rise in the federal funds rate ... This finding is consistent with the presence of a strong liquidity effect.... After a delay of 2 quarters, there is a sustained decline in real GDP.... The GDP deflator is flat for roughly a year and a half after which it declines.

The main takeaway here is that a *decrease* in reserves (which means a decrease in the monetary base) *increases* the fed funds rate and leads to a *contraction* in output. In terms of the movement in the monetary base and output, this is consistent with

2. Christiano et al. in chapter 2 of the *Handbook of Macroeconomics*, volume 1(A), 1999, pages 65–148.

our New Keynesian model if we squint a bit, since there is quite a delay here. But this is the opposite of what we have going on between interest rates (at least as measured by the fed funds rate) and output. In our model increases in interest rates come about primarily through higher anticipated inflation and this in turn discourages current effort.

We are interested in trying to see if our model can be adapted so as to include this kind of mechanism. To do so, we will need to change our model of workers/firms to have them use cash. This way, injections of cash can "lubricate" the wheels of commerce and, as a result, lower interest rates and raise output. It will turn out to be a great simplification to assume that money growth rates are i.i.d.[3]

1. NEW GOODS MARKET

Remember that in our old model each household splits into a buyer and a seller before heading off to the goods market. Now we will assume that each seller has to hire other sellers to produce her goods while, at the same time, selling her own labor to other sellers. Thus, each seller has become a combination of a worker and a producer. We will also assume that the seller must pay cash to these other workers before she can sell the goods she has produced. As a result, each seller faces a cash-in-advance constraint with respect to the workers she hires. We will denote the amount of cash that the seller has by N_t. We will assume that she can either pay for her workers using her own funds or borrow (lend) funds D_t from (to) other sellers at interest rate R_t. These borrowed funds are to be paid back in the asset market at the end of the period. The c.i.a. constraint of the seller is given by

$$N_t + D_t \geq W_t \hat{L}_t,$$

where $\hat{L}_t$ denotes the amount of labor she hires. Note here that $D_t > 0$ means that the seller borrowed funds and $D_t < 0$ means that she lends funds. The total amount of funds with which the seller shows up in the asset market is given by

$$W_t L_t + P_t Z_t \hat{L}_t + N_t - R_t D_t - w_t \hat{L}_t,$$

where $W_t L_t$ denotes the amount she earns from working for others, $P_t Z_t \hat{L}_t$ denotes the amount she earns from selling her produced goods, $w_t \hat{L}_t$ denotes the

3. The original formulation of this sort of model is Fuerst, Timothy S. "Liquidity, loanable funds, and real activity." Journal of Monetary Economics 29.1 (1992): 3–24. See also Christiano, Lawrence J., and Martin Eichenbaum. Liquidity effects and the monetary transmission mechanism. No. w3974. National Bureau of Economic Research, 1992.

amount she pays her workers, and $R_t D_t$ denotes her loan costs (and $1 + R_t$ is the gross interest rate).

Consider increasing $\hat{L}_t$ by $d\hat{L}_t$ and generating the funds to do this by borrowing $dD_t = W_t d\hat{L}_t$. Clearly, this is a feasible thing to do and the net impact on the seller's funds is

$$P_t Z_t d\hat{L}_t - W_t d\hat{L}_t - R_t W_t d\hat{L}_t.$$

So, if this expression is positive, the seller should hire more workers, and if it is negative she should hire fewer workers. Thus, it must equal 0, or

$$P_t Z_t - (1 + R_t) W_t = 0. \tag{76}$$

This is our first key equation.

Next, consider the decision of whether the seller should use her funds N_t to hire workers or lend funds to someone else. If she uses her funds to hire workers she hires

$$\hat{L}_t = \frac{N_t}{W_t}$$

and earns

$$P_t Z_t \frac{N_t}{W_t}.$$

If she lends these funds she earns

$$(1 + R_t) N_t.$$

For her to be indifferent, these numbers must be equal, and this just implies (76) again.

If we look at (76), it says that the gap between wages and earnings is equal to the interest rate, or

$$\frac{P_t Z_t}{W_t} = 1 + R_t. \tag{77}$$

Note that if the l.h.s. ratio were less than one, no seller would hire a worker and no one would lend out funds. Hence, we get the following: The interest rate is determined by (77) and this ratio is bounded below by 1.

What happens if the amount of money N_t is so big that the c.i.a. constraint does not bind. It follows that no one will have to pay any interest on money, or $R_t = 0$.

But, in this case, competition among the sellers to hire workers will bid up wages to the point where a seller just breaks even on her workers, or $P_t Z_t = W_t$.

We are now ready to characterize the equilibrium outcomes in the goods market conditional on the amount of labor that a seller wants to work L_t and the price level P_t. Because we have a representative agent model, it follows that $L_t = \hat{L}_t$ and no one lends any money, so $D_t = 0$. Hence, we get the following characterization of the production market.

Proposition 2. *Given the equilibrium level of labor L_t, if the c.i.a. constraint holds as an equality, then*

$$\frac{N_t}{L_t} = W_t \text{ and } \frac{P_t Z_t}{W_t} = 1 + R_t.$$

If the c.i.a. condition is slack, then $R_t = 0$, and $P_t Z_t = W_t$.

Remark 18. *We are discussing the equilibrium of a linear model here. In this linear model the seller/producer is exactly breaking even on each worker she hires, which is another way of saying she is completely indifferent between hiring many or hiring 0. In this case, the allocation of workers among the different seller/producers is not pinned down. We could modify the model by assuming that production was subject to decreasing returns-to-scale as in*

$$P_t Z_t \left(\hat{L}_t\right)^\gamma \text{ where } 0 < \gamma < 1.$$

This would give us a f.o.c. that would pin down employment given $(1 + R_t)W_t$, and it would be equal across all sellers. However, the extra insight that we get from this does not seem worth the complication. So we will simply take it as a convention that each seller hires an equal number of workers.

2. HOUSEHOLD'S PROBLEM IN THE REVISED MODEL

Our households start the period with M_t units of money. We are going to assume that they always split their money holding into χM_t units going with the buyer and $(1 - \chi)M_t$ units going with the seller. The household at this point knows both the productivity shock g_t, and hence the productivity level $Z_t = (1 + g_t)Z_{t-1}$. It also knows the current monetary injection $T_t = \tau_t \bar{M}_{t-1}$, where $\bar{M}_{t-1}$ is the money supply at the beginning of the period. This monetary injection will be received by the seller on her way to the goods market, and hence $N_t = (1 - \chi)M_t + \tau_t \bar{M}_{t-1}$.[4]

---

4. Remember that our timing is a bit strained here between the household's beginning of period money holdings M_t and the beginning of period aggregate money stock, which is $\bar{M}_{t-1}$ before

The seller's c.i.a. constraint is

$$(1 - \chi)M_t + \tau_t \bar{M}_{t-1} \geq W_t \hat{L}_t \tag{78}$$

In the goods market the buyer will spend his money on consumption subject to his c.i.a. constraint

$$\chi M_t \geq P_t C_t. \tag{79}$$

The buyer and seller get back together in the asset market, where they face the budget constraint

$$W_t L_t + P_t Z_t \hat{L}_t + (1 - \chi)M_t + \tau_t \bar{M}_{t-1} - R_t D_t - w_t \hat{L}_t$$
$$+ \chi M_t - P_t C_t + B_t - q_t B_{t+1} - M_{t+1} \geq 0. \tag{80}$$

The household's problem is to maximize its payoff subject to both c.i.a. constraints and various nonnegativity constraints, such as it cannot lend more than it has. Since these nonnegativity constraints will not bind, we will ignore them.

The household's state at the beginning of each period is its initial money and bond positions (M_t, B_t). The aggregate state is given by $(\bar{M}_{t-1}, Z_{t-1}, \tau_t, g_t)$. It will turn out to be convenient to probability weight the multiplier conditions (which is equivalent to setting the multiplier $\lambda(s^t) = \tilde{\lambda}(s^t)\Pr(s^t)$). The household's Lagrangian is then given by

$$\mathcal{L} = \max_{\{L(s^t), \hat{L}(s^t), C(s^t), M(s^t), B(s^t), D(s^t)\}_{t=1}^2} \min_{\{\mu(s^t), \lambda(s^t), \phi(s^t)\}_{t=1}^2}$$

$$E\left\{ \sum_{t=1,2} \beta^{t-1}[u(C(s^t)) - v(L(s^t))] + \beta^2 V(M(s^2), B(s^2), s_3) \right\}$$

$$+ E\left\{ \sum_{t=1,2} \lambda(s^t)\{\chi M(s^{t-1}(s^t)) - P(s^t)C(s^t)\} \right\}$$

$$+ E\left\{ \sum_{t=1,2} \phi(s^t)\{(1 - \chi)M(s^{t-1}(s^t)) + \tau_t \bar{M}(s^t) + D(s^t) - W(s^t)\hat{L}(s^t)\} \right\}$$

$$+ E\left\{ \sum_{t=1,2} \mu(s^t) \left\{ \begin{array}{c} P(s^t)Z(s^t)\hat{L}(s^t) + [M(s^{t-1}(s^t)) - P(s^t)C(s^t)] \\ W(s^t)L(s^t) - W(s^t)\hat{L}(s^t) + B(s^{t-1}(s^t)) + T(s^t) \\ -R(s^t)D(s^t) - M(s^t) - q(s^t)B(s^t) \end{array} \right\} \right\}$$

the new money injection changes it to $\bar{M}_t = (1 + \tau_t)\bar{M}_{t-1}$. We did this to line up the money and productivity transition equations.

The f.o.c. for our standard choice variables C_t, L_t, M_{t+1} and B_{t+1} are

$$\beta^{t-1} u'(C(s^t)) = [\lambda(s^t) + \mu(s^t)] P(s^t),$$
$$\beta^{t-1} v'(L(s^t)) = \mu(s^t) W(s^t),$$
$$-\mu(s^t) + E\{\chi\lambda(s^{t+1}) + (1-\chi)\phi(s^{t+1}) + \mu(s^{t+1}) | s^t\} = 0,$$
$$-q(s^t)\mu(s^t) + E\{\mu(s^{t+1}) | s^t\} = 0.$$

The nice feature of probability weighting the multipliers is that the probabilities drop out of static conditions, though conditional probabilities show up in expectational conditions.

In addition, we have our f.o.c. for hired labor $\hat{L}_t$ or

$$\mu(s^t) P(s^t) Z(s^t) - (\mu(s^t) + \phi(s^t)) W(s^t) = 0.$$

And our f.o.c. for borrowing D_t

$$\phi(s^t) - \mu(s^t) R(s^t) = 0.$$

If we make use of this condition on D_t in our hired labor condition, we get a nice expression that is easy to interpret:

$$\mu(s^t) P(s^t) Z(s^t) - \mu(s^t)(1 + R(s^t)) W(s^t) = 0.$$

The nominal marginal product of labor is being equated to the full cost of labor taking account of the opportunity cost of funds in the goods market on the producer side, which is $1 + R_t$.

> Remark 19. *We are assuming that the allocation of money, which is controlled by χ, is exogenous. To understand what would happen if we allowed the household to choose this parameter, consider differentiating our Lagrangian with respect to it, and note that we get that*
>
> $$\lambda(s^t) - \phi(s^t) = 0,$$
>
> *which says that we would equate the shadow prices of money in on the buyer's and producer's sides of the market.*

3. CONSTRUCTING THE EQUILIBRIUM

To construct an equilibrium of our model, start first with prices and wages. If we assume that the c.i.a. constraint binds in the goods market, then we get that

$$P_t = \frac{\chi \bar{M}(s^t)}{Z_t L_t},$$

where in a bit of confusing notation, $\bar{M}(s^t) = \bar{M}_{t-1}$ is the beginning of period money supply in history state s^t.

Turn next to the wage. From our proposition, we know that $W_t \leq Z_t P_t$. If this inequality is strict and $R_t > 0$ then the c.i.a. constraint in the labor market must hold. If, on the other hand, the two are equal then there may be excess cash in the labor market, in which case $R_t = 0$. So, we get that W_t is either equal to

$$W_t = \frac{(1 - \chi)\bar{M}(s^t) + \tau(s^t)\bar{M}(s^t)}{L_t}$$

if the c.i.a. constraint determines things, or is

$$W_t = P_t Z_t$$

if the c.i.a. constraint does not bind and $R_t = 0$. Both of these conditions put limits on how large the wage can be, so the tighter of these two conditions will end up pinning down the wage. Hence, we get that

$$W_t = \min \left[\frac{(1 - \chi)\bar{M}(s^t) + \tau(s^t)\bar{M}(s^t)}{L_t}, P_t Z_t \right]$$

$$= \min \left[\frac{(1 - \chi)\bar{M}(s^t) + \tau(s^t)\bar{M}(s^t)}{L_t}, \frac{\chi \bar{M}(s^t)}{Z_t L_t} Z_t \right]$$

$$= \frac{\bar{M}(s^t)}{L_t} \min \left[(1 - \chi) + \tau(s^t), \chi \right].$$

Then, note that

$$1 + R_t = \frac{P_t Z_t}{W_t} = \frac{\chi \bar{M}(s^t)/L_t}{\bar{M}(s^t)\min\left[(1 - \chi) + \tau(s^t), \chi\right]/L_t}$$

$$= \frac{\chi}{\min\left[(1 - \chi) + \tau(s^t), \chi\right]}.$$

These results imply that we can rewrite our f.o.c.'s for labor and consumption as

$$\beta^{t-1} v'(L(s^t)) = \mu(s^t)\frac{\bar{M}(s^t)}{L_t} \min\left[(1 - \chi) + \tau(s^t), \chi\right], \text{ and}$$

$$\beta^{t-1} u'(Z_t L_t) = [\lambda(s^t) + \mu(s^t)]\frac{\chi \bar{M}(s^t)}{Z_t L_t}.$$

If we make our log preference assumption our consumption condition simplifies further to

$$\beta^{t-1} = [\lambda(s^t) + \mu(s^t)] \chi \bar{M}(s^t).$$

These results suggest that a change in variables is in order. So define

$$\lambda(s^t)\bar{M}(s^t) = \beta^{t-1}\hat{\lambda}(s^t),$$

$$\mu(s^t)\bar{M}(s^t) = \beta^{t-1}\hat{\mu}(s^t).$$

Moreover, I am going to guess and later verify the following conjectures.

Conjecture 1. *If $\{\tau_t\}$ is an i.i.d. sequence of random variables, then $\hat{\lambda}(s^t) = \hat{\lambda}(\tau_t)$ and $\hat{\mu}(s^t) = \hat{\mu}(\tau_t)$.*

This conjecture means that under our assumption about τ_t, the expectation of $\hat{\lambda}(s^{t+1})$ and $\hat{\mu}(s^{t+1})$ conditional on s^t are both time-invariant constants. Denote these two constants by

$$\lambda^* = E\{\hat{\lambda}(s^{t+1})|s^t\},$$

$$\mu^* = E\{\hat{\mu}(s^{t+1})|s^t\}.$$

Now, we can rewrite our f.o.c.'s for consumption as

$$1 = [\hat{\lambda}(\tau_t) + \hat{\mu}(\tau_t)]\chi,$$

labor as

$$v'(L(\tau_t))L(\tau_t) = \hat{\mu}(\tau_t)\min[(1-\chi)+\tau_t, \chi],$$

and bonds as

$$q(\tau_t)\hat{\mu}(\tau_t) = \beta \frac{\mu^*}{1+\tau_t}.$$

The f.o.c. for money is a bit trickier. Start with

$$-\mu(s^t) + E\{\chi\lambda(s^{t+1}) + (1-\chi)\phi(s^{t+1}) + \mu(s^{t+1})|s^t\} = 0.$$

Then make use of our results that $\phi(s^t) = \mu(s^t)R(s^t)$ to get

$$-\mu(s^t) + E\{\chi\lambda(s^{t+1}) + (1-\chi)\mu(s^{t+1})R(s^{t+1}) + \mu(s^{t+1})|s^t\} = 0.$$

If we make our change in variables and use our result for $R(s^t)$, we get that

$$\hat{\mu}(\tau_t) = \frac{\beta}{1+\tau_t}E\left\{\begin{array}{c}\chi[\hat{\lambda}(\tau_{t+1}) + \hat{\mu}(\tau_{t+1})] \\ +(1-\chi)\hat{\mu}(\tau_{t+1})[1+R(s^{t+1})]\end{array}\middle|s^t\right\}$$

$$= \frac{\beta}{1+\tau_t}E\left\{\begin{array}{c}\chi[\hat{\lambda}(\tau_{t+1}) + \hat{\mu}(\tau_{t+1})] \\ +(1-\chi)\hat{\mu}(\tau_{t+1})\left[\frac{\chi}{\min[(1-\chi)+\tau_{t+1},\chi]}\right]\end{array}\middle|s^t\right\}$$

$$= \frac{\beta}{1+\tau_t}\left[\begin{array}{c}\chi[\lambda^* + \mu^*] + \\ (1-\chi)E\left\{\frac{\chi\hat{\mu}(\tau_{t+1})}{\min[(1-\chi)+\tau_{t+1},\chi]}\right\}\end{array}\right].$$

Note here that everything in the expectation term is a function of τ_{t+1}, which, given our i.i.d. assumption, is just a constant. So call this term

$$X^* = E\left\{\frac{\chi\hat{\mu}(\tau_{t+1})}{\min[(1-\chi)+\tau_{t+1},\chi]}\right\}.$$

Now, we can write our system of equations as

$$1/\chi = \hat{\lambda}(\tau_t) + \hat{\mu}(\tau_t)$$

$$\hat{\mu}(\tau_t) = \frac{\beta}{1+\tau_t}[1 + (1-\chi)X^*]$$

$$v'(L(\tau_t))L(\tau_t) = \hat{\mu}(\tau_t)\min[(1-\chi)+\tau_t,\chi]$$

$$q(\tau_t)\hat{\mu}(\tau_t) = \beta\frac{\mu^*}{1+\tau_t}.$$

Note that in this system everything, and $\hat{\mu}(\tau_t)$ and $\hat{\lambda}(\tau_t)$, just depends on the current realization of τ_t. This verifies our conjecture.

To characterize things a bit further, note that

$$X^* = E\left\{\frac{\chi\hat{\mu}(\tau_{t+1})}{\min[(1-\chi)+\tau_{t+1},\chi]}\right\}$$

$$= E\left\{\frac{\chi\frac{\beta}{1+\tau_{t+1}}[1+(1-\chi)X^*]}{\min[(1-\chi)+\tau_{t+1},\chi]}\right\},$$

or

$$\frac{X^*}{[1+(1-\chi)X^*]} = E\left\{\frac{\chi\frac{\beta}{1+\tau_{t+1}}}{\min\left[(1-\chi)+\tau_{t+1},\chi\right]}\right\}.$$

This gives us a fairly simple expression to solve for X^*. Once we have this value we can determine our fundamental equation for labor, or

$$v'(L(\tau_t))L(\tau_t) = \frac{\beta}{1+\tau_t}[1+(1-\chi)X^*]\min\left[(1-\chi)+\tau_t,\chi\right].$$

From this expression, we can see that the response of labor to the growth rate of money depends on which of the two expressions in the $\min[\cdot]$ is operative. If it is the first, then

$$v'(L(\tau_t))L(\tau_t) = \frac{\beta[(1-\chi)+\tau_t]}{1+\tau_t}[1+(1-\chi)X^*].$$

Since

$$\frac{d}{d\tau_t}\left[\frac{1-\chi+\tau_t}{1+\tau_t}\right] = \frac{\chi}{(1+\tau_t)^2} > 0.$$

This term is positive. Then, since

$$\frac{d}{dL}[v'(L)L] = v'(L)+v''(L)L > 0,$$

it follows that an increase in τ_t increases labor. This positive response will certainly change by the point where

$$1+\tau_t = 2\chi,$$

at which point the *response switches sign*. This is because the derivative of the r.h.s. term w.r.t. to τ_t becomes

$$\frac{d}{d\tau_t}\left[\frac{1}{1+\tau_t}\right] = \frac{-1}{(1+\tau_t)^2}.$$

This is our standard response-type term and it comes from the depressing effects of anticipated inflation tomorrow. This inflation arises when the increase in the money supply today shows up in the hands of tomorrow's buyers leading to a higher P_{t+1}.

4. SIMULATING OUR MODEL

Computing an equilibrium of our model is not simple because the model's response to shocks is not smooth and, even worse, not monotone. For these reasons we cannot use linearization. Instead, we will have to solve our model using our analytic characterization of labor and then use that to determine the rest of the components.

To do this, start by specifying a probability distribution over money growth rates $F(\tau; \bar{\tau}, \sigma_\tau)$ where $\bar{\tau}$ is the mean and σ_τ is the standard deviation (s.d.). Then draw a bunch of shocks from this distribution, which we arrange in a vector T. You want to truncate τ from below to make sure that it doesn't get too low, so probably you want to set

$$\tilde{\tau}_j = \max\left[-.25, \tau_j\right]$$

and construct a revised set of growth rates $\tilde{T}$. We use these henceforth.

We need to construct the realized $L's$ for each τ. To do that, we need to know X^* since, given this, we can construct $L(\tau)$ by using

$$L(\tau)^{1+\gamma} = \frac{\beta}{1+\tau}\left[1 + (1-\chi)X^*\right]\min\left[(1-\chi) + \tau, \chi\right].$$

This turns out to be straightforward. Just use our draws to construct the outcomes of the

$$\frac{\chi \frac{\beta}{1+\tau_j}}{\min\left[(1-\chi) + \tau_j, \chi\right]}$$

for each $\tau_j \in \tilde{T}$ and compute the mean. Then use this mean to solve for the X^* that satisfies the following equation

$$\frac{X^*}{[1 + (1-\chi)X^*]} = E\left\{\frac{\chi \frac{\beta}{1+\tau_{t+1}}}{\min\left[(1-\chi) + \tau_{t+1}, \chi\right]}\right\}.$$

Now we are ready to simulate our model.

Exercise 21. *How does the response of our model change with τ? To determine this, construct a grid of possible τ values. If τ is taking on values between $-.25$ and 1.0, then our grid would be something like $T = [-.25 : .05 : 1.00]$; Then for each value of τ in our grid compute the equilibrium value of L. Plot these values against the values of τ to trace out a response function. Are their values of our parameters for which there response to τ by L is nonmonotonic?*

Exercise 22. *Draw a sequence of truncated $\tau's$ and $g's$ and use our computed X^* to determine L, P, R, π, and q. Report on what you find. What is the relationship between L and R? Do you find an indication of our nonlinearity in L?*

5. QUANTITATIVE EASING AND THE LIQUIDITY MODEL

The standard approach to monetary policy is to buy and sell short-term government debt, and thereby expand and contract the level of reserves in the banking system. Under certain circumstances central banks have felt that this is no longer an effective method for stimulating the economy and have resorted to other methods. For example, when the short-term interest rate on government debt gets close to 0, lowering it further may not have much effect. Another example is when there is a lot of uncertainty about the solvency of many of the major participants in financial markets. In this case no one may be willing to make loans or transact with each other.

One group of these other methods goes under the banner of quantitative easing. Under quantitative easing the central bank switches the financial assets it is buying from short-term government debt to either (i) long-term government debt, or (ii) private financial assets. When the central bank does this, it is thought that the prices of these assets rise, which lowers their yield. At the same time, since these purchases are done with reserves, the monetary base also expands. In Figure 2 we can see evidence of the very vigorous extent to which the Federal Reserve conducted a quantitative easing policy during the Great Recession. Quantitative easing was also used by the European Central Bank during the euro crisis, and has been used by the of Japan during its long period of stagnation.

When the central bank buys longer-term government debt, it is effectively shortening the maturity distribution of the government's outstanding liabilities. Longer-term debt is being reduced and reserves, which are a very short-term liability, are being increased. From Figure 2 we can see that the Federal Reserve started doing this very aggressively after 2012. When the central bank buys private financial assets, it is not just providing liquidity, it is also directly acting to support the prices of these securities. At the same time, it is taking the risk associated with these assets off the private agents' balance sheet and onto its own. In Figure 2

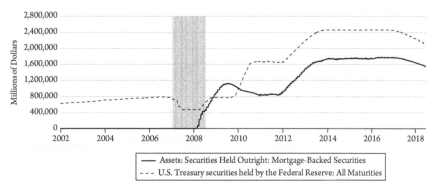

Figure 2. Quantitative Easing by the Federal Reserve
SOURCE: Board of Governors of the Fed. Res. System (U.S.)
Retrieved from FRED, Federal Reserve Bank of St. Louis.

we can see that the Federal Reserve started supporting the mortgage-backed securities markets very aggressively even earlier, starting in 2009.[5] Moreover, for both of these types of securities, the Fed has continued holding them at unprecedented levels since those interventions started.

We can use our liquidity model to think through how quantitative easing done using private financial assets might affect the outcomes we see. To do this, we need a version of our model in which private loans are taking place in positive quantities and playing an important role. We therefore modify our existing model to generate more of a role for loans and a new type of agent, the financier.

Assume that half of the producers find out that they cannot produce anything when they get to the goods market in the middle of the period. These producers turn into financiers from our perspective. They cannot produce, but they have funds they can loan to those who do. Each of our financiers has $(1 - \chi)M_t + \tau_t \bar{M}_{t-1}$ to lend at rate $1 + R_t$. When they do this, the remaining producers will have twice as much cash as before, but since there are only half as many, the total amount of cash available to hire workers is the same as before. Because our model features linear production, if each of these producers hires $2\hat{L}_t$ units of labor, the total amount of labor and the total wage bill will be the same. Also, the total amount of output produced will be the same. Since each of our producers just breaks even on his production (but makes money on his liquid funds), the net return to a producer or a financier is the same. Thus, these changes do not fundamentally change the outcomes from our model and the overall c.i.a. constraint for hiring labor is still given by

5. Source is Board of Governors of the Federal Reserve System (US), Assets: Securities Held Outright: Mortgage-Backed Securities [WSHOMCB], and U.S. Treasury Securities (DISCONTINUED) [WSHOTS] retrieved from FRED, Federal Reserve Bank of St. Louis.

$$(1 - \chi)M_t + \tau_t \bar{M}_{t-1} \geq W\hat{L}_t.$$

To accommodate normal open market operations, imagine that we also give the investment bankers some government bonds that are coming due in the asset market. The central bank could buy these bonds from or sell these bonds to the investment bankers and thereby affect the amount of cash they have to lend to the producers. If the overall c.i.a. constraint on labor binds, and $R_t > 0$, then buying bonds would stimulate the equilibrium amount of labor being hired because it would relax the aggregate c.i.a. constraint, while selling bonds would have the opposite effect. However, if the c.i.a. constraint does not bind and $R_t = 0$, then this sort of operation would not have any effect.

Now imagine that our financiers come to believe that the producers have some large liabilities in the form of IOUs and large risky assets on their balance sheet. This means that our producers will be bankrupt in the asset market at the end of the period and unable to pay off their loans if the returns on the risky assets turn out to be poor. As a result, while the producers are still willing to borrow, the financiers may be unwilling to lend, even at a quite high interest rate on these short-term loans. If this occurred, then the producers would only have their own funds with which to pay for labor. This would lead to a dramatic tightening of the c.i.a. constraint for labor and a sharp fall in the amount of labor being hired in equilibrium, even once we take into account that the equilibrium wage will fall.

What can the central bank do to stimulate the economy in this case? If it bought up its outstanding bonds from the financiers, thereby giving them more cash, it is likely that this operation would have no effect on the amount of loans the financiers were willing to make to the producers, since the financiers would still be worried about producer solvency. What could the central bank do instead of a standard open market operation? Well, it could sell bonds to the financiers and buy up IOUs from the producers. In doing this, the central bank would be taking on the financing role normally played by the financiers. In particular, it would be absorbing the producers' bankruptcy risk. Under the proposed operation, there would be no change in the overall amount of money $(1 - \chi)M_t + \tau_t \bar{M}_{t-1}$. It is just that the central bank would be acting to ensure that all of this money got into the hands of the producers.

Something like this scenario is thought to have played out in the Great Recession when investors, and money market mutual funds, lost faith in the solvency of the investment banks. This led them to cease buying the investment banks' commercial paper, which, in turn, left the investment banks unable to roll over their liabilities and continue to hold the large amounts of mortgage-backed securities (MBS) on their balance sheets. This crisis led the Federal Reserve and the U.S. Treasury (through the Troubled Asset Relief Program (TARP)) to buy up large amounts of MBS, thereby preventing their price from collapsing and sending many financial institutions into bankruptcy. Despite this, a fair number of the investment banks ended up in fairly extreme financial difficulty. However, a complete market collapse was thought to have been prevented by the Fed's actions.[6]

6. See my other book, *Finance and Financial Intermediation: A Modern Treatment of Money, Credit, and Banking*, where this is discussed in more detail in the chapter on the financial meltdown that occurred during the Great Recession.

## PART 2

Capital and Fiscal Policy

## 14

A Model of Money and Capital

Thus far we have assumed that output is produced only with labor. Now we are going to introduce capital into our model. This way, we can think about some of the basic issues in fiscal policy such as how much to tax labor and capital and how much the government should spend.

We will assume that the final good (output) can now be used either in the form of consumption C_t or in the form of investment X_t. This investment augments the household's capital stock. We will denote the household's beginning-of-period capital stock as K_t so that the date t state has date t variables. The equation of motion for the capital stock is

$$K_{t+1} = (1 - \delta)K_t + X_t.$$

We will assume that households produce the final good according to a standard Cobb-Douglas production function which is subject to a labor-augmenting productivity growth factor Z_t. With this, the resource constraint for the economy is given by

$$[Z_t L_t]^{1-\alpha} K_t^\alpha = C_t + X_t.$$

Remark 20. *The Cobb-Douglas production function* $[Z_t L_t]^{1-\alpha} K_t^\alpha$ *has many nice features. First, if labor and capital double, then so does output; this is called constant returns to scale. The marginal products are given by*

Monetary and Fiscal Policy through a DSGE Lens. Harold L. Cole, Oxford University Press (2020).
© Oxford University Press. DOI: 10.1093/oso/9780190076030.001.0001

$$MPL = (1 - \alpha)Z_t^{1-\alpha}L_t^{-\alpha}K_t^{\alpha},$$
$$MPK = \alpha\left[Z_t L_t\right]^{1-\alpha}K_t^{\alpha-1}.$$

If labor is constant and both capital and productivity grow at the same rate, then the marginal product of capital, is constant while the marginal product of labor grows with productivity. This will turn out to lead to nice long-run growth predictions. Also, the shares paid out to labor and capital, which are

$$MPL * L = (1 - \alpha)Y_t$$
$$MPK * K = \alpha * Y_t,$$

are constant over time. Finally, when we look at how capital and labor inputs respond to price changes; since $MPL = w$, the equilibrium rental rate of labor, and $MPK = r$, the equilibrium rental rate of capital, in an optimal program, it follows that

$$\frac{MPL}{MPK} = \frac{w}{r} = \frac{(1-\alpha)K}{\alpha L} \quad \text{and hence}$$
$$dlog\left(\frac{w}{r}\right) = dlog\left(\frac{K}{L}\right).$$

In words, a 1% change in the ratio of input prices changes the relative inputs by 1%. This is called a unit elasticity.

Note here that just as in our pure labor model, productivity shocks make labor more productive. This is called the labor-augmenting version, though the more productive labor ends up making capital more productive too. This version will turn out to be convenient because along a balanced growth path, K will end up growing at the same rate as Z. As a result, output will also grow at this rate too because our production function exhibits constant returns to scale.

Because we have a representative agent economy again (since there is only a single good and all households end up being the same), we will not distinguish between a household's choice of labor, investment, and capital, and the aggregate choices. This is a serious abuse of notation and we need to be careful not to confuse ourselves. The transition equation for capital holds at the level of the household. However, the resource constraint holds at the level of the economy. A household simply takes prices as given and chooses its optimal plan.

We will start with a perfect foresight version of the model, which means that households know the future path of productivity growth and money growth. With this said, the household's problem is choosing a sequence of quantities $\{C_t, L_t, M_t, B_{t+1}, K_{t+1}\}_{t=1}^2$ so as to maximize

$$\max \sum_{t=1,2} \beta^{t-1} \left[u(C_t) - v(L_t) \right] + \beta^2 V(M_3, B_3, K_3)$$

subject to

$$M_t \geq P_t C_t \text{ and}$$

$$P_t \left[[Z_t L_t]^{1-\alpha} K_t^{\alpha} - \delta K_t \right] + [M_t - P_t C_t] + B_t + T_t$$

$$\geq M_{t+1} + q_t B_{t+1} + P_t [K_{t+1} - K_t] \text{ for all } t \leq 2.$$

Note here that only consumption shows up in the household's c.i.a. constraint because we are thinking that new investment is transacted in the asset market. Another way to think about this is that the household has other and more efficient means of making large purchases such as capital. We could also think that because capital is a long-lived asset, the household can essentially borrow in the goods market to acquire it, pledging its capital as collateral on this loan. Then it can simply pay up in the asset market. All of these formulations will lead to the set of constraints we have above. In the budget constraint we have dealt with capital depreciation by subtracting the depreciated component of capital from output and assuming that the household picks the new capital stock. So, X_t is not a choice variable, K_{t+1} is, and we don't have to worry about the transition equation for capital since it will be satisfied by construction.

The household's f.o.c.'s now include our original constraints plus a new one for investment. The consumption condition is unchanged and given by

$$\beta^{t-1} u'(C_t) - P_t [\lambda_t + \mu_t] = 0.$$

The f.o.c. for L_t has changed:

$$-\beta^{t-1} v'(L_t) + \mu_t P_t Z_t^{1-\alpha} (1-\alpha) L_t^{-\alpha} K_t^{\alpha} = 0.$$

This is very similar to before except that the marginal product of labor now depends on the level of labor, the level of capital and the productivity shock rather than just the productivity shock. The f.o.c. for money and bonds are also unchanged and are given by

$$-\mu_t + \lambda_{t+1} + \mu_{t+1} = 0$$

and

$$-\mu_t q_t + \mu_{t+1} = 0.$$

Finally, we have our new condition coming from the presence of capital. Our choice here is simply with respect to the capital stock at the end of period t, which will determine the level of capital that we start with in period $t + 1$:

$$-\mu_t P_t + \mu_{t+1} P_{t+1} \left[[Z_{t+1} L_{t+1}]^{1-\alpha} \alpha K_{t+1}^{\alpha-1} + 1 - \delta \right] = 0.$$

These f.o.c.'s along with the c.i.a. constraint, the budget constraint, the resource constraint, and the market clearing conditions for money and bonds give the constraints that our equilibrium must satisfy. Once again, the presence of money growth and productivity growth means that our economy is not going to be stationary. Money growth means that nominal balances will be nonstationary, productivity growth means that output and capital will be nonstationary, and the combination of these two effects means that prices will generally be nonstationary.

1. BALANCED GROWTH PATH

Assume that both productivity and the money supply grow at constant rates given by

$$Z_t = (1 + g)Z_{t-1},$$

and

$$M_t = (1 + \tau)M_{t-1}$$

respectively. If we make the normalization that $Z_1 = 1$, then $Z_t = (1 + g)^{t-1}$, so it is just the accumulated growth factor. This will turn out to be notationally convenient.

Conjecture 2. *Conjecture that capital grows at the same rate as productivity and that labor is constant, which implies that output will grow at rate g since*

$$Y_t = [Z_t L]^{1-\alpha} K_t^{\alpha}$$
$$Y_{t-1} = [Z_{t-1} L]^{1-\alpha} K_{t-1}^{\alpha}$$

and hence

$$Y_t = (1 + g)Y_{t-1} = Z_t Y_1$$

given our normalization of $Z_1 = 1$. We will also conjecture that our standard assumption that the c.i.a. constraint holds as an equality is true.

Since capital is assumed to grow at the same rate as productivity,

$$K_t = (1+g)K_{t-1} = Z_t K_1.$$

Making use of the fact that capital grows at rate g, we can pin down investment as

$$X_t = (1+g)K_t - (1-\delta)K_t = (g+\delta)Z_t K_1.$$

Taking account of this in the resource constraint, we get that

$$[Z_t L]^{1-\alpha}K_t^\alpha = C_t + [(g-\delta)]K_t$$
$$Z_t L^{1-\alpha}K_1^\alpha = C_t + [g+\delta]Z_t K_1.$$

Note that since output and capital are growing at rate g, this implies that consumption must also grow at rate g too. If we take account of the fact that everything except labor grows at rate g, then we get that

$$L^{1-\alpha}K_1^\alpha = C_1 + [g+\delta]K_1.$$

Turn next to our c.i.a. constraint which we are again assuming holds with equality. This yields

$$P_t = \frac{M_t}{C_t} = \frac{(1+\tau)}{(1+g)}P_{t-1}.$$

This is essentially the same result we derived previously when output was just produced with labor.

Assuming log utility, we can rewrite our f.o.c. for consumption as

$$\beta^{t-1}\frac{1}{C_t} = [\lambda_t + \mu_t]P_t = [\lambda_t + \mu_t]\frac{M_t}{C_t}.$$

This leads to

$$\beta^{t-1} = [\lambda_t + \mu_t](1+\tau)^{t-1}M_1.$$

So once again, we make a change in variables, setting

$$\tilde{\lambda}_t = \lambda_t \frac{(1+\tau)^{t-1}}{\beta^{t-1}},$$

$$\tilde{\mu}_t = \mu_t \frac{(1+\tau)^{t-1}}{\beta^{t-1}}.$$

This gives us

$$1 = [\tilde{\lambda}_t + \tilde{\mu}_t] M_1,$$

indicating that their sum is invariant and suggesting that just as we found before they are both time invariant.

The f.o.c. for labor can be written as

$$\beta^{t-1}(L_t)^\gamma = \mu_t P_t Z_t^{1-\alpha}(1-\alpha)L_t^{-\alpha}K_t^\alpha$$
$$= \mu_t \frac{(1+\tau)^{t-1}}{(1+g)^{t-1}} P_1 Z_t^{1-\alpha}(1-\alpha)L_t^{-\alpha}K_t^\alpha$$

once we substitute in for P_t. Note that both Z_t and K_t are growing at rate g and labor is constant. So, this can be simplified to

$$\beta^{t-1}(L)^{\gamma+\alpha} = \mu_t \frac{(1+\tau)^{t-1}}{(1+g)^{t-1}} P_1 Z_1^{1-\alpha}(1-\alpha)K_1^\alpha(1+g)^{t-1}$$

which, since $Z_1 = 1$, simplifies to

$$L^{\gamma+\alpha} = \tilde{\mu}_t P_1(1-\alpha)K_1^\alpha$$

The f.o.c.'s for money and bonds can be written as

$$\frac{\beta}{1+\tau}[\tilde{\lambda}_{t+1} + \tilde{\mu}_{t+1}] = \tilde{\mu}_t$$

and

$$\tilde{\mu}_t q_t = \frac{\beta}{1+\tau}\tilde{\mu}_{t+1}.$$

The f.o.c. for capital,

$$\mu_t P_t = \mu_{t+1} P_{t+1}\left([Z_{t+1}L_{t+1}]^{1-\alpha}\alpha K_{t+1}^{\alpha-1} + 1 - \delta\right),$$

can be rewritten as follows once we substitute out for prices

$$\mu_t = \mu_{t+1} \frac{1+\tau}{1+g} \left\{ \alpha \left[\frac{Z_{t+1} L_{t+1}}{K_{t+1}} \right]^{1-\alpha} + 1 - \delta \right\}.$$

Then, making use of the fact that Z_t and K_t grow at the same rate and that labor is constant, we get

$$\mu_t = \mu_{t+1} \frac{1+\tau}{1+g} \left\{ \alpha \left[\frac{Z_1 L}{K_1} \right]^{1-\alpha} + 1 - \delta \right\}.$$

Finally we put in our change in variables to get that

$$\tilde{\mu}_t = \tilde{\mu}_{t+1} \beta \frac{1}{1+g} \left\{ \alpha \left[\frac{Z_1 L}{K_1} \right]^{1-\alpha} + 1 - \delta \right\}.$$

If we collect our expressions and recognize that the multipliers will be time-invariant, we get the following set of equations. The first is our resource constraint

$$[Z_1 L]^{1-\alpha} K_1^\alpha = C_1 + [g + \delta] K_1.$$

The second is our optimal labor condition,

$$L^{\gamma + \alpha} = \tilde{\mu} P_1 (1 - \alpha) Z_1^{1-\alpha} K_1^\alpha. \tag{81}$$

The third is our optimal capital condition,

$$1 = \frac{\beta}{1+g} \left\{ \alpha \left[\frac{Z_1 L}{K_1} \right]^{1-\alpha} + 1 - \delta \right\}. \tag{82}$$

The fourth is our optimal consumption condition,

$$1 = [\tilde{\lambda} + \tilde{\mu}] M_1.$$

The fifth is our optimal money condition,

$$\frac{\beta}{1+\tau} [\tilde{\lambda} + \tilde{\mu}] = \tilde{\mu}.$$

The sixth is our optimal bond condition, which pins down the discount rate,

$$q = \frac{\beta}{1+\tau}.$$

The last is our price condition from the c.i.a. constraint

$$P_1 = \frac{M_1}{C_1}.$$

We have seven variables to solve for $\left[C_1, L, P_1, \tilde{\mu}, \tilde{\lambda}, q, K_1 \right]$ and we do so taking as given Z_1 and M_1 along with g and τ. The one surprise is that we have to "solve" for K_1. This is because even the initial level of the capital stock must be consistent with balanced growth if we are going to be on a balanced growth path from the start, which we are assuming. Fortunately, our system is again block recursive so we can solve things in steps.

Step 1: Start with the resource constraint and note that it implies that

$$C_1 = [Z_1 L]^{1-\alpha} K_1^{\alpha} - [g + \delta] K_1,$$

hence if we know K_1 and L we know C_1. Then, move to the price condition and note that we can use our expression for C_1 to get that

$$P_1 = \frac{M_1}{[Z_1 L]^{1-\alpha} K_1^{\alpha} - [g + \delta] K_1}.$$

Hence the initial price level is also determined by K_1 and L.

Step 2: Solve for $\tilde{\mu}$. To do this, use our optimal money condition and our optimal consumption condition to get that

$$\frac{\beta}{1+\tau} \frac{1}{M_1} = \tilde{\mu}.$$

Step 3: We can solve for K_1 and L as a simultaneous block given these results. Start with our optimality condition for capital,

$$1 = \frac{\beta}{1+g} \left\{ \alpha \left[\frac{Z_1 L}{K_1} \right]^{1-\alpha} + 1 - \delta \right\}.$$

This depends only on K_1 and L to begin with. Moreover, it really just serves to pin down the ratio of productive labor— $Z_1 L$ —and capital K.

$$\frac{Z_1 L}{K_1} = \left\{ \frac{1}{\alpha} \left(\frac{1+g}{\beta} - 1 + \delta \right) \right\}^{1/(1-\alpha)}. \tag{83}$$

Remark 21. *Note that productive-labor-to-capital ratio depends on the discount rate, the level of productivity growth, and the depreciation rate. It does not depend on the rate of inflation. Since the ratio of productive labor to capital is pinned down, this implies that increases in productivity Z_1 raise the level of capital-to-labor, or K_1/L. At the same time, increases in the depreciation rate or the growth rate raise the ratio of productive labor to capital and hence lower the capital-to-labor ratio, while increases in the discount rate β (which means we are more patient) raise it. The fact that the capital-to-labor ratio is negatively affected by growth is the real surprise here.*

To simplify things further, substitute for P_1 and for $\tilde{\mu}$ in our optimal labor condition to get that

$$L^{\gamma+\alpha} = \left[\frac{\beta}{1+\tau}\frac{1}{M_1}\right](1-\alpha)Z_1^{1-\alpha}K_1^\alpha \left[\frac{M_1}{[Z_1L]^{1-\alpha}K_1^\alpha - [g+\delta]K_1}\right].$$

This condition is fairly complicated, but remember, we already have pinned down the capital-to-labor ratio using (83). To take advantage of this, focus on the last term, and note that

$$\left[\frac{M_1}{[Z_1L]^{1-\alpha}K_1^\alpha - [g+\delta]K_1}\right] \times \frac{L^{-1}}{L^{-1}} = \frac{M_1 L^{-1}}{[Z_1]^{1-\alpha}\left[\frac{K_1}{L}\right]^\alpha - [g+\delta]\frac{K_1}{L}}.$$

Plugging into the original equation, converting our last K_0 into K_1/L and simplifying yields

$$L^{1+\gamma} = \left[\frac{\beta}{1+\tau}\right](1-\alpha)Z_1^{1-\alpha}\left[\frac{K_1}{L}\right]^\alpha \left[\frac{1}{[Z_1]^{1-\alpha}\left[\frac{K_1}{L}\right]^\alpha - [g+\delta]\frac{K_1}{L}}\right]. \qquad (84)$$

This expression says that once we have pinned down the capital-to-labor ratio, we can just substitute that value into (84) and then determine the level of labor.

Remark 22. *Once again we see money growth depressing labor in essentially the exact same way as in our simple model, in which output was produced with labor.*

Step 4: Once we have solved for L and K_1, we can easily determine the rest of our variables.

Exercise 23. *Why didn't money growth discourage capital formation, just labor?* *[Hint: check out the c.i.a. constraint.] Why does money growth end up discouraging labor effort in essentially the exact same way as in our original simple model? [Hint: check out the c.i.a. constraint.]*

2. KALDOR'S GROWTH FACTS

In the early 1960s, Nicholas Kaldor came up with a list of six "facts" to summarize what economists had learned from national income and product accounts during the past decade or more. Much of the growth theory that followed was aimed at coming up with a model that could reasonably account for these facts.

Kaldor's long-run growth facts were:

1. The growth rate of output per worker is roughly constant over time.
2. The growth rate of capital per worker is roughly constant over time but varies a lot across countries.
3. The capital-to-output ratio is roughly constant over time.
4. The return on investment is roughly constant over time.
5. The real wage grows over time.
6. The shares of national income paid to labor and capital are roughly constant over time.

For more information on Kaldor's facts see https://en.wikipedia.org/wiki/ Kaldor%27s_facts.

The growth rates we typically see for different countries' output are between 2 and 6%. The U.S. output has grown at roughly 2% since 1900, which is a long time. This sort of growth is very much a modern fact. Prior to the industrial revolution, growth in output per worker was *extremely* slow. While we do see dramatic growth rates for a while, those are typically for countries whose output per capita is quite a bit lower than the U.S. output, say, 20% of ours. And while these high-growth-rate periods can last for quite a while, growth tends very strongly to slow down as these countries get close to the U.S. level of output per worker.

Exercise 24. *Write a program to compute the balanced growth path levels of capital K_1 and labor L_1 for different growth rates in productivity and money. In your program you should also compute the balanced growth path levels of output, Y_1, and wages, w_1, and rental rates on capital r_1. Then, compute outcome paths for output, capital, the capital-output ratio, the rental rate on capital, the wage rate, and the shares of national income paid to labor and capital. Discuss whether your model is consistent with Kaldor's facts.*

Exercise 25. *Use your program of this model to try to see how the key variables along a balanced growth path depend on the parameters. Discuss how you would expect the capital-to-labor ratio to differ between a high-growth country, where $g = 0.8$; a medium-growth country, where $g = 0.2$; and a low-growth country, where $g = 0$.*

## 15

Taxes

In this chapter we want to examine the implications of different forms of taxation for our model. We are mainly concerned with how differences in the taxation of labor and capital can affect the predictions of our model. To get a start on things, it is useful to first lay out how labor and capital are taxed. Then, we will discuss how we want to go about putting some version of these taxes into our model.

1. OVERVIEW OF THE FEDERAL GOVERNMENT

We are going to start with an overview of the U.S. government's spending and receipts. In the first panel of Figure 1 we can see that the gap in expenditures and receipts opens up a bit during the 1960s when the U.S. was seeking to fight the Vietnam War while not raising taxes to fund it.[1]

This gap persists past the end of the war. The gap widens substantially during the Reagan presidency. It closes during the very strong economic years of the Clinton presidency, and we even get a positive surplus for several years (1998–2001) at the end of Clinton's administration. Then, there is a reversal of this surplus, and another big deficit opens up during the early phase of George W. Bush's presidency, which starts in 2001. There is another, even bigger widening

---

1. The source is U.S. Bureau of Economic Analysis, Federal Government Current Receipts and Expenditures, retrieved from FRED, Federal Reserve Bank of St. Louis.

Monetary and Fiscal Policy through a DSGE Lens. Harold L. Cole, Oxford University Press (2020).
© Oxford University Press. DOI: 10.1093/oso/9780190076030.001.0001

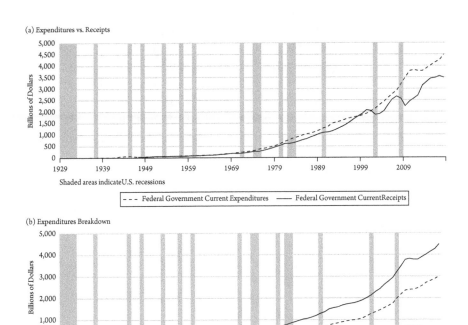

(a) Expenditures vs. Receipts

Shaded areas indicateU.S. recessions

- - - Federal Government Current Expenditures —— Federal Government CurrentReceipts

(b) Expenditures Breakdown

Shaded areas indicate U.S. recessions

—— Federal Government Current Expenditures   ⋯⋯ Government current expenditures: Federal: National defense
- - - Government current transfer payments   -·-·- Federal government current expenditures: Interest payments

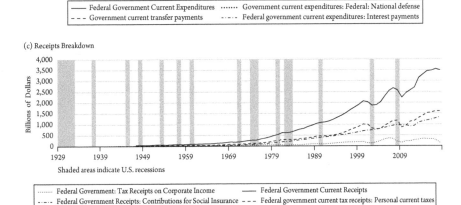

(c) Receipts Breakdown

Shaded areas indicate U.S. recessions

⋯⋯ Federal Government: Tax Receipts on Corporate Income   —— Federal Government Current Receipts
-·-·- Federal Government Receipts: Contributions for Social Insurance - - - Federal government current tax receipts: Personal current taxes

Figure 1. U.S. Ferderal Government Expenditures and Receipts.

SOURCE: U.S. Bureau of Economic Analysis
Retrieved from FRED, Federal Reserve Bank of St. Louis
SOURCE: U.S. Bureau of Economic Analysis
Retrieved from FRED, Federal Reserve Bank of St. Louis
SOURCE: U.S. Bureau of Economic Analysis
Retrieved from FRED, Federal Reserve Bank of St. Louis

during the later years of the Bush presidency and that widening continues into the Obama presidency, before closing somewhat lately.

The second panel of Figure 1 breaks that down by showing some of the key components. These components include defense spending and interest on payments on the government's accumulated debt. While both of those series rise a bit, and defense spending bulges up during the main Middle Eastern wars of Bush II, they are not what's driving the big rise in expenditures. That is mainly coming from the rise in transfer payments, which include things like Social Security and Medicare.

The third panel of Figure 1 shows the breakdown of the key sources of revenue for the federal government. The biggest contributors are personal income taxes and social insurance taxes, which primarily includes social security taxes. As you can see from the figure the importance of these two components has grown substantially, while the other sources of income for the government have grown at slower rates, leading to a decline in their importance. The third biggest component is corporate income taxes. To put this figure in a bit of perspective, in 2015 44% of government revenue came from personal income taxes, 34.8% came from contributions to social insurance, and 12.1% came from corporate income taxes.

2. TAXATION OF INDIVIDUALS IN THE U.S.

Households in the United States are subject to the personal income tax. Income taxes are collected mainly at the federal and state levels, but there are a few cities, such as Philadelphia, that also have some form of an income tax. Taxation of income, although it began formally during the Civil War, only really begins to show up during WWI. Before this, the dominant source of tax revenue was from excise taxes. Income taxation goes up sharply during WWII and has largely stayed between 15 and 20% of GDP since then.[2]

The tax rate that a household pays in a given year depends on its marital status and its income level. This means that different people are taxed very differently. To get a handle on this, we plot in Figure 2 the marginal tax rate at the highest and lowest income brackets. While the income tax goes way back to the War of 1812, we start our graph in 1913.

What is striking in Figure 2 is the variation in the highest tax bracket. The top rate went up a lot during WWI, only to fall back before being ratcheted up sharply during Great Depression. The rate stayed around 80–90% until Ronald

---

2. Source is the Wikipedia entry on "Income tax in the United States."

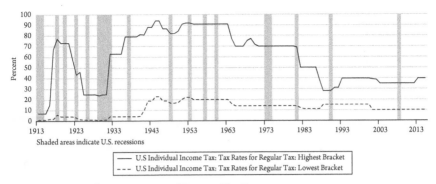

Figure 2. Top and Bottom Marginal Income Tax Rates.
SOURCE: U.S. Department of Treasury, IRS
Retrieved from FRED, Federal Reserve Bank of St. Louis.

Reagan cut it sharply. The first cut came in 1981 and the second came with the Tax Reform Act of 1986. It is fair to say that a tax rate as high as 90% can only be rationalized by a very low estimate of the elasticity of work effort with respect to after-tax income. In contrast, the lowest marginal tax bracket has generally been around 10% since the end of the Great Depression, though it did get up to 20% for a couple of decades.

The personal income tax is applied to taxable income less some allowed deductions. These deductions include a personal exemption on personal expenses such as moving costs or mortgage interest payments, as well as state tax payments and charitable contributions. Business expenses can also be deducted. In addition, while capital gains and dividend receipts are also taxed, the tax rate on them is set at a lower rate. High-earning households are now subject to a second tax calculation, called the alternative minimum tax, if their income exceeds certain limits.

To get a sense of how things play out for households in different parts of the income distribution, I reproduce a table from the Congressional Budget Office (CBO) in figure 3.[3] One can see that there is a huge amount of variation in income, government transfers, and taxes paid. Because of the large disparity in income and taxes paid, the top one-fifth of U.S. households end up with roughly 60% of before-tax income and pay almost 70% of federal taxes.

This variation led to a wide difference in the average tax rate that households paid on their before-tax income, which includes government transfers. In figure 4 I have reproduced a figure on average tax rates from the CBO. What this shows is that since 1980, tax rates at the top of the income distribution appear fairly stable,while those at the bottom have generally declined somewhat. In 2015, the top 1% had an average tax rate of 33.3%, the rest of the top quintile had an average

3. See https://www.cbo.gov/publication/51361 for more information.

**Average Household Income, Transfers, and Taxes, by Before -Tax Income
Group, 2013**

Dollars

	Lowest Quintile	Second Quintile	Middle Quintile	Fourth Quintile	Highest Quintile	All Households
Market Income	15, 800	31, 300	53, 000	88, 700	253, 000	86, 400
Government Transfers	9, 600	16, 200	16, 700	15, 000	12, 000	13, 900
Before- Tax Icome	25, 400	47, 400	69, 700	103, 700	256,000	100, 200
Federal Taxes	800	4, 000	8, 900	17, 600	69, 700	20, 100
After-Tax Income	24, 500	43, 400	60, 800	86, 100	195, 300	80, 100

Figure 3. Income, Transfer, and Tax Levels by Income Groups.
SOURCE: Congressional Budget Office.

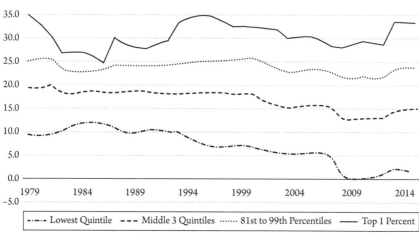

Figure 4. Average Tax Rates by Income Groups.
SOURCE: Congressional Budget Office.

tax rate of 23.8%, the middle three quintiles had an average tax rate of 14.9%, and
the bottom quintile had an average tax rate of 1.5%.[4]

The income tax code distinguishes between long- and short-term capital gains.
Short-term capital gains (which are earned within a year) are treated as regular
income and taxed accordingly. Long-term capital gains, along with dividends, are
taxed at lower rates. These lower rates are capped at 28%. Business and partner-

---

4. Source for figure and data is "The Distribution of Household Income," 2015, published by the
Congressional Budget Office, November 2018.

ship income is generally treated like regular income. However, corporations face their own version of the income tax system.

3. CORPORATE TAXATION

Corporations face their own income tax schedule. The federal schedule has a variety of statutory marginal rates. Prior to the Trump tax cut, they began at a low of 15% and rose to a high of 39%. These statutory rates are very high relative to those in the rest of the world. However, the actual or "effective" rate at which corporations are taxed varies considerably from these statutory rates.

The U.S. Treasury estimated the effective tax rate by year between 2007 and 2011. It ranges from a high of 26% in 2007 to a low of 20% in 2010 and 2011. When we look across industries during this period, there is an even bigger range in the average effective tax rates for this period. It starts from a low of 10% for utilities. Manufacturing's effective tax rate is 22%, while finance and real estate had rates of 19% and 20%, respectively. (See https://www.treasury.gov/resource-center/tax-policy/tax-analysis/Documents/Average-Effective-Tax-Rates-2016.pdf for more information on these rates.) Note that since corporations can deduct their interest payments from their taxable income, paying out through dividends is more expensive than paying out through interest payments.

## 16

Taxes in Our Model: Take 1

We are going to begin studying taxes within a standard representative agent framework. This means that we cannot analyze the distributional impact of taxes. However, we can use this model to think about the impact of taxes on capital vs. labor and the overall level of taxation.

Since we have a representative agent model, it does not make sense to worry about issues such as the progressivity of taxation or the impact on wealthy vs. poor people. Hence, our focus will be solely on their aggregate impact. For this reason, we will restrict ourselves to flat rate taxes, leaving more exciting forms of taxation for another day.

We want to consider labor and capital taxation, but in a world in which all production is done by households in their own plant using their own capital and labor, the households will see through this. As a result, they pay everything to whichever factor gets the lowest level of taxation. In addition, since tax revenue will be refunded to the households, if they got back exactly what they paid in, then they see through this and do not worry about their taxes. So we are going to make two conceptual changes to get around this: (i) all factors are rented, and (ii) the tax rebate depends on the aggregate level of per capita revenue.

Change (i) means that each household employs the labor and capital of other households. We will assume that these factors are traded in competitive markets with w_t and r_t being the rental rates of labor and capital, respectively. Change (ii) means that at the household level tax payments are viewed as lost, even though in equilibrium everyone gets back exactly what they paid in.

Let τ_l and τ_k denote the tax rates on capital and labor. Then the after-tax level of labor income is given by $(1 - \tau_l)w_t L_t$ and tax receipts are given by $\tau_l w_t L_t$. Capital

Monetary and Fiscal Policy through a DSGE Lens. Harold L. Cole, Oxford University Press (2020).
© Oxford University Press. DOI: 10.1093/oso/9780190076030.001.0001

taxation is normally done net of depreciation, but we are going to ignore that nicety. So, if r_t is the rental rate on capital, then after-tax capital income is given by $(1 - \tau_k)r_t K_{t-1}$ and tax receipts are given by $\tau_k r_t K_{t-1}$.

The government transfers its receipts back to the public on a per capita basis, so

$$T_t = \tau_l w_t L_t + \tau_k r_t K_{t-1} + \bar{M}_{t+1} - \bar{M}_t$$

This includes both the revenue from taxation and the revenue from money creation.

A household running a production plant using hired labor $\bar{L}_t$ and capital $\bar{K}_t$ will just seek to maximize its net revenue which is given by

$$P_t \left[Z_t \bar{L}_t \right]^{1-\alpha} \bar{K}_t^\alpha - w_t \bar{L}_t - r_t \bar{K}_t$$

Fixing the inputs, the marginal product of a factor is simply the derivative of the revenue w.r.t. that factor. The household will optimally choose to set the marginal product equal to the rental price. If we assume that markets are competitive and hence that factors are paid their marginal products, we get that

$$w_t = P_t \left[(1 - \alpha) Z_t^{1-\alpha} \bar{L}_t^{-\alpha} \bar{K}_t^\alpha \right]$$

and that

$$r_t = P_t \left[\alpha \left[Z_t L_t \right]^{1-\alpha} \bar{K}_t^{\alpha-1} \right]$$

Putting this together with our taxes yields a different income term in the household's budget constraint in the asset market.

Remark 23. *But wait, note that*

$$P_t \left[(1 - \alpha) Z_t^{1-\alpha} L_t^{-\alpha} K_t^\alpha \right] L_t = (1 - \alpha) P_t Y_t$$

and that

$$P_t \left[\alpha \left[Z_t L_t \right]^{1-\alpha} K_t^{\alpha-1} \right] K_t = \alpha P_t Y_t$$

Putting this together would imply that the output term Y_t in the old budget constraint is now replaced by

$$\left[(1 - \alpha)(1 - \tau_l) + \alpha(1 - \tau_k) \right] \left[Z_t L_t \right]^{1-\alpha} K_t^\alpha .$$

But then, what is the difference between labor and capital taxes? The answer is that in making its labor decision a household takes w_t and r_t as given and does not internalize the impact its choices would have on these returns. If the household took account of the impact of their choice of labor effort on w_t alone, then it would want to act like monopsonists and hold back its labor. However, if it also took account of the impact on r_t then it would not want to do so. If all households were integrated and hence owned their own capital and worked in the family business, there would not be much difference between the two taxes. They would all just boil down to a tax on output.

In light of this remark, we are going to need to distinguish very carefully between the aggregate levels of capital and labor, $\bar{K}_t$ and $\bar{L}_t$, over which the household has no control, and the household's choice variables over which it does have control. The marginal products will depend only on the aggregates. Of course in equilibrium $\bar{K}_t = K_t$ and $\bar{L}_t = L_t$.

Given this, we can write the household's choice problem as choosing a sequence of quantities $\{C_t, L_t, M_t, B_t, K_{t+1}\}_{t=1}^{2}$ so as to maximize

$$\max \sum_{t=1,2} \beta^{t-1}\left[u(C_t) - v(L_t)\right] + \beta^2 V(M_3, B_3, K_3)$$

subject to

$$M_t \geq P_t C_t \text{ and}$$

$$P_t\left\{ \begin{array}{l} (1-\tau_l)\left[(1-\alpha)Z_t^{1-\alpha}\bar{L}_t^{-\alpha}\bar{K}_t^{\alpha}\right]L_t + \\ (1-\tau_k)\left[\alpha\left[Z_t\bar{L}_t\right]^{1-\alpha}\bar{K}_t^{\alpha-1}\right]K_t - \delta K_t \end{array} \right\}$$

$$+ \left[M_t - P_t C_t\right] + B_{t-1} + T_t$$

$$\geq M_{t+1} + q_t B_{t+1} + P_t\left[K_{t+1} - K_t\right] \text{ for all } t \leq 2.$$

From this problem, we can see right away that only the f.o.c.'s for labor and capital will be affected by the tax policy variables. Moreover, since we will assume for now that all of the proceeds of the tax are rebated through T_t, it follows that the resource constraint will be the same too. So, let's just focus on these two key f.o.c.'s and see how things change as a result of taxation. The f.o.c. for labor is given by

$$-\beta^{t-1}v'(L_t) + \mu_t P_t(1-\tau_l)Z_t^{1-\alpha}(1-\alpha)\bar{L}_t^{-\alpha}\bar{K}_t^{\alpha} = 0.$$

The f.o.c. for capital is given by

$$-\mu_t P_t + \mu_{t+1} P_{t+1} \left[(1-\tau_k)[Z_{t+1}\bar{L}_{t+1}]^{1-\alpha} \alpha \bar{K}_{t+1}^{\alpha-1} + 1 - \delta \right] = 0.$$

Here we see the tax wedges affecting the individual's choices. Moreover, each tax affects only its own marginal condition so labor and capital taxes here are playing a distinct role.

If we undertake the same sort of analytics as we did in the balanced growth section, and set the aggregate equal to the individual choice values for capital and labor, we will get the following variants on our two conditions (81) and (82):

$$L^{\gamma+\alpha} = \tilde{\mu} P_1 (1-\tau_l)(1-\alpha) Z_1^{1-\alpha} K_1^{\alpha} \tag{85}$$

and

$$1 = \frac{\beta}{1+g} \left\{ (1-\tau_k)\alpha \left[\frac{Z_1 L}{K_1} \right]^{1-\alpha} + 1 - \delta \right\}. \tag{86}$$

Remark 24. *Equation (86) is the key result with respect to understanding capital taxation. It indicates that the after-tax return on capital is pinned down by things such as the discount rate β and the growth rate g, and that any change in the tax rate is offset by changes in the capital-to-labor ratio. This result follows fundamentally from our using an infinitely lived representative framework with additively separable preferences.*

We can use expression (86) to pin down the ratio of productive labor to capital just as we did without taxes,

$$\frac{Z_1 L}{K_1} = \left\{ \frac{1}{\alpha(1-\tau_k)} \left(\frac{1+g}{\beta} - 1 + \delta \right) \right\}^{1/(1-\alpha)}. \tag{87}$$

From (87) we can see that an increase in the tax rate on capital works exactly like making people more impatient (i.e., lower β). Hence, it will increase the ratio of productive labor to capital, but this in turn implies that it will depress the capital-to-labor ratio.

Now let's return to our optimal labor condition (85) and we will use our prior results to generate a nice condition to work with. Remember that

$$P_1 = \frac{M_1}{C_1}$$

and that

$$\tilde{\mu} = \frac{\beta}{1+\tau} \frac{1}{M_1}.$$

We then use these two results just as we did before when we did not have taxes in our optimal labor condition to get that

$$L^\gamma = \left[\frac{\beta}{1+\tau}\right]\left[\frac{1}{[Z_1 L]^{1-\alpha} K_1^\alpha - [g+\delta]K_1}\right](1-\tau_l)(1-\alpha)Z_1^{1-\alpha}\left(\frac{K_1}{L}\right)^\alpha.$$

Now all we need to do is follow the same steps as in the case without taxes to get the analog of (84) to get

$$L^{1+\gamma} = \left[\frac{\beta}{1+\tau}\right]\left[\frac{1}{[Z_1]^{1-\alpha}\left(\frac{K_1}{L}\right)^\alpha - [g+\delta]\frac{K_1}{L}}\right](1-\tau_l)(1-\alpha)Z_1^{1-\alpha}\left(\frac{K_1}{L}\right)^\alpha.$$

$$(88)$$

and then we can just substitute in for the capital-to-labor ratio which is pinned down by (87).

The capital-to-labor ratio is also important for labor productivity. To see this, note that

$$\frac{Y_t}{L_t} = \frac{Y_1(1+g)^{t-1}}{L}$$

where Y is initial output when $t = 1$ and hence the level of productivity is Z. This then leads to

$$\frac{Y_1}{L} = \frac{(Z_1 L)^{1-\alpha}K_1^\alpha}{L} = Z_1^{1-\alpha}\left(\frac{K_1}{L}\right)^\alpha.$$

$$(89)$$

From (87) and (89) we can see that capital taxes are important for labor productivity, but labor taxes are not. From (87) and (88) we can see that both capital taxes (through the capital-to-labor ratio) and labor taxes are important for the level of labor effort.

1. QUANTITATIVE FINDINGS

This has been a lot of work, but we are now in a position to answer some important questions:

1. How much do labor and capital taxes distort the optimal levels of labor and capital? Are they equally sensitive or is one of these two key inputs more sensitive?
2. Lowering taxes will raise the level of the associated input and indirectly the other input. Can this positive effect be enough to offset the direct loss of revenue? And, if not, how much are we losing?

The last question has been highly debated of late in Congress. We are ready to put in some numbers and begin to sort this out. I am going to start our debate on this issue by providing some results of my own. To do this, I programmed the solution to our model. The key parameters in my computed solutions are reported in Table 1. I set $\gamma = 0.5$, which implies a Frisch elasticity of 2. This is pretty high by micro standards and at the low end for macro.

I graphed the results on tax revenue in Figure 1. The first panel gives total tax revenue for a range of labor and capital taxes. The second panel gives labor tax revenue. Let's start with the first panel. There are several key features to note. First, starting from 0 for both tax rates, total revenue is increasing in both rates. This is close to a tautology, since revenue has to start at 0 and has no place to go but up. However, revenue, while increasing for low values of a tax rate, eventually starts decreasing at high values. In other words, tax revenue is hump-shaped with respect to an individual tax fixing the other tax. Third, looking at adjusting both tax rates, total revenue is dome-shaped, indicating that there is an interior optimum for maximizing revenue. Next, turn to the second panel and note that labor tax revenue is decreasing in the level of capital taxation, and hump-shaped with respect to the labor tax rate. A similar result holds for capital taxes. The reason is that each tax steals a bit from the revenue of the other tax by discouraging capital accumulation for capital taxes or labor effort for labor taxes.

One aspect of the debate on taxes is how responsive the level of output is. After all, if output shoots up enough, then tax revenue rises in response to a cut in the rates. To get some preliminary insight into this question, I computed the taxes that maximize total tax revenue. This is reported at the bottom of Table 1. It turns out that a quite low level of capital taxation and a moderately high level of labor taxation maximize revenue. This clearly indicates the limits of assuming

Table 1. EQUILIBRIUM TAX CALCULATIONS:
PARAMETERS AND KEY RESULTS

Parameter	Value	Parameter	Value
γ	0.5	α	1/3
β	1/(1.01)	g	1.01
τ	1.02	δ	0.08
Maximum Total Revenue			
τ_K	0.1	τ_L	0.6

(a) Total Tax Revenue

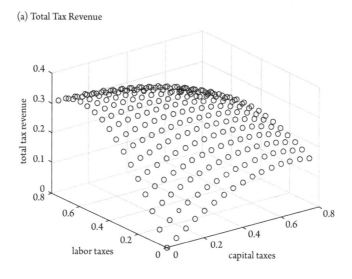

(b) Labor Tax Revenue

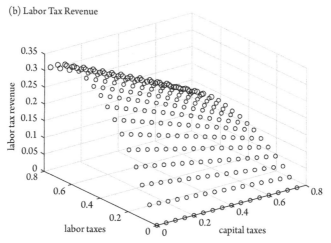

Figure 1. Tax Revenue by Tax Rates.

that output increases will make up for tax cuts with respect to labor taxation, but suggests that the gains with respect to capital taxation are considerably higher.

However, unless you are some kind of ruthless dictator, the normal goal is not to raise the most revenue, but to raise it *efficiently*, by which I mean giving the highest welfare level for a given amount of revenue raised. To examine this issue, I fixed the amount of revenue raised to be the total revenue we get when $\tau_K = 0.3$ and $\tau_L = 0$. This is just to give us a feasible interior revenue level. Then, for each of the capital tax rates we considered in our original plots, I computed the labor tax rate that would allow me to raise the same amount of revenue. The combination of the level of taxes that hit the targeted revenue amount and the implied consumption and labor effort levels are plotted in Figure 2.

The results in Figure 2 are particularly striking with respect to consumption. It is monotonically declining in the extent to which we rely on capital taxes to raise revenue. Moreover, at high levels of capital taxation, we end up subsidizing labor by having a negative tax rate. The results with respect to labor are a bit more nuanced; however, low capital taxes are associated with both high consumption and low labor effort. Thus, our model, under the current parameterization is clearly saying that capital taxes are a bad way to raise revenue. A natural question here is to what extent this is fundamental to the model or a product of the particular parameterization? And if it is fundamental to this model, what aspect of the model is driving this result?

(a) Consumption

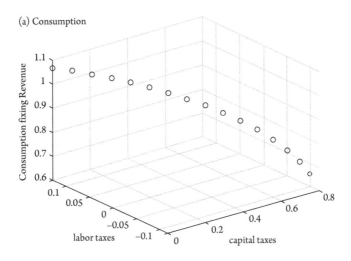

(b) Labor

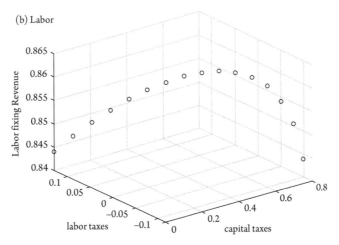

Figure 2. Outcomes Fixing Government Revenue.

Remark 25. *To produce these 3D plots, I used the Matlab plotting function "scatter3." To compute the labor tax rate that hit my revenue goal given the capital tax rate, I used the Matlab nonlinear equation solver "fsolve."*

Exercise 26. *Write a program to compute the balanced growth path levels of capital K_1 and labor L_1 given our tax rates τ_l and τ_k. In your program you should also compute the balanced growth path levels of output, Y_1, and wages, w_1, and the rental rates on capital r_1. Consider taxes rates $\tau_i \in [0 : .1 : .8]$ for each of our two taxes. Use your program to solve for how all of these variables change with the different tax rates. In particular, note how an increase in labor taxes affects capital and the return to capital, and how an increase in capital taxes affects labor and the return to labor.*

Exercise 27. *In a famous article, Christophe Chamley argued that capital taxes should be set to 0 in the long run.[1] Discuss this claim in light of your results. Organize your discussion around the efficient way to raise a given amount of revenue using our two tax channels.*

Exercise 28. *In a well-known paper, Edward Prescott has argued that taxation can explain the following facts: (1) labor productivity is roughly the same in Europe and the United States, but (2) Europeans work substantially fewer hours than Americans. Try to use your results to suggest how this outcome might occur. Then look at his article to see if your explanation is consistent with the facts he cites. Organize your discussion around the impact of the overall level of revenue raised.[2]*

2. CAPITAL'S RESPONSE

How much does capital responsd to changes in taxes? This issue is at the heart of any predictions that we make. Unfortunately, it turns out to depend on the model one assumes. In Equation 87 the combination of a Cobb-Douglas aggregate production function and our infinitely lived representative household with

1. Chamley, Christophe. "Optimal taxation of capital income in general equilibrium with infinite lives." Econometrica: Journal of the Econometric Society (1986): 607–622.

2. Prescott, Edward C. Why do Americans work so much more than Europeans? No. w10316. National Bureau of Economic Research, 2004. This claim by Prescott is not without controversy. See Ljungqvist, Lars, et al. "Do taxes explain European employment? Indivisible labor, human capital, lotteries, and savings [with Comments and Discussion]." NBER Macroeconomics Annual 21 (2006): 181–246.

additively separable preferences generates a fairly stark prediction. We can boil down the essence of this equation by noting that it implies that the term

$$(1 - \tau_k)\alpha \left(\frac{ZL}{K}\right)^{1-\alpha}$$

is equal to a constant pinned down by the other parameters of the model. Given this, the impact of a change in capital taxes and the ratio of productive labor to capital must offset within this condition. This expression says that the MPK of capital will respond to exactly offset the impact of a change in taxation on the after-tax MPK. In other words, if the after-tax share of capital income rises by 10%, then the marginal product of capital is predicted to fall by 10%, indicating a response coefficient of -1 with respect to this comparison.

Let's consider what this implies for the recent changes in taxes on capital. If we were to assume that labor was not going to respond, then the proposed statutory tax cut on corporate income taxation from 35% to 22% would imply that the capital stock should increase by 30%. This seems very large.

What do the data say? Figure 3 plots the share of private domestic investment in GDP, and the ratio of corporate tax receipts to corporate profits, which is a crude measure of the effective tax rate on capital.[3]

The procyclical pattern on investment is very distinct in the data. This is the sort of strong response our theory would predict. However, this is a short-run

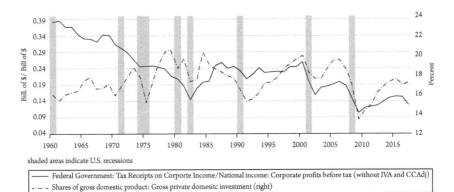

shaded areas indicate U.S. recessions

—— Federal Government: Tax Receipts on Corporte Income/National income: Corporate profits before tax (without IVA and CCAdj)
-·-·- Shares of gross domestic product: Gross private domesitc investment (right)

Figure 3. Investment Spending and Taxes.
SOURCE: U.S. Bureau of Economic Analysis.

3. Sources are: U.S. Bureau of Economic Analysis, Shares of gross domestic product: Gross private domestic investment [A006RE1Q156NBEA], retrieved from FRED, Federal Reserve Bank of St. Louis. U.S. Bureau of Economic Analysis, Federal Government: Tax Receipts on Corporate Income [FCTAX] and National income: Corporate profits before tax (without IVA and CCAdj) [A053RC1Q027SBEA], retrieved from FRED, Federal Reserve Bank of St. Louis.

response, and truth be told, we are looking at some sort of long-run response to a change in the tax rate on capital and this is very hard to tease out of the data. I emphasize the long run because it often takes time for investment projects to ramp up, and some forms of capital take investments over time to generate them.

Generally, attempts to estimate investment response equations suggest a much smaller response coefficient than our theory predicts. This small response is consistent with the fact that although our crude measure of the tax rate on corporate capital has been trending down in Figure 3, investment does not seem to exhibit a trend. The data in Figure 3 only show investment's share of output through the first quarter of 2018. Enough time probably has not passed yet to gauge the full response of investment to the Trump tax cut. Investment is forward looking, but as mentioned earlier, it takes time for projects to be developed and come online.

Another prediction of our theory is that the realized real rate of return on a risk-free bond should be pretty close to our discount rate β^{-1} on average. At least for the United States, real rates have been pretty close to 1% throughout the post-WWII period. They were a bit low around 1975 and again more recently, and a bit high around 1985, but these fluctuations are fairly modest: plus or minus 1%.[4] To really sort all of this out, we would ideally look for some sort of cross-country comparison. However, there are always so many differences between countries that it is very hard to make a sharp inference. Also, we have not allowed for any sort of response to productivity. One might think that things like R&D spending would also go up in response to a cut in capital taxes.

Exercise 29. *Examine the implications of our model for a cut in capital taxes from .35 to .22 when labor taxes are held fixed at .35. Then, redo your analysis assuming that capital does not change in response to the tax cut. These two experiments bracket the responses that we can reasonably expect to see in the data. Finally, redo it assuming that capital responds by only half of what our model predicts. Discuss how different these outcomes are. Does this suggest that our positive predictions about the benefits of cutting capital taxation are sensitive or insensitive to this aspect of the model?*

4. See Yi, K.-M., and Zhang, J., "Real Rates over the Long Run." Economic Policy Papers Federal Reserve Bank of Minneapolis, 2016. On a cautionary note, the real rates in many other countries are not nearly so smooth, especially for Italy. However, the debt for these countries seems far from risk-free.

## 17

Taxes in Our Model: Take 2

Our baseline model of taxation provided some very interesting results. However, it was completely silent on one of the key parts of any debate on the impact of changing taxes: its distributional consequences. The distributional aspect of the tax debate looms large because both income and tax receipts are heavily skewed in the United States, and total federal receipts are very dependent on individual taxes. About one-half of total federal tax receipts come from income taxes. However, those earning less than $50,000 contribute only 7% of revenue but make up roughly two-thirds of total filers, while those making over $1 million make up 27% of revenue but constitute 0.3% of filers.[1] This skewness can also be seen Figure 3 in chapter 15.

Given the importance of distributional issues, in this chapter we want to extend our baseline tax model to allow for different income groups. To match the data in any realistic manner, we will need these groups to differ in terms of the wages they earn, the transfers they receive, and the amount of capital they own. That's a tall order, and it's going to require some cleverness on our part in order to be able to construct a model with these features that we can realistically hope to analyze. Figuring out how to construct a model that is both rich enough to address the issues you want to analyze but simple enough to actually analyze is the real art of economic analysis.

---

1. See F. Martin's "A Closer Look at Federal Income Taxes," Economic Synopsis Federal Reserve Bank of St. Louis 2016, No. 23.

Monetary and Fiscal Policy through a DSGE Lens. Harold L. Cole, Oxford University Press (2020).

1. ADDING HETEROGENEITY TO THE MODEL

We will extend our model by assuming that we have two different groups of individuals which we denote by h and l. The h individuals have high initial productivity Z^h, the low productivity l individuals have low initial productivity Z^l, where $Z^h > Z^l$. We will assume that the productivity of each type grows at the same rate $(1+g)$. So this relative productivity differential is persistent. Let η_i denote the fraction of households that are type $i \in \{l, h\}$.

If we are going to be able to solve this model, we will need it to follow a balanced growth path, just as it did in the economy with only one type of household. So, let's make some guesses consistent with this fundamental assumption.

> Conjecture 3. *For there to exist a balanced growth path for this economy, we need the following to be true:*
>
> 1. *Guess that the level of labor for each type will be constant; hence, the effective labor input for each type will be growing at rate $1+g$ and thus, the overall effective labor input, denoted by $\bar{L}_t$, will also be growing at this rate, or*
>
> $$\bar{L}_{t+1} = (1+g)^{t-1}\bar{L}.$$
>
> 2. *Guess that the marginal product of capital will be constant over time, and hence, the overall capital stock must grow at the same rate as effective labor so*
>
> $$K_{t+1} = (1+g)^{t-1}K,$$
>
> *just as in our representative economy with only one type of household.*
> 3. *Guess that overall consumption and consumption for each type of household will also grow at this same rate. Hence, the consumption of an individual of type i will be given by $C^i_t = (1+g)^{t-1}C^i$.*

To see what these assumptions imply, let's start with the big picture. Total output will be given by

$$Y_t = \bar{L}_t^{1-\alpha}K_t^\alpha,$$

and hence, the marginal product of effective labor, w, will be given by

$$w = (1-\alpha)\left(\frac{K_t}{\bar{L}_t}\right)^\alpha. \tag{90}$$

Since the capital-to-effective-labor ratio is constant, this term will be constant. However, since the amount of effective labor is growing at rate $1 + g$, the marginal product of labor will be growing at this rate. At the same time, since there is no effective capital, the marginal product of capital, r, will be given by

$$r = \alpha \left(\frac{\bar{L}_t}{K_t} \right)^{1-\alpha}, \tag{91}$$

and this will be constant over time. These two results are exactly what we saw in our representative economy with one type of household.

In each period the total payments to labor and the total payments to capital must equal output, while total consumption is equal to output less depreciation and adjusted for the extra investment needed to keep up with growth:

$$\eta_h C_h + \eta_l C_l = w(\eta_h Z_h L_h + \eta_l Z_l L_l) + (r - g - \delta)K, \tag{92}$$

(where we need to multiply by $(1 + g)^{t-1}$ to get the actual levels). At the same time, if we know the effective-labor-to-capital ratio and hence both r and w, we can use all this to determine K according to

$$K(1+g)^{t-1} = \frac{K_t}{\bar{L}_t}(1+g)^{t-1}(\eta_h Z_h L_h + \eta_l Z_l L_l) \tag{93}$$

We turn now to a household of type i's problem. We will implicitly allow the households to differ by type in terms of their productivity, the marginal tax rate on labor they face and the transfers they receive. Because it has no bearing on the derivations, we suppress the dependence on type for everything except productivity for now. Given this, we can express the generic household's problem as

$$\max \sum_{t=1,2} \beta^{t-1}[u(C_t) - v(L_t)] + \beta^2 V(M_3, B_3, K_3)$$

subject to

$$M_t \geq P_t C_t \text{ and}$$

$$P_t \left\{ \begin{array}{c} (1 - \tau_l)w(1+g)^{t-1}Z_i L_t + \\ (1 - \tau_k)rK_t - \delta K_t \end{array} \right\}$$

$$+ [M_t - P_t C_t] + B_t + T_t^i$$

$$\geq M_{t+1} + q_t B_{t+1} + P_t[K_{t+1} - K_t] \text{ for all } t \leq 2.$$

In writing the household's problem, we have taken advantage of our results on the marginal product of effective labor and the marginal product of capital. Note that the problems for our two types of households differ only w.r.t. the productivity of effective labor Z_i (and all the other stuff we suppressed like its transfers or its labor tax rate). The first-order condition for C_t, given log utility, is

$$\beta^{t-1}/C_t - [\lambda_t + \mu_t]P_t = 0.$$

The f.o.c. for L_t, given our standard disutility function, is

$$-\beta^{t-1}L_t^\gamma + \mu_t P_t (1+g)^{t-1} Z_i (1 - \tau_l)w = 0.$$

The f.o.c. for M_t is

$$-\mu_t + \lambda_{t+1} + \mu_{t+1} = 0.$$

The f.o.c. for B_t is

$$-\mu_t q_t + \mu_{t+1} = 0.$$

The f.o.c. for K_t is

$$-\mu_t P_t + \mu_{t+1} P_{t+1}[(1 - \tau_k)r + 1 - \delta] = 0.$$

These conditions are essentially the same as in our single household-type economy. This suggests that the same set of derivations, including the change-in-variables step, can be used to reduce them down to a set of tractable conditions. The c.i.a. constraint implies that

$$P_t = \frac{M_t}{C_t},$$

where this conditions holds at the aggregate level w.r.t. the aggregate money supply and aggregate consumption

$$C_t = [\eta_h C_h + \eta_l C_l](1+g)^{t-1},$$

and at the level of the household type. So, it is also true using the per capita money holdings of a household of type i and the per capita consumption level as well. This last insight means that we can essentially go through just as before. If we substitute for the price level using the per capita values for households of this type, we have that

$$\beta^{t-1} - [\lambda_t + \mu_t]M_t = 0.$$

Now the money supply here is the individual household's money holdings and not the aggregate level. But in a balanced growth path, the share of total consumption and hence total money held by each type will have to be constant. So, this will imply that M_t is growing at the same rate as the money supply. Hence, we will want to make our standard change in variables to render the multipliers stationary:

$$\tilde{\mu} = \mu_t M_t / \beta^{t-1}$$

and similarly for $\tilde{\lambda}$. Doing this yields the following version of our consumption f.o.c.

$$1 = \left(\tilde{\lambda} + \tilde{\mu}\right). \tag{94}$$

Remark 26. *Let's be careful not to be too sloppy here. What we've shown is that for both types of households, our preference and balanced growth assumptions imply that their multipliers are growing at the same rate. Hence, we can apply the same change in variables to render them stationary. But the levels of these multipliers will generally not be the same across the two households.*

Let's turn next to the f.o.c. for capital, and note that we can rewrite this given our change in variables as

$$1 = \frac{\beta}{1+g}[(1 - \tau_k)r + 1 - \delta], \tag{95}$$

where we have divided through by $\tilde{\mu}$. This equation implies that the exogenous parameters of the model pin down the marginal product of capital, which we have denoted by r. Since the marginal product of capital is still a simple function of the ratio of effective labor to capital from (91), we have pinned down this crucial ratio, just as we did before. The good news does not stop here, since this same ratio determines the marginal product of effective labor, and hence the wage per unit of effective labor through (90). So this too is pinned down.

Remark 27. *It is pretty amazing that satisfying one of our household intertemporal capital conditions pins down all of our return variables. But it comes at a price. Who holds the capital stock is not pinned down. This is because all this follows from the growth rate of consumption, not the level of consumption.*

Let's turn next to the one other major f.o.c. we have not yet considered: labor. Making our change in variables, we get that

$$
\begin{aligned}
L_t^\gamma &= \frac{\tilde{\mu}}{(1+g)^{t-1}C_1} Z_i(1+g)^{(t-1)}(1-\tau_l)w, \\
&= \frac{\beta}{1+\tau}\frac{Z_i}{C_1}(1-\tau_l)w,
\end{aligned}
\tag{96}
$$

where we substituted in for $\tilde{\mu}$ using the f.o.c. for money with our change in variables, and then use the fact that the sum of the normalized multipliers is 1 from our consumption f.o.c.

Remark 28. *This is an important result since it implies that labor effort will be constant, so effective labor will be growing at rate $(1+g)$, just as we assumed. Since we have already shown that the effective-labor-to-capital ratio will be constant too, we have now verified our first two conjectures. However, note that the level of labor will depend upon the ratio of labor productivity to consumption through the Z_1/C_1 term. Hence, the level of labor effort can differ across our two households. Another source of possible variation could come through the marginal tax rate on labor, which can also be allowed to be different.*

Now it's time to confront the monster under the bed. The allocation of consumption, even given aggregate consumption is not pinned down. This is true because the allocation of capital is indeterminate and because of government transfers. To get around this, we are going to posit how consumption is allocated and then determine outcomes and the allocation of capital and government transfers that will make this so. To do this, start from the accounting identity that if C_t is total consumption, where $C_t = (1+g)^{t-1}C$ and C is normalized consumption, then

$$
\eta_h C_h + \eta_l C_l = C = w(\eta_h Z_H L_h + \eta_l Z_l L_l) + (r - g - \delta)K.
\tag{97}
$$

Then, if $C_h = \theta_h C$ and $C_l = \theta_l C$, we need them to satisfy the following adding up condition

$$
\eta_h \theta_h + \eta_l \theta_l = 1.
\tag{98}
$$

Another allocation rule we could use is to allocate income. For example, we could allocate some or all of an individual's pretax labor income to that person and some or all of the net capital income.

So now we are in a position to put all of the pieces together and solve our model.

1. Posit values for $\{\theta_h, \theta_l\}$ that are consistent with our adding up condition.
2. Solve for the effective-labor-to-capital $\bar{L}/K$ ratio using (95). This determines r and w too.
3. Given guess values for $\{L_h, L_l\}$, we can determine normalized effective labor

$$\bar{L} = \eta_h Z_h L_h + \eta_l Z_l L_l$$

and with this K.
4. Our guess also determines consumption, C. The allocation of consumption between our two types is not pinned down, so we need to use our allocation rule to determine consumption for each type.
5. Once we have consumption for each type, we can plug this into our labor condition (96) to determine the implied level of labor for each type $\{\tilde{L}_h, \tilde{L}_l\}$.
6. If our initial guess was correct, then it should be the case that

$$\tilde{L}_i = L_i.$$

7. We can then iterate using a nonlinear equation solver to solve for the guess values such that we get out what we put in.

Once we know what an equilibrium of our model looks like, we can figure out how this could arise given appropriate choices for holding capital and government transfers. Assume for simplicity that no one borrows, so debt is equal to 0. Then, note that the c.i.a. constraint holds as an equality. Then, divide through by $(1+g)^{t-1} P_t$ and we get that

$$(1-\tau_l) w Z^i L^i + [(1-\tau_k)r - \delta - g] K^i + \frac{T_t^i}{(1+g)^{t-1} P_t} = \frac{M_t}{(1+g)^{t-1} P_t} = (1+\tau)C^i,$$

where we used the $t+1$ c.i.a. constraint to rewrite real balances in terms of consumption plus the residual inflation adjustment. Note that the growth rate of output lowers prices and raises consumption in an offsetting manner. Equation (1) lays out the combinations of capital allocations and transfers that we can use to support our particular outcome.

If we assume that the high-productivity h types hold all (or most all) of the capital, we can see how a shift from relying on capital taxation to labor taxation is likely to pay out from equation (1). Holding fixed labor and capital, the benefit from this shift will go completely to h types, while the cost in terms of the increase in labor taxes will be shared across the two groups. At the same time, the increase in capital holdings will also most directly benefit the h types, but may, through an increase in w, help both types in terms of their labor income. The big remaining question is: How big is this spillover effect?

2. QUANTITATIVE RESULTS

To examine the potential impact of such a spillover effect, we need to get some reasonable numbers upon which to base our calculations. The Census Bureau provides us with some estimates of income dispersion. From its website we can download a table of the income shares by quintile (fifths) for the United States. These income shares for 2016 can be seen in Table 1. The results, unsurprisingly, show that income in the United States is very uneven, with the top fifth earning half of all income. To get a handle on the wealth distribution, I looked to the CBO's "Trends in Family Wealth, 1989 to 2013" online report, which gives wealth levels in 5% increments of the wealth distribution. I aggregated these into deciles for the second set of entries in Table 1. The wealth distribution is even more skewed, with the top 20% of owning 75% of the wealth in the country.

In our computation we will try to roughly match these results. We will seek to choose relative labor productivity values such that the top fifth earn 50% of all wage income. We will have them own 75% of the capital stock. We will assume that government revenue is just rebated back to the groups that paid it, so there are no transfers between groups. We will set the tax rate on labor to 35%, since it is supposed to cover all labor taxes, including Social Security and Medicare taxes. Then we will compute what will happen if we lower the capital tax rate from the statutory level of 35% down to the proposed level of 22%.

The outcomes from our computations are displayed in Table 2. The absolute values of the numbers do not mean much, since it is unclear what our units are. So, we should focus on the relative values. In our computation we set the labor productivities to 1 for the poor and 5 for the rich. So the important point here is

Table 1. DISTRIBUTION OF INCOME AND WEALTH IN THE U.S.

Quintile	Lowest	Second	Third	Fourth	Highest
2016 Income Share	3.1	8.3	14.2	22.9	51.5
2013 Wealth Share	−0.3	1.0	5.7	17.8	75.9

SOURCE: Census Bureau website for income data and Congressional Budget Office for wealth data.

Table 2. CAPITAL TAXATION EXPERIMENT

Initial Outcome

τ_L	τ_K	w	r	K	G
.35	.35	0.9348	0.1695	3.1746	0.5651
Z_h	L_h	C_h	Z_L	L_l	C_l
5	0.6071	3.7847	1	0.6805	0.7150

Alternative Outcome

τ_L	τ_K	w	r	K	G
.35	.22	1.0240	0.1413	4.5832	0.5584
Z_h	L_h	C_h	Z_L	L_l	C_l
5	0.6322	4.0630	1	0.6915	0.7770

that the rich are 5 times as productive as the poor. This generated a 53% share of labor income going to the rich, which is pretty close to ideal. The reason that this difference in productivities had to be so high is that there are four poor people for each rich person. If we look at the marginal product of labor before and after we lowered the capital tax rate, we see that it rose by almost 10%. This rise occurs because the capital stock increases by 40%. On a somewhat negative note, the level of government revenue falls by 1%. So at the aggregate level, things look positive for individuals but not so positive for government revenue. Next, we turn to looking at things across our two groups.

Let's start by comparing the situation of the richest 20% to the poorest 80%. First, note that it is much better to be rich than poor in this world. The rich consume 5 times as much as the poor, while working slightly less. Now let's see what happens when we lower the tax rate on capital from 35% to 22%. The labor-effort level of the poor rises slightly (1.5%), however their consumption level rises by 8.6%. For the rich, their labor-effort level rises slightly (4%), while their consumption rises by 7%. Of course the rich in quantity terms are reaping most of the gains since the increase in their consumption relative to that of the poor is 4.4 times larger than the poor.

2.1. But Wait a Minute

After I did this calculation, I went back and looked at the before- and after-tax income table in Figure 3 of chapter 15 on tax facts. I noticed that the bottom three quintiles have *higher* after-tax income once the various transfers are added back in, while the fourth quintile's income is only very slightly lower. At the same time, for the top quintile, the after-tax income is much lower than the before-tax, even after we have factored in all of their benefits. These facts really call into question the assumption I made about each group getting back their own

Table 3. MORE PROGRESSIVE CAPITAL TAXATION
EXPERIMENT

Initial Outcome

τ_L	τ_K	w	r	K	G
.35	.35	0.9348	0.1695	3.1811	0.5663
Z_h	L_h	C_h	Z_L	L_l	C_l
5	0.7017	2.3727	1	0.5653	1.0714

Alternative Outcome

τ_L	τ_K	w	r	K	G
.35	.22	1.0240	0.1413	4.2976	0.5586
Z_h	L_h	C_h	Z_L	L_l	C_l
5	0.6939	3.8782	1	0.6150	0.8239

paid taxes. Remember, in the real world government revenue does not just go
for transfers but also for goods and services. So these facts suggest that net of
expenditures, the allocation of benefits (i.e., transfers and such) is really pretty
progressive. This made me rethink how I should do this experiment and I came
up with an alternative progressive version. In the progressive version I assumed
that every group gets back their own labor taxes (since much of this goes for Social
Security and Medicare) but the poor get all of the capital tax revenue, including
that of the rich. This is probably a bit extreme too, but in the other direction
from the first experiment. To make everything comparable I just kept all of the
parameters the same, and just resolved the new equilibrium values given the new
government transfer rule.

The new results are reported in Table 3. Now things are a bit more extreme, as
the rich get 60% of labor income because the extra transfers depress work effort by
the poor and increase the labor effort of the rich relative to the original benchmark
in Table 2. At the same time, consumption of the poor is higher, while that of
the rich is lower. The wage rate is the same between the two initial benchmarks
because the condition that pins down the capital-to-effective-labor ratio does not
depend on the level of consumption. When we cut taxes on capital, we now get a
very different dispersion in the benefits. All of this lost revenue is coming at the
expense of the poor, who are implicitly seeing their transfers drop. This leads to
their consumption actually falling under the tax cut, despite the fact that the wage
rate rises just as it did in the first experiment. For the rich, this tax cut is great, since
their consumption rises by 60%, while their labor effort falls slightly.

The fundamental point of our second "more progressive" tax experiment is that
the details of the tax and transfer scheme are going to matter a lot in terms of who
exactly benefits and how much. This should makes us skeptical of any modeling
that leaves out important elements. In the model I have constructed, we did not
explicitly model government expenditures, or even take account of how they

reduce consumption, because they too use up output. I have also not accounted for the fact that taxes on labor vary with your income level. Especially since we are interested in the distribution of gains and loses, one might also want to account for a finer degree of heterogeneity than the simple two-group decomposition we have here. Finally, since we are focusing on capital taxation, one would want to take account of how exactly capital is taxed in more detail. For example, we might want to think about deducting depreciation and how different kinds of capital are taxed differently. One can see from this discussion that a lot of thought and detail needs to go into a good model to predict policy outcomes.

2.2. Code Used

Here I report on the code I used for the calculations in Tables 2 and 3.[2]

```
function Taxes2 % This program computes the steady state of our model
with capitial and
% linear taxes when there are two types of households. The code
examines
% the impact of changing the tax rate on labor and capital and the
% distribution of income and wealth across the two groups
% By Harold Cole

% Parameters
gama = 0.5; % Frisch elasticity (1/gama) parameter for labor micro
(0,0.5) macro (2,4)
 g = .01; % growth rate of labor productivity
 beta = 1/1.02; % discount rate given risk-free rate
 alpha = 1/3; % capital's share
 tau = g; % growth rate of money, inflation is 1+tau / 1+g
 % Z has been normalized to 1.
 delta = .08; % depreciation rate of capital
 Zl = 1; Zh = 5; % relative productivity of the two groups.
 global Param
 tK = .35
 tL = .35
 Param = [gama g beta tau alpha delta Zl Zh tK tL];
```

---

2. I often misspell the Greek characters in my code because there can be well known functions with these names that are preprogrammed into Matlab. For example, there is the gamma function which is associated with a statistical model.

```
%
% Guess values
Ll = .7; Lh =.7; X = [Ll Lh];

% Solving for the EQ L's given tK and tL
sol = fsolve(@LEQ X)
Ll = sol(1); Lh = sol(2);

% EQ outcomes given labor
L = .8*Zl*Ll + .2*Zh*Lh; LabCap(tK,g,beta,alpha,delta,tau);
[LK r w] = LabCap(tK,g,beta,alpha,delta,tau);
K = L/LK;
(1-tK)*r-g-delta
G = tL*w*L + tK*r*K;

% We allocate the tax revenue here to determine consumption.
% The assumptions made about this allocation will affect
% our outcomes. If you want the tax revenue to just go
% back to whichever group paid it choose this and comment
% out the other choice. BE CAREFUL you need to fix
%Cl = Ll*w*Zl + (1/.8)*.25*K*(r-g-delta);
%Ch = Lh*w*Zh + (1/.2)*.75*K*(r-g-delta);
% If you want all of the tax revenue to go to the poor
% choose this and comment out the earlier choice. BE CAREFUL
% you need to fix it below in the subroutine too.

Cl = (1-tL)*Ll*w*Zl + (1/.8)*.25*K*((1-tK)*r-g-delta) + (1/.8)*G;
Ch = (1-tL)*Lh*w*Zh + (1/.2)*.75*K*((1-tK)*r-g-delta);

disp(' Here are the Equilibrium Outcomes')
disp('Frisch Parameter and Taxes for capital and labor')
[tK tL gama]
disp('High productivity/rich outcome - cons & labor')
[Ch Lh]
disp('Low productivity/poor outcome - cons & labor')
[Cl Ll]
disp('capital stock, wage rate and return on capital')
[K w r]
disp('Government Revenue')
G
disp('Share of labor income going to top group')
(.2*Lh*w*Zh)/(.2*Lh*w*Zh + .8*w*Zl*Ll)
```

```
% Alternative Tax Plan Scenario
tK = .22
tL = .35
Param = [gama g beta tau alpha delta Zl Zh tK tL];

% Solving for the EQ L's given tK and tL
sol = fsolve(@LEQ, X);

Ll = sol(1); Lh = sol(2);
% EQ outcomes given labor
L = .8*Zl*Ll + .2*Zh*Lh; LabCap(tK,g,beta,alpha,delta,tau);
[LK r w] = LabCap(tK,g,beta,alpha,delta,tau);
K = L/LK;
(1-tK)*r-g-delta
G = tL*w*L + tK*r*K;
% If you want the tax revenue to just go back to which
% ever group paid it choose this and comment out the
% other choice
%Cl = Ll*w*Zl + (1/.8)*.25*K*(r-g-delta);
%Ch = Lh*w*Zh + (1/.2)*.75*K*(r-g-delta);
% If you want all of the capital tax revenue to go to the
% poor choose this and comment out the earlier choice
Cl = Ll*w*Zl + (1/.8)*.25*K*((1-tK)*r-g-delta) + (1/.8)*tK*r*K;
Ch = Lh*w*Zh + (1/.2)*.75*K*((1-tK)*r-g-delta);
disp(' Here are the Equilibrium Outcomes under the Alternative Plan')
disp('Frisch Parameter and Taxes for capital and labor')
[tK tL gama]
disp('High productivity/rich outcome - cons & labor')
[Ch Lh]
disp('Low productivity/poor outcome - cons & labor')
[Cl Ll]
disp('capital stock, wage rate and return on capital')
[K w r]
disp('Government Revenue')
G
disp('Share of labor income going to top group')
(.2*Lh*w*Zh)/(.2*Lh*w*Zh + .8*w*Zl*Ll)
end
% Sub-Functions
function [LK r w] = LabCap(tK,g,beta,alpha,delta,tau)
LK = ( (1+g)/beta -1 +delta )/(alpha*(1-tK));
LK = LK (1/(1-alpha)); % effective labor to capital ratio
```

```
% and labor to capital ratio given Z=1
r = alpha*LK(1-alpha); % MPK
w = (1-alpha)*LK(-alpha); % MPL of effective labor
end
function labor = FOCL(Z,C,r,w,tL,g,beta,tau,gama)
Factor = (beta/(1+tau))*(Z/C)*(1-tL)*w;
labor = Factor(1/gama);
end
function LEQout = LEQ (X);
Ll = X(1); Lh = X(2);
global Param %Param = [gama g beta tau alpha delta Zl
% Zh tK tL]
gama = Param(1); g = Param(2); beta = Param(3);
tau = Param(4); alpha = Param(5); delta = Param(6);
Zl = Param(7); Zh = Param(8); tK = Param(9); tL = Param(10);
L = .8*Zl*Ll + .2*Zh*Lh; LabCap(tK,g,beta,alpha,delta,tau);
[LK r w] = LabCap(tK,g,beta,alpha,delta,tau);
K = L/LK;
K = L/LK;
G = tL*w*L + tK*r*K;
% If you want the tax revenue to just go back to which
% ever group paid it choose this and comment out
% the other choice
%Cl = Ll*w*Zl + (1/.8)*.25*K*(r-g-delta);
%Ch = Lh*w*Zh + (1/.2)*.75*K*(r-g-delta);
% If you want all of the capital tax revenue to go to the
% poor choose this and comment out the earlier choice
Cl = Ll*w*Zl + (1/.8)*.25*K*((1-tK)*r-g-delta) + (1/.8)*tK*r*K;
Ch = Lh*w*Zh + (1/.2)*.75*K*((1-tK)*r-g-delta);
Laborl = FOCL(Zl,Cl,r,w,tL,g,beta,tau,gama);
Laborh = FOCL(Zh,Ch,r,w,tL,g,beta,tau,gama);
LEQout = [X(1)-Laborl X(2)-Laborh];
end
```

Exercise 30. *Construct a version of our model with at least two income groups. For additional realism you could push things to three for extra credit: the poor, the middle class, and the rich. Use your model to undertake a tax experiment as we did here. In a famous article, Kenneth Judd argued that capital taxation just ends up hurting workers, so they too should want 0 long-run capital taxation.*[3] *Discuss*

3. Judd, Kenneth L. "Redistributive taxation in a simple perfect foresight model." Journal of public Economics 28.1 (1985): 59–83.

your results and how they reflect on Judd's claim. Discuss how your results depend on the parameters you assume. (To be fair to Judd, he was explicitly calculating the gains and losses along the transition path, and not just the steady state outcomes. Also, he fixed labor effort in line with the very low labor elasticities estimated in the micro literature. Finally, his point was more akin to saying that fixing the amount of revenue you want to raise from the rich, the poor are better off doing this through labor taxes rather than capital taxes. This is probably true here too.)

Exercise 31. *Next we want to revisit the responsiveness-of-capital issue to see how our results depend on it. Redo your calculations assuming no response in capital and only half as large a response as our model predicts.*

## 18

Modeling Government Expenditures

Thus far, we have simply assumed that government tax revenue is rebated to the households as a lump sum. As a result, the optimal level of taxation is 0 when taxes are distortionary. Here we want to make more realistic assumptions about the social value of government expenditures and examine how changes in taxation can affect the provision of government services, and through this, economic outcomes and overall welfare.

Government spending can have many different positive benefits, such as: (i) a direct utility benefit, such as public television or national defense; (ii) a productive input such as roads and bridges and the legal system; (iii) insurance through various transfers; (iv) spending on education; and (v) spending on basic research, which affects productivity growth. All of these are potentially important, but the easiest to accommodate are the first two channels. So, we will limit the roles we consider, while recognizing that, clearly, this is not anywhere close to the last word on this subject.

1. ADJUSTING OUR MODEL

We will simplify our tax system so that taxes are one-dimensional and are simply a flat rate output tax τ_Y. We will also do away with government debt and assume that spending is just equal to revenue. This leads to the following form of the government budget constraint

$$\omega G_{t+1} = \tau_Y Y_t,$$

Monetary and Fiscal Policy through a DSGE Lens. Harold L. Cole, Oxford University Press (2020).
© Oxford University Press. DOI: 10.1093/oso/9780190076030.001.0001

where $\omega > 1$ is our model of government waste or inefficiency, and revenue that is collected today funds expenditure in the next period.

We will assume that government spending is divided into a fraction ψ of spending that works as a consumption good and a fraction $1 - \psi$ that works as a production input. This leads us to modify our flow utility to be

$$u(C) - v(L) + h(\psi G),$$

and our production function to be

$$Y = f(ZL, K, (1 - \psi)G).$$

To do anything quantitative, we are going to have to take a stand on $h(\cdot)$ and $f(\cdot)$. Clearly, we can get almost any kind of answer if we make "creative" enough assumptions. So thinking of a way to rationalize our assumptions and thereby discipline them vis-à-vis the data is going to be important.

With respect to preferences, we have gone with a constant-elasticity or power-function type of preferences. These preferences have nice properties. In addition, unless we want either consumption or government spending to crowd out the other, the functional form should be the same. This suggests that $u(\cdot) = a \times h(\cdot)$. This is going to lead us to log preferences over government consumption.

With respect to production, it is common to use constant-returns-to-scale production functions, which also exhibit a constant elasticity of inputs. At the same time, we have found that a special version of this, Cobb-Douglas, works well for private inputs. This suggests something like the following:

$$Y_t = \left\{ \omega \left[(Z_t L_t)^{1-\alpha} K_t^{\alpha} \right]^{\rho} + (1 - \omega)[(1 - \psi)G_t]^{\rho} \right\}^{1/\rho}. \tag{99}$$

To understand this production function, note that if the cost of a unit of private value added is W_P and the cost of a unit of government input is W_g, then we get that

$$Y_t^{1-\rho} \omega \rho P^{\rho-1} = W_P,$$
$$Y_t^{1-\rho}(1-\omega)\rho(1-\psi)^{\rho} G^{\rho-1} = W_G.$$

This implies that

$$dlog\left(\frac{W_P}{W_G}\right) = (\rho - 1)dlog\left(\frac{P}{G}\right).$$

A special case is $\rho = 0$, which corresponds to Cobb-Douglas and gives us the following production function:

$$Y = (ZL)^{1-\alpha-\nu}K^{\alpha}((1-\psi)G)^{\nu}. \tag{100}$$

If we assume log preferences over government consumption and a Cobb-Douglas aggregator over private and public inputs, we get a fairly tractable model with which to begin our analysis. This representation gives us a four-parameter system within which to think about government spending.

2. ANALYZING OUR MODEL

The household's problem is fairly standard since G is exogenous to the household. We can write it as choosing a sequence of quantities $\{C_t, L_t, M_t, B_{t+1}, K_{t+1}\}_{t=1}^{2}$ so as to maximize

$$\max \sum_{t=1,2} \beta^{t-1}[u(C_t) - v(L_t) + h(\psi G_t)] + \beta^2 V(M_3, B_3, K_3)$$

subject to

$$M_t \geq P_t C_t \text{ and}$$

$$P_t\left[(1-\tau_Y)[Z_t L_t]^{1-\alpha-\nu}K_t^{\alpha}((1-\psi)G_t)^{\nu} - \delta K_t\right] + [M_t - P_t C_t] + B_t + T_t$$
$$\geq M_{t+1} + q_t B_{t+1} + P_t[K_{t+1} - K_t] \text{ for all } t \leq 2.$$

The household's f.o.c.'s are very similar to what we had in the simple model with capital. The consumption condition is given by

$$\beta^{t-1}u'(C_t) - P_t[\lambda_t + \mu_t] = 0.$$

The f.o.c. for L_t is

$$-\beta^{t-1}v'(L_t) + \mu_t P_t(1-\tau_Y)Z_t^{1-\alpha-\nu}(1-\alpha-\nu)L_t^{-\alpha-\nu}K_t^{\alpha}((1-\psi)G_t)^{\nu} = 0.$$

The f.o.c. for capital is given by

$$-\mu_t P_t + \mu_{t+1}P_{t+1}\left[(1-\tau_Y)[Z_{t+1}L_{t+1}]^{1-\alpha-\nu}((1-\psi)G_t)^{\nu}\alpha K_{t+1}^{\alpha-1} + 1 - \delta\right] = 0.$$

The f.o.c. for money is given by

$$-\mu_t + \lambda_{t+1} + \mu_{t+1} = 0$$

and the f.o.c. for bonds is given by

$$-\mu_t q_t + \mu_{t+1} = 0.$$

These f.o.c.'s along with the c.i.a. constraint, the budget constraint, the resource constraint, and the market clearing conditions for money and bonds, give the constraints that our equilibrium must satisfy. Once again, the presence of money growth and productivity growth means that our economy is not going to be stationary. Money growth means that nominal balances will be nonstationary, productivity growth means that output and capital will be nonstationary, and the combination of these two effects means that prices will generally be nonstationary. As usual this will lead us to solve out for a balanced growth path.

To do this, we again assume that both productivity and the money supply grow at constant rates given by

$$Z_t = (1+g)Z_{t-1}, \quad \text{with } Z_1 = 1,$$

and

$$M_t = (1+\tau)M_{t-1} \quad \text{with } M_1 = 1.$$

Conjecture that capital and government spending grow at the same rate as productivity and that labor is constant which implies that output will grow at rate g. This means that tax revenue grows at this rate and hence so does government spending, so these conjectures are at least consistent. Since capital is assumed to grow at the same rate as productivity,

$$K_t = (1+g)K_{t-1} = Z_t K_1.$$

Making use of the fact that capital grows at rate g, we can pin down investment as

$$X_t = (1+g)K_t - (1-\delta)K_t = (g+\delta)Z_t K_1.$$

Similarly, since

$$G_t = (1+g)G_{t-1} = Z_t G_1.$$

Taking account of this in the resource constraint, we get that

$$[Z_t L]^{1-\alpha-\nu} K_t^\alpha ((1-\psi)G_t)^\nu = C_t + [(g+\delta)] K_t + (1+g)G_t$$
$$Z_t L^{1-\alpha-\nu} K_1^\alpha ((1-\psi)G_1)^\nu = C_t + [g+\delta] Z_t K_1 + (1+g)Z_t G_1.$$

Note that since output and capital are growing at rate g, this implies that consumption must also grow at rate g. If we take account of the fact that everything except labor grows at rate g, then we get that

$$L^{1-\alpha-\nu} K_1^\alpha ((1-\psi)G_1)^\nu = C_1 + [g+\delta] K_1 + (1+g)G_1.$$

Turn next to our c.i.a. constraint which we are again assuming holds with equality. This yields the same result as before,

$$P_t = \frac{M_t}{C_t} = \frac{(1+\tau)}{(1+g)} P_{t-1}.$$

We can rewrite our f.o.c. for consumption as

$$\beta^{t-1} \frac{1}{C_t} = [\lambda_t + \mu_t] P_t = [\lambda_t + \mu_t] \frac{M_t}{C_t}.$$

This leads to

$$\beta^{t-1} = [\lambda_t + \mu_t](1+\tau)^{t-1} M_1.$$

So once again, we make a change in variables, setting

$$\tilde{\lambda}_t = \lambda_t \frac{(1+\tau)^{t-1}}{\beta^{t-1}},$$

$$\tilde{\mu}_t = \mu_t \frac{(1+\tau)^{t-1}}{\beta^{t-1}}.$$

This gives us

$$1 = [\tilde{\lambda}_t + \tilde{\mu}_t],$$

indicating that their sum is invariant and suggesting that just as we found before they are both time invariant.

With this change in variables, the f.o.c.'s for money and bonds can be written as

$$\tilde{\mu}_t = \frac{\beta}{1+\tau} [\tilde{\lambda}_{t+1} + \tilde{\mu}_{t+1}] = \frac{\beta}{1+\tau},$$

where we used our consumption condition, and

$$\tilde{\mu}_t q_t = \frac{\beta}{1+\tau} \tilde{\mu}_{t+1} \implies q_t = \frac{\beta}{1+\tau}$$

The f.o.c. for labor can be written as

$$\beta^{t-1} L_t^{\gamma} = \mu_t (1-\tau_Y) P_t Z_t^{1-\alpha-\nu} (1-\alpha-\nu) L_t^{-\alpha-\nu} K_t^{\alpha} ((1-\psi)G_t)^{\nu}$$

$$\implies L_t^{\gamma} = \tilde{\mu}_t (1-\tau_Y) \frac{1}{C_1} (1-\alpha-\nu) L_t^{-\alpha-\nu} K_1^{\alpha} ((1-\psi)G_1)^{\nu}$$

$$\implies L^{\gamma+\alpha+\nu} = \frac{\beta}{1+\tau} \frac{(1-\tau_Y)}{C_1} (1-\alpha-\nu) K_1^{\alpha} ((1-\psi)G_1)^{\nu},$$

where I have dropped the time subscript for labor, since clearly it will be constant on our balanced growth path.

The f.o.c. for capital,

$$\mu_t P_t = \mu_{t+1} P_{t+1} \left((1-\tau_Y) [Z_{t+1} L_{t+1}]^{1-\alpha-\nu} \alpha K_{t+1}^{\alpha-1} ((1-\psi)G_{t+1})^{\nu} + 1 - \delta \right),$$

can be rewritten as follows once we substitute out for prices

$$\mu_t = \mu_{t+1} \frac{1+\tau}{1+g} \left\{ (1-\tau_Y)\alpha [Z_{t+1} L_{t+1}]^{1-\alpha-\nu} K_{t+1}^{\alpha-1} ((1-\psi)G_t)^{\nu} + 1 - \delta \right\}.$$

Then, making use of the fact that Z_t, G_t, and K_t all grow at the same rate and that labor is constant, we get

$$\mu_t = \mu_{t+1} \frac{1+\tau}{1+g} \left\{ (1-\tau_Y)\alpha L^{1-\alpha-\nu} K_1^{\alpha-1} ((1-\psi)G_1)^{\nu} + 1 - \delta \right\}.$$

Finally, we put in our change of variables to get that

$$1 = \frac{\beta}{1+g} \left\{ (1-\tau_Y)\alpha L^{1-\alpha-\nu} K_1^{\alpha-1} ((1-\psi)G_1)^{\nu} + 1 - \delta \right\}.$$

If we collect our expressions we get the following set of equations: The government spending condition, where we have taken account of the fact that the revenue was raised in the prior period and deflated by $1+g$ to get

$$G_1^{1-\nu} = \frac{1}{1+g} \frac{\tau_Y}{\omega} L^{1-\alpha-\nu} K_1^{\alpha} (1-\psi)^{\nu}; \qquad (101)$$

the resource constraint

$$C_1 = (1-\tau_Y) L^{1-\alpha-\nu} K_1^{\alpha} ((1-\psi)G_1)^{\nu} - [g+\delta] K_1; \qquad (102)$$

the labor condition

$$L^{\gamma+\alpha+\nu} = \frac{\beta}{1+\tau}\frac{(1-\tau_Y)}{C_1}(1-\alpha-\nu)K_1^\alpha((1-\psi)G_1)^\nu; \qquad (103)$$

and the capital condition

$$1 = \frac{\beta}{1+g}\{(1-\tau_Y)\alpha L^{1-\alpha-\nu}K_1^{\alpha-1}((1-\psi)G_1)^\nu + 1 - \delta\}. \qquad (104)$$

This is a two-variable system, since given L and K_1 we can determine G_1 from equation (101). Given these three variables, we can determine C_1 from (102). Given these four variables, we use conditions (103) and (104) to check that our two original values were correct. The derivation of this system also verifies our assumption that there existed a balanced growth path with capital and government spending growing at the same rate as labor productivity.

3. QUANTITATIVE RESULTS

This model gives us a nice laboratory to explore the impact of different policy choices for τ_Y and ψ, along with different levels of efficiency, on the outcomes a country might experience. If we take the view that government-provided consumption is nice, but probably not as nice as regular consumption, a utility function of the form

$$h(\psi G_t) = .5log(\psi G_t)$$

might seem reasonable. Clearly, the government cannot create goods magically, so values of ω between 1 and 2 (for a fairly inefficient government) might seem plausible. With respect to government spending that goes to something we might call a productive input, given that Social Security and Medicare take up about 1/2 of expenditures, with military spending coming in for another 15%, a plausible range here is probably between 3.5 and 5%. But back in time, these values might have been higher.

We need to adjust our view of the Cobb-Douglas share in production given government inputs. To be conservative, let us take a production parameter value of $\nu = .05$, and adjust down $\alpha = 0.25$, so we still have a labor share of 0.7. We can think that the returns on government-provided inputs probably flow to the owners of capital, who control the firm, rather than the workers, who provide labor.

Exercise 32. *Given our assumptions with respect to parameters and functional forms, we are now in a position to explore the impact of government policy choices* *on outcomes, particularly the level of government spending, output, consumption, labor effort, and welfare along the balanced growth path. To do this, compute the solutions to our model for an efficient government with $\omega = 1$, $\psi = .5$, and tax rates between .1 and .5. Then, do this exercise again, but assume that the government wastes a fair amount of revenue, so set $\omega = 1.5$, and uses a lot of it on consumption-type spending, so set $\psi = .75$. Graph your results and discuss the extent to which government policy along this simple dimension could have an important impact on our key variables.*

Here is an example of what I found from doing this exercise plotted in Figure 1. The figure suggests that the overall level of government spending should be low, with taxes optimally around 17% of output. (Of course, this level leaves out some other important aspects of government spending, so even within the context of this model, this is probably at the low end.) At the same time, the figure suggests that while altering the efficiency of government spending or the allocation had some impact on output and welfare, lowering output by around 8% and welfare by around 6 percent. This impact is quite large relative to many quantitative experiments, but is small relative to output differentials that we observe internationally. If in addition, we thought that the level of government spending was efficient in the first experiment, and inefficient in the second, we can get a much larger difference. For example if we make $\tau_Y = .45$, which is consistent with the spending levels we see in many countries, we get an output gap of around 14%, which is a good bit larger. Despite this, I was a bit disappointed at the magnitude of the impact, since I had thought that this channel might be useful to explain some of the extreme differences we see across countries.

In a well-known accounting exercise for cross-country differences, Hall and Jones (1999) examined the factors affecting the observed differences in output per worker within a production accounting framework, much like we have here.[1] In their data the differences are very large, in the most extreme case by a factor of 35 between the United States and Niger. Their accounting framework is more sophisticated than ours since it includes human capital as well as physical capital. Their framework essentially implies that they will be able to account for the differences in output with differences in productivity along with physical and human capital accumulation. What is really interesting then is the roles each component plays. They find that differences in productivity are the most important factor, but differences in the accumulation of physical and human capital are also quite important. They then examine differences in "social infrastructure":

---

1. Hall, Robert E., and Charles I. Jones. "Why do some countries produce so much more output per worker than others?." The Quarterly Journal of Economics 114.1 (1999): 83–116.

(a) Solution g = 0

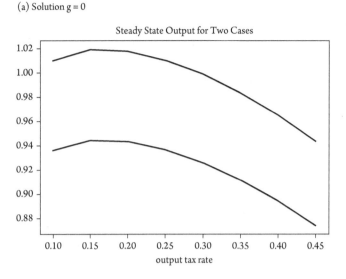

(b) Solution g = 0.02

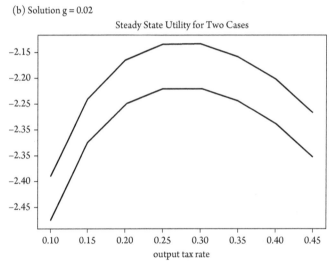

Figure 1. Outcomes in Our Two Experiments

By social infrastructure we mean the institutions and government policies that determine the economic environment within which individuals accumulate skills, and firms accumulate capital and produce output. (p. 84)

They conclude that this was the decisive factor in explaining the physical and human capital gaps. Their results suggest that we need to come up with a broader vision of the role of government and social institutions.

While this broader model is outside the scope of what we are doing here, I want to illustrate how, within the context of our model, we can explore other setups that might make the impact of government spending larger. For example, we could go back to our CES production aggregator (99) and choose a value of ρ above 0, which reduces the elasticity of substitution and thereby makes the level of government spending more crucial. For another example, we might want to take into account what the government charges producers for many services. This would reduce private value-added by subtracting some amount to account for the government's contribution. In that case, we would be comparing private factor payments relative to output less government payments, or $Y - P_G$. For labor this would make the factor share

$$\frac{\frac{\partial}{\partial L}\left[(ZL)^{1-\alpha-\nu}K^{\alpha}((1-\psi)G)^{\nu}\right] \times L}{(ZL)^{1-\alpha-\nu}K^{\alpha}((1-\psi)G)^{\nu} - P_G}.$$

This would allow us to raise ν and lower both α and $1 - \alpha - \nu$ without getting unreasonable factor payment shares.[2]

2. To explore this last possibility, I increased ν to 0.1, and set $\alpha = 0.2$. Now the optimal level of the output tax appears to be higher, roughly around 0.3, and the output gap at this tax rate between my two experiments is 10%.

## PART 3

Dynamic Models with Capital

## 19

Dynamic Adjustment with Capital

When we look at the data on output per capita, we often see countries moving along something that looks like a balanced growth path. However, we also see countries making fairly rapid transitions from low to high levels of output per capita. These are often called "growth miracles" when they seem to come about because of substantial economic reforms or transitions toward the "modern world." In Figure 1 I have plotted two well-known growth miracles.[1] The first is Spain, and the figure shows its dramatic growth path after WWII. The second is South Korea and after the Korean War it too shows a dramatic growth path. In both cases, I have plotted real output per capita relative to the level of this series in the United States. This allows us to account for growth in population, and growth in the overall frontier level of technological development. Hence, what we see in this figure is simply the movement from a level of output per capita that is well below the most advanced countries of the time, to one that is fairly close to the frontier (as measured by the U.S.). In the figure one can see how Spain, started from 30% of the U.S. level after WWII, and grew to almost 70% of the U.S. level. One can see an even more dramatic transition for South Korea. It went from 10% of the U.S. level after the end of the Korean War, and has similarly closed to almost 70% of the U.S. level.

---

1. Source is University of Pennsylvania, Purchasing Power Parity Converted GDP Per Capita Relative to the United States, retrieved from FRED, Federal Reserve Bank of St. Louis.

Monetary and Fiscal Policy through a DSGE Lens. Harold L. Cole, Oxford University Press (2020). © Oxford University Press. DOI: 10.1093/oso/9780190076030.001.0001

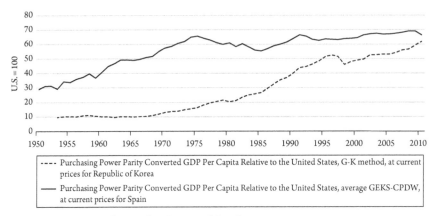

Figure 1. Two Growth Miracles: Spain and South Korea.
SOURCE: University of Pennsylvania.

How should we think about such a transition occurring in our model? There are two natural mechanisms. The first is that the technological level, which was well below the frontier level, suddenly started catching up. The second is that there were various frictions that discouraged the use of labor and capital, and thereby reduced output. We are going to extend our model to enable us to construct dynamic adjustment paths. We want to do this so that we can use the extended model to consider both of these mechanisms.

1. EXTENDING THE MODEL

Let us start by returning to the basic representative agent model of our first take on taxes. Assume that we have some arbitrary initial value of the capital stock K_1. Assume again that productivity and the money supply grow at constant rates given by

$$Z_t = (1+g)Z_{t-1},$$

and

$$M_t = (1+\tau)M_{t-1},$$

respectively. Also, let us again make the normalization that $Z_1 = 1$, so $Z_t = (1+g)^{t-1}$. In that model the household's choice problem was choosing a sequence of quantities $\{C_t, L_t, M_t, B_t, K_{t+1}\}_{t=1,2}$ so as to maximize

$$\max \sum_{t=1,2} \beta^{t-1}\left[u(C_t) - v(L_t)\right] + \beta^2 V(M_3, B_3, K_3)$$

subject to

$$M_t \geq P_t C_t \text{ and}$$

$$P_t \left\{ \begin{array}{l} (1-\tau_l)\left[(1-\alpha)Z_t^{1-\alpha}\bar{L}_t^{-\alpha}\bar{K}_t^{\alpha}\right]L_t + \\ (1-\tau_k)\left[\alpha\left[Z_t\bar{L}_t\right]^{1-\alpha}\bar{K}_t^{\alpha-1}\right]K_t - \delta K_t \end{array} \right\}$$
$$+ \left[M_t - P_t C_t\right] + B_{t-1} + T_t$$
$$\geq M_{t+1} + q_t B_{t+1} + P_t \left[K_{t+1} - K_t\right] \text{ for all } t \leq 2.$$

The consumption condition is given by

$$\beta^{t-1} u'(C_t) - P_t \left[\lambda_t + \mu_t\right] = 0.$$

The f.o.c. for labor is given by

$$-\beta^{t-1} v'(L_t) + \mu_t P_t (1-\tau_l) Z_t^{1-\alpha} (1-\alpha) \bar{L}_t^{-\alpha} \bar{K}_t^{\alpha} = 0.$$

The f.o.c. for capital is given by

$$-\mu_t P_t + \mu_{t+1} P_{t+1} \left[(1-\tau_k)\left[Z_{t+1}\bar{L}_{t+1}\right]^{1-\alpha} \alpha \bar{K}_{t+1}^{\alpha-1} + 1 - \delta\right] = 0.$$

The f.o.c. for money and bonds are given by

$$-\mu_t + \lambda_{t+1} + \mu_{t+1} = 0$$

and

$$-\mu_t q_t + \mu_{t+1} = 0.$$

Because we will assume that the c.i.a. constraint binds in each period, we again get that

$$P_t = \frac{M_t}{C_t},$$

where the numerator is the aggregate money stock at the beginning of the period and the denominator is real consumption. If we impose this result in our f.o.c.'s for consumption, along with log preferences, we get that

$$\beta^{t-1} = M_t \left[\lambda_t + \mu_t\right].$$

Note that this condition holds even though consumption may not be growing at a constant rate. This result implies that we can use a similar change in variables to help render the long-term model stationary, even though in the short-term these new multipliers may be time-varying. So, exploit this insight and define the following new variables

$$\tilde{\lambda}_t = \lambda_t M_t / \beta^{t-1}, \text{ and } \tilde{\mu}_t = \mu_t M_t / \beta^{t-1}.$$

If we now impose our price equation and our change in variables in our f.o.c.'s for consumption, we get

$$1 = \tilde{\lambda}_t + \tilde{\mu}_t.$$

If we use this result in our f.o.c. for money we get that

$$\tilde{\mu}_t = \frac{\beta}{1+\tau}.$$

These two conditions imply that our multipliers will not be time-varying despite the fact that we are on a transition path. This is a special product of having log preferences.

With these results, let's turn to the f.o.c. for capital. Making our substitutions we get that

$$-\tilde{\mu}_t \frac{M_t}{C_t} + \frac{\beta}{1+\tau} \tilde{\mu}_{t+1} \frac{M_{t+1}}{C_{t+1}} \left[[(1-\tau_k)Z_{t+1}\bar{L}_{t+1}]^{1-\alpha} \alpha \bar{K}_{t+1}^{\alpha-1} + 1 - \delta \right] =$$

$$-\frac{1}{C_t} + \frac{1}{C_{t+1}} \beta \left[[(1-\tau_k)Z_{t+1}\bar{L}_{t+1}]^{1-\alpha} \alpha \bar{K}_{t+1}^{\alpha-1} + 1 - \delta \right] = 0. \quad (105)$$

Next, the f.o.c. for labor is given by

$$-v'(L_t) + \frac{\tilde{\mu}_t}{C_t} (1-\tau_l)Z_t^{1-\alpha}(1-\alpha)\bar{L}_t^{-\alpha}\bar{K}_t^{\alpha} =$$

$$-v'(L_t) + \frac{\beta}{(1+\tau)C_t}(1-\tau_l)Z_t^{1-\alpha}(1-\alpha)\bar{L}_t^{-\alpha}\bar{K}_t^{\alpha} = 0. \quad (106)$$

Finally, note that the resource constraint says that

$$C_t = [Z_t L_t]^{1-\alpha} K_t^{\alpha} + K_t(1-\delta) - K_{t+1}.$$

Hence, the capital (105) and labor (106) f.o.c.'s form a two-equation block (once we substitute out for consumption), which we can use to solve for our fundamentals.

2. A SPECIAL ANALYTIC CASE

To construct a version of the model that we can solve analytically, we assume that taxes are 0, and depreciation of capital is 100%, so $\delta = 1$. Next, we are going to conjecture and verify a key aspect of the solution, which is that consumption and investment are constant fractions of output. Given this conjecture, it follows that

$$C_t = \psi Y_t, \quad K_{t+1} = (1 - \psi)Y_t \quad Y_t = (Z_t L_t)^{1-\alpha} K_t^{\alpha}. \qquad (107)$$

Plugging this first into our consumption equation (105), we get that

$$\frac{1}{\psi Y_t} = \frac{\alpha \beta}{\psi Y_{t+1}} \left[\frac{Z_{t+1} L_{t+1}}{K_{t+1}} \right]^{1-\alpha}$$

$$\implies \frac{1}{\psi Y_t} = \frac{\alpha \beta}{\psi Y_{t+1}} \frac{Y_{t+1}}{K_{t+1}} = \frac{\alpha \beta}{\psi Y_{t+1}} \frac{Y_{t+1}}{(1 - \psi)Y_t}$$

$$\implies 1 - \psi = \alpha \beta \qquad (108)$$

This both verifies our conjecture and pins down the value of ψ. This neat result— that savings is a constant fraction of income when depreciation is 100%—follows from our log assumption.

Next, we turn to our labor equation (106) to get that

$$v'(L_t) = \frac{\beta}{(1+\tau)\psi Y_t} Z_t^{1-\alpha}(1-\alpha)L_t^{-\alpha} K_t^{\alpha}$$

$$v'(L_t) = \frac{\beta}{(1+\tau)\psi Y_t}(1-\alpha)\frac{Y_t}{L_t}$$

$$\implies v'(L_t)L_t = \frac{\beta(1-\alpha)}{(1+\tau)\psi} \qquad (109)$$

This result also follows from our log assumption. It is both very neat and some-what troubling. With 100% depreciation we get that labor is constant. This suggests that we might have trouble matching the volatility of labor that we see in our data with this simple model. Our analytic solution gives us a nice case with which to test any code we might write for solving the full model.

Exercise 33. *Derive a similar result when we have constant labor and capital taxes. Discuss how these taxes will or will not affect our solution.*

3. SOLVING THE FULL MODEL

To solve our model, we are going to conjecture that, after a reasonable amount of time, both labor and capital will settle down to their balanced growth path levels. This will occur *because* capital has (approximately) converged to its balanced growth path level and hence so will labor. Let L^* and $Z_t K^*$ denote the balanced growth path levels of labor (which is constant) and capital (which grows with Z_t). Then what we are conjecturing is that up until time T, there is a sequence of values of $\{L_t, K_{t+1}\}_{t=1,2,\dots,T-1}$ and then for all $t \geq T$, $L_t = L^*$ and $K_{t+1} = Z_{t+1} K^*$. Solving for a solution in this fashion is often referred to as a "shooting method."

In Table 1 I report on the parameters I used, and the "steady state" solutions for several cases. I considered two different growth rates, g equal to 0 and 0.02. For each growth rate I computed the balanced growth path levels of labor, and the level of the capital stock for the normalized value of $Z_1 = 1.0$. I did this computation for an initial high level of taxation of capital and labor, which was set to 75%, and a low level of taxation, which was set to 35%. There are several interesting aspects to note with respect to Table 1. First, the reduction in taxation leads to a rough doubling of labor effort, and roughly a factor 8.5 increase in capital. These are big changes. Second, labor and capital are lower in the faster-growing economy than in the slower one, fixing the level of taxation. This is because growth raises future consumption directly and discourages savings a bit. The lower level of capital then discourages labor effort.

I then computed the transition paths given that the economy started at the high level of taxation and suddenly switched to the low level of taxation. These

Table 1. TWO DYNAMIC SOLUTIONS

Common Parameters			
γ	α	β	δ
0.05	1/3	1/1.02	0.08

Steady States $g = 0 = \tau$			
τ_L	τ_K	L	K
.75	.75	0.3129	0.2381
τ_L	τ_K	L	K
.35	.35	0.6416	2.0462

Steady States $g = .02 = \tau$			
τ_L	τ_K	L	K
.75	.75	0.3094	0.1782
τ_L	τ_K	L	K
.35	.35	0.6366	1.5368

solutions to the transition path are displayed in Figure 2. The transition in panel (A) is coming about purely through the dynamics of the capital stock adjustment to the reduction in taxation. One can see how the capital stock quickly rises and then levels off at its new steady-state level (since there is no long growth) well before the end of the transition period. This indicates that all of the transition has essentially been accomplished within the window we considered. The transition path in panel (B) combines the transition coming from the reduction in taxation, with the transition coming from long-run growth in productivity. This induces an

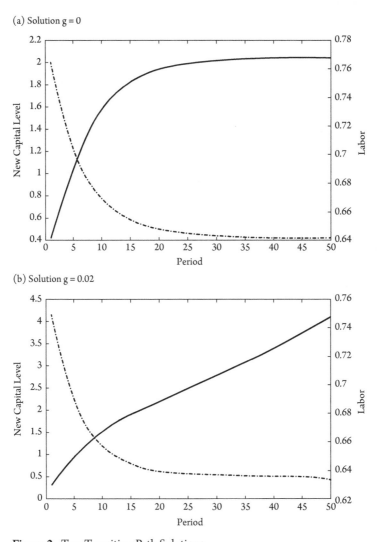

Figure 2. Two Transition Path Solutions

exponential curve in the capital stock, which can be seen toward the end of the transition period.[2]

4. SHOOTING ALGORITHM CODE

Here I want to talk through how one constructs the shooting algorithm code. The key part is getting the timing right.

We start with an initial level of labor and capital from the initial normalized balanced growth path. Denote by L_1 and K_1 the labor and capital level in the initial balanced growth path with high taxes when the level of labor productivity is normalized to $Z_1 = 1$. Denote the transition horizon by T with the understanding being that, in period 1, we start the transition with K_0 units of capital and labor productivity of Z_1, and we end the transition in period T. In each period from $t = 1, ..., T$ we will be determining the level of labor input L_t and the next period's initial capital stock K_{t+1}. In period $T + 1$, we will be assuming that the new level of the capital stock picked in period $T + 1$ is $K_{T+2} = (1 + g)^{T+1} K_{ss}$, where K_{ss} is the balanced growth level of the capital stock with low taxation that we are converging to, when productivity is normalized to 1. Given this,

$$C_t = [Z_t L_t]^{1-\alpha} K_t^{\alpha} + K_t(1 - \delta) - K_{t+1} \text{ for } t = 1, ..., T \text{ and}$$
$$C_{T+1} = [Z_{T+1} L_{ss}]^{1-\alpha} K_{T+1}^{\alpha} + K_{T+1}(1 - \delta) - (1 + g)^{T+1} K_{ss}.$$

These are the consumption levels we will want to be plugging into our two conditions: capital (105) and labor (106).

One slightly redundant way to do this is to construct the matrix

$$Q = \begin{bmatrix} K_1 & L_1 & K_2 \\ \vdots & \vdots & \vdots \\ K_T & L_T & K_{T+1} \\ K_{T+1} & L_{ss} & (1+g)^{T+1} K_{ss} \end{bmatrix} \tag{110}$$

The first column of Q is the capital input in the current period, which is a state variable from the point of view of this period. The second column is the labor input, and the third is the new capital level that is being chosen for next period.

2. In their classic article King and Rebelo pointed out that the transition dynamics in a suitably calibrated growth model was very short. See King, Robert G., and Sergio T. Rebelo. Transitional dynamics and economic growth in the neoclassical model. No. w3185. National Bureau of Economic Research, 1989.

These last two variables are being determined within the current period. The last row is for the outcomes beyond the last period of the transition. We need this row to determine the anticipated outcomes in $T + 1$ that we use in constructing the forward-looking condition (105) for K_T. The idea here will be to construct a function F that takes in the values of L and K that we are solving for, forms Q, and then computes the errors in zeroing out (105) and (106), given that we are constructing consumption as we just discussed.

It is useful to think of this function F as checking whether or not we have a solution, and, in fact, this is one of its uses. A natural way to verify your code is to share a solution with someone else, who then checks your answer using her version of F.

To construct the guess values of te capital stock, K_t^G (which is chosen in period $t - 1$), one can just posit that it will gradually move from the level implied by the initial high-tax balanced growth path to that implied by the final low-tax balanced growth path. For example

$$K_t^G = K_0(1+g)^{t-1}\frac{1}{1.2^t} + K_{ss}(1+g)^{t-1}\left[1 - \frac{1}{1.2^t}\right]$$

The choice of 1.2 is, of course, pretty arbitrary here, and you might need to play around with it. Presumably the slower and longer the transition, the closer this number should be to 1. For the guess values of labor, I just set $L_t = L_{ss}$, which is pretty crude but all we generally need to do is get close enough for our equation solver to work.

Here is an example of the code I used to construct my guess values. I could not get Latex to reproduce the up-arrow symbol that we use for exponentiation in Matlab, so I just wrote in "up-arrow" in its place.

```
T = 50; % Shooting horizon
ZT = (1+g)."up-arrow" [0:(T-1)]; % growth factor to adjust capital stock
   Fudge = (1/1.2)."up-arrow" [0:(T-1)]; % use this to adjust closeness to Kss
for guess
   Kguess = (ZT.*K0).*Fudge + (ZT.*Kss).*(1-Fudge);
   Lguess = Lss*ones(1,T);
   Guess = [Lguess' Kguess'];
```

I constructed my version of F in a subroutine that I labeled TransEQ. This subroutine needed to have the parameters of the model passed to it. So running it looks like

$$TransEQ(Guess, Param)$$

Unfortunately, Matlab is not as open to having variables passed when using the nonlinear equation solver, fsolve. One way around this is to declare a parameter vector as a global variable. Another is through a dummy function that has the parameter vector embedded in it. I chose the latter, and here is an example of this from my code. I also like to make sure that fsolve will work hard for me, so I set its options to make sure that happens.

```
options = optimset('MaxFunEvals',1e5,'TolFun',1e-10,'MaxIter',1e4);
    Param = [alpha gama g beta tau delta tK tL T L0 K0 Lss Kss]; %
parameters passed to equation solver
    fundummy = @(y) TransEQ(y,Param); % function of dummy variable
y, use to pass in Param
    sol = fsolve(fundummy,Guess,options)
```

Finally, I want to construct a nice graph of the transition solution I have computed. In this graph I plot both capital and labor, and use a two-sided figure with different scales on each of the two y axes.

```
figure(1)
yyaxis left
plot([1:length(sol)]',sol(:,2),'-k')
xlabel('Period')
ylabel('New Capital Level')
yyaxis right
plot([1:length(sol)]',sol(:,1),'-.k')
ylabel('Labor')
```

Exercise 1. *The first step is to find numbers on (i) GDP/hour, (ii) capital-to-labor ratios, and (iii) hours worked per capita for a developed country (DC), like the U.S., and a less developed country (LDC) like, say, Indonesia. A good source is the Penn World Tables. There you can find data on:*

emp = Number of persons engaged (in millions)
avh = Average annual hours worked by persons engaged
cgdpo = Output-side real GDP at current PPPs (in mil. 2011US$)
ck = Capital stock at current PPPs (in mil. 2011US$)

From these data it is easy to infer, L, Y/L and K/L. Then, compute the balanced growth paths for the DC for the following tax and productivity values: Z = 1,

$\tau_L^D = 0.2$ and $\tau_K^D = 0.2$. *The balanced growth path for the developed country will look like*

$$L_t^D = L^D, \quad K_t^D = (1+g)^{t-1}K^D, \quad Y_t^D = (1+g)^{t-1}Y^D.$$

Then, you want to determine a productivity factor, Z^L, labor tax rate, τ_L^L, and capital tax rate, τ_K^L, for our LDC, such that when you solve for the associated balanced growth path values,

$$Z_t^L = Z^L(1+g)^{t-1} \quad L_t^L = L^L, \quad K_t^L = (1+g)^{t-1}K^L, \quad Y_t^L = (1+g)^{t-1}Y^L,$$

the relative values of the three comparison facts are matched reasonably closely. To be precise, we want

$$\frac{Y_t^L/L_t^L}{Y_t^D/L_t^D}, \quad \frac{K_t^L/L_t^L}{K_t^D/L_t^D}, \quad \frac{L_t^L}{L_t^D}$$

to look like these ratios in the data. How important is it to have an initial productivity difference in order to match our three comparison facts? To answer this, you could simply fit facts (ii) and (iii) with $Z^D = Z^L$ and show how far off you would be. To do this, it is useful to return to equations (87), (88), and (89) in the chapter on balanced-growth with taxes. Note that we can determine the level of productivity, given the capital-to-labor ratio we have targeted off of (89). Given this, and our targeted capital-to-labor ratio, we can use (87) to determine the level of capital taxation. Finally, given productivity, we can see that capital taxes are important for labor productivity, but labor taxes are not. From (87) and (88) we can see that both capital taxes (through the capital-to-labor ratio) and labor taxes are important for the level of labor effort.

Exercise 2. *Start from the parameters and balanced growth path solutions from the prior problem. We are going to compute several transitions for the LDC. In the first, assume that the LDC suddenly switches to the tax rates of the DC. Do this assuming that the productivity factor does not change. You probably will want a transition length of, say, 50 periods. How close do the come in terms of output per capita from this reform? In the second transition, do the same thing assuming that the tax rates do not change but productivity gradually rises to the same level as in the DC. To do this, assume that*

$$Z_t^L = Z^L(1+g)^{t-1}\frac{1}{1.1^t} + Z^D(1+g)^{t-1}\left(1-\frac{1}{1.1^t}\right).$$

Increase the transition length to 100 periods just to be safe, and assume that from that point onward, $Z_t^L = Z_t^D$. In the third and final case, compute the transition assuming that the tax rates change immediately, but productivity changes slowly. Discuss how important changing productivity differences are relative to tax differences, relative to differences in both.

## 20

A Business Cycle
Model with Capital

Thus far, we have only dealt with perfect-foresight models of capital. To extend our analysis to a genuine business cycle model, we need to incorporate uncertainty. This is hard because we will have both an exogenous state in terms of the shocks and an endogenous state in terms of capital. The endogenous state will be evolving in response to past shocks. And when the agents in our model try to forecast the future, they will need to forecast the evolution of both the exogenous and the endogenous state variables. All in all, this is pretty complicated. For this reason, we will try to make our model as simple as possible. In particular, we will neglect taxes and work within a representative family version of our model.[1]

1. BUSINESS CYCLE MODEL

The aggregate state consists of the productivity shock Z_t, money growth rate τ_t, the money supply before the shock M_t, and the aggregate capital stock K_t. In addition, there is a private state that consists of the individual's money holdings, bond position, and capital holdings. Of course, in equilibrium these must line up

---

1. This sort of model was first used to study business cycles in Kydland, Finn E., and Edward C. Prescott. "Time to build and aggregate fluctuations." Econometrica: Journal of the Econometric Society (1982): 1345–1370. Much of what we do here follows this famous article quite closely. However, we simplify things along a number of dimensions along the lines of Hansen, Gary D. "Indivisible labor and the business cycle." Journal of Monetary Economics 16.3 (1985): 309–327.

Monetary and Fiscal Policy through a DSGE Lens. Harold L. Cole, Oxford University Press (2020).
© Oxford University Press. DOI: 10.1093/oso/9780190076030.001.0001

with the aggregates, but that is an equilibrium result. For now, we will denote the individual's state by s with the understanding that this includes both the aggregate and the private state variables. Later, when we do the equilibrium analysis, we can drop the private variables with the understanding that they are redundant then.

The household's problem is choosing a sequence of functions $\{C_t, L_t, M_{t+1}, B_{t+1}, K_{t+1}\}_{t=1}^{2}(s_t)$ (which are functions of the aggregate state and the individual's private state) so as to maximize

$$\max \mathbb{E}_1 \left\{ \sum_{t=1,2} \beta^{t-1}\left[u(C_t) - v(L_t)\right] + \beta^2 V(M_3, B_3, K_3) \right\}$$

subject to

$$M_t \geq P_t C_t \text{ and}$$
$$P_t\left[\left[Z_t L_t\right]^{1-\alpha}K_t^\alpha - \delta K_t\right] + \left[M_t - P_t C_t\right] + B_t + T_t$$
$$\geq M_{t+1} + q_t B_{t+1} + P_t\left[K_{t+1} - K_t\right] \text{ for all } t \leq 2.$$

The household's f.o.c.'s for consumption condition is static and hence remains simply

$$\beta^{t-1}u'(C_t) - P_t\left[\lambda_t + \mu_t\right] = 0.$$

This is also true of the f.o.c. for L_t:

$$-\beta^{t-1}v'(L_t) + \mu_t P_t Z_t^{1-\alpha}(1-\alpha)L_t^{-\alpha}K_t^\alpha = 0.$$

Note here that all prices are implicitly functions of the current aggregate state, while all multipliers are implicitly functions of both the aggregate and the private state.

The f.o.c. for money and bonds are exactly like what we saw in our stochastic model without capital and are given by

$$-\mu_t + \mathbb{E}_t\{\lambda_{t+1} + \mu_{t+1}\} = 0$$

and

$$-\mu_t q_t + \mathbb{E}_t\{\mu_{t+1}\} = 0.$$

Finally, we have the stochastic version of our optimal investment condition, which is given by

$$-\mu_t P_t + \mathbb{E}_t\left\{\mu_{t+1}P_{t+1}\left[\left[Z_{t+1}L_{t+1}\right]^{1-\alpha}\alpha K_{t+1}^{\alpha-1} + 1 - \delta\right]\right\} = 0.$$

These f.o.c.'s along with the c.i.a. constraint, the budget constraint, the resource constraint, and the market clearing conditions for money and bonds, give the constraints that our equilibrium must satisfy.

Imposing the c.i.a. constraint pins down the price level as the ratio of the money supply to consumption, just as before. So, using this result along with our standard log utility assumption also allows us to reduce the consumption f.o.c. to the following

$$\beta^{t-1} = M_t [\lambda_t + \mu_t].$$

which, once we make our standard change in variables, yields our familiar condition

$$\tilde{\lambda}_t + \tilde{\mu}_t = 1. \tag{111}$$

Using this result in our f.o.c. for money gives us another familiar expression

$$\tilde{\mu}_t = \frac{\beta}{1 + \tau_t}. \tag{112}$$

In this last expression, remember that the time $t+1$ multipliers are being normalized by $M_{t+1} = M_t(1 + \tau_t)$, and that both of these variables are known at time t.

Turn now to the labor condition, and note that if we make our standard preference specification, and use our prior results, we get that

$$\beta^{t-1} L_t^{\gamma} = \mu_t \frac{M_t}{C_t} Z_t^{1-\alpha}(1 - \alpha) L_t^{-\alpha} K_t^{\alpha} \text{ or}$$

$$L_t^{\gamma} = \tilde{\mu}_t \frac{1}{C_t} Z_t^{1-\alpha}(1 - \alpha) L_t^{-\alpha} K_t^{\alpha}$$

$$= \frac{\beta}{(1 + \tau_t)C_t} Z_t^{1-\alpha}(1 - \alpha) L_t^{-\alpha} K_t^{\alpha} \tag{113}$$

We cannot easily reduce this further, as we could in a world without capital where consumption was equal to output. So, onward to our capital equation.

Using our prior results again, we can rewrite the capital condition as follows:

$$\mu_t P_t = \mathbb{E}_t \left\{ \mu_{t+1} P_{t+1} \left[[Z_{t+1} L_{t+1}]^{1-\alpha} \alpha K_{t+1}^{\alpha-1} + 1 - \delta \right] \right\} \text{ or}$$

$$\tilde{\mu}_t \frac{\beta^{t-1}}{M_t} \frac{M_t}{C_t} = \mathbb{E}_t \left\{ \tilde{\mu}_{t+1} \frac{\beta^t}{M_{t+1}} \frac{M_{t+1}}{C_{t+1}} \left[[Z_{t+1} L_{t+1}]^{1-\alpha} \alpha K_{t+1}^{\alpha-1} + 1 - \delta \right] \right\} \text{ or}$$

$$\frac{\beta^t}{(1+\tau_t)C_t} = \mathbb{E}_t\left\{\frac{\beta^{t+1}}{(1+\tau_{t+1})C_{t+1}}\left[[Z_{t+1}L_{t+1}]^{1-\alpha}\alpha K_{t+1}^{\alpha-1} + 1 - \delta\right]\right\} \text{ or}$$

$$1 = \mathbb{E}_t\left\{\frac{\beta(1+\tau_t)C_t}{(1+\tau_{t+1})C_{t+1}}\left[[Z_{t+1}L_{t+1}]^{1-\alpha}\alpha K_{t+1}^{\alpha-1} + 1 - \delta\right]\right\} \quad \textbf{(114)}$$

Our final condition is the consumption equation (which is just the resource constraint)

$$C_t = [Z_tL_t]^{1-\alpha}K_t^{\alpha} + (1-\delta)K_t - K_{t+1} \quad\quad\quad \textbf{(115)}$$

Our labor condition (113), our capital condition (114), and our consumption equation (115) form our three-equation block. Let us write this three-equation block in the following manner:

$$F^L(\cdot) = L_t^{\gamma} - \frac{\beta}{(1+\tau_t)C_t}Z_t^{1-\alpha}(1-\alpha)L_t^{-\alpha}K_t^{\alpha} = 0 \quad\quad\quad \textbf{(116)}$$

$$F^K(\cdot) = \mathbb{E}_t\left\{\frac{\beta(1+\tau_t)C_t}{(1+\tau_{t+1})C_{t+1}}\left[[Z_{t+1}L_{t+1}]^{1-\alpha}\alpha K_{t+1}^{\alpha-1} + 1 - \delta\right]\right\} - 1 = 0 \quad \textbf{(117)}$$

$$F^C(\cdot) = C_t - [Z_tL_t]^{1-\alpha}K_t^{\alpha} + (1-\delta)K_t - K_{t+1} = 0 \quad\quad\quad \textbf{(118)}$$

The labor and consumption conditions depend only on current values, but the capital condition has a much richer pattern of dependence. We are seeking a sequence of functions $\{C_t, L_t, K_{t+1}\}_{t=1}^{\infty}(s_t)$ that satisfy these three conditions at each point in time.

1.1. Special Case

To gain some insight into how this model works, let us return to the simple 100% depreciation case we considered before in chapter 19, section 2. Assume also that money growth is i.i.d., and since we have seen that money growth can affect labor and potentially consumption, conjecture that $C_t = \psi(\tau_t)Y_t$, and therefore $K_{t+1} = (1 - \psi(\tau_t))Y_t$; that is, the savings rate depends only on current money growth. With these changes, our capital condition can be written as

$$1 = \mathbb{E}_t\left\{\frac{\beta(1+\tau_t)\psi(\tau_t)Y_t}{(1+\tau_{t+1})\psi(\tau_{t+1})Y_{t+1}}\left[\alpha\frac{Y_{t+1}}{(1-\psi(\tau_t))Y_t}\right]\right\}$$

$$= \frac{\alpha\beta(1+\tau_t)\psi(\tau_t)}{1-\psi(\tau_t)}\mathbb{E}_t\left\{\frac{1}{(1+\tau_{t+1})\psi(\tau_{t+1})}\right\}$$

If you stare at this equation for a while, you will realize that our i.i.d. assumption on τ_t implies that

$$\mathbb{E}_t \left\{ \frac{1}{(1 + \tau_{t+1})\psi(\tau_{t+1})} \right\}$$

is going to be some unknown constant. Thus, the form of this equation implies that we are seeking an unknown coefficient X that satisfies

$$\frac{1 - \psi(\tau_t)}{\psi(\tau_t)} = X(1 + \tau_t) \implies \psi(\tau_t) = [1 + X(1 + \tau_t)]^{-1}. \tag{119}$$

This implies that the ratio of the savings share over the consumption share will rise in proportion to the gross current monetary shock but not respond to the productivity shock.[2]

Turn next to our labor condition and note that it can be written as

$$L_t^\gamma = \frac{\beta}{(1 + \tau_t)\psi(\tau_t)Y_t}(1 - \alpha)\frac{Y_t}{L_t} = \frac{\beta}{(1 + \tau_t)\psi(\tau_t)}(1 - \alpha)\frac{1}{L_t}$$

or

$$L_t^{1+\gamma} = \frac{\beta}{(1 + \tau_t)\psi(\tau_t)} = \frac{\beta[1 + X(1 + \tau_t)]}{(1 + \tau_t)} \tag{120}$$

It seems that we are going to get a dampened response of labor to our money shock relative to the model without capital. However, the key point to note here is that labor is not going to respond to the productivity shock. This implies that any response of labor to productivity in our full model is going to come through capital not depreciating fully. This seems like a weak reed on which to build a strong labor response.

1.2. Back to the General Model

Solving the full model analytically is very difficult, if not impossible. However, we are going to follow a much easier road using linearization. The first step is to solve for the steady state given that productivity is 1 and money growth is $\bar{\tau}$. We need to solve for $\bar{L}$, $\bar{K}$, and $\bar{C}$ so that

2. Plugging this into our condition gives an equation to solve for X,

$$1 = \frac{\alpha\beta(1 + \tau_t)[1 + X(1 + \tau_t)]^{-1}}{1 - [1 + X(1 + \tau_t)]^{-1}} \mathbb{E}_t \left\{ \frac{1}{(1 + \tau_{t+1})[1 + X(1 + \tau_{t+1})]^{-1}} \right\}.$$

$$F^L(\cdot) = \bar{L}^\gamma - \frac{\beta}{(1+\bar{\tau})\bar{C}}(1-\alpha)\bar{L}^{-\alpha}\bar{K}^\alpha = 0 \qquad (121)$$

$$F^K(\cdot) = \beta\left[\bar{L}^{1-\alpha}\alpha\bar{K}^{\alpha-1} + 1 - \delta\right] - 1 = 0 \qquad (122)$$

$$F^C(\cdot) = \bar{C} - \bar{L}^{1-\alpha}\bar{K}^\alpha - \delta\bar{K} = 0 \qquad (123)$$

If we define the real return on capital as $r = \alpha\bar{L}^{1-\alpha}\bar{K}^{\alpha-1}$, from the capital equation we get that in the steady state

$$r = 1/\beta + \delta - 1 \implies \frac{L}{K} = \left(\frac{r}{\alpha}\right)^{\frac{1}{1-\alpha}}.$$

This in turn implies that the real return on labor is given by

$$w = (1-\alpha)\bar{L}^{-\alpha}\bar{K}^\alpha = (1-\alpha)\left(\frac{\alpha}{r}\right)^{\frac{\alpha}{1-\alpha}}.$$

Next, note that we can use the fact that we have pinned down the capital-labor ratio to express the consumption condition as

$$C = L*(K/L)^\alpha - \delta*L*(K/L) = L\left[\left(\frac{\alpha}{r}\right)^{\frac{\alpha}{1-\alpha}} - \delta\left(\frac{\alpha}{r}\right)^{\frac{1}{1-\alpha}}\right].$$

If we plug this result into the labor condition, we get that

$$L^{\gamma+1} = \left[\left(\frac{\alpha}{r}\right)^{\frac{\alpha}{1-\alpha}} - \delta\left(\frac{\alpha}{r}\right)^{\frac{1}{1-\alpha}}\right]^{-1}\frac{\beta w}{1+\tau}.$$

Next, we are going to linearize our three conditions around the steady state.[3] For the labor condition this is given by

$$dF^L(\cdot) = \left[\gamma\bar{L}^{\gamma-1} - \frac{\beta}{(1+\bar{\tau})\bar{C}}(1-\alpha)(-\alpha)\bar{L}^{-\alpha-1}\bar{K}^\alpha\right]\partial L_t + [0]\partial K_{t+1}$$

$$+ \left[\frac{\beta}{(1+\bar{\tau})\bar{C}^2}(1-\alpha)\bar{L}^{-\alpha}K^\alpha\right]\partial C_t + \left[\frac{\beta}{(1+\bar{\tau})^2\bar{C}}(1-\alpha)\bar{L}^{-\alpha}K^\alpha\right]\partial\tau_t$$

$$+ \left[-\frac{\beta}{(1+\bar{\tau})\bar{C}}(1-\alpha)(1-\alpha)\bar{L}^{-\alpha}K^\alpha\right]\partial Z_t + \left[-\frac{\beta}{(1+\bar{\tau})\bar{C}}(1-\alpha)\bar{L}^{-\alpha}\alpha K^{\alpha-1}\right]\partial K_t$$

$$(124)$$

3. Remember here that we are seeking a first-order approximation to $f(x) \approx f(\bar{x}) + f'(\bar{x})(x - \bar{x})$. And since we are evaluating these conditions at the steady state, where $f(\bar{x}) = 0$, we only have the first-order deviation component.

Note here that we have carefully distinguished between changes in the choice variables (the first three partials) and changes in the state variables (the second three partials). Note also that all of the partials are in terms of the deviation from the steady-state value.

Let's turn next to the consumption condition because it is easier. The deviations are given by

$$dF^C(\cdot) = [-(1-\alpha)\bar{L}^{-\alpha}\bar{K}^{\alpha}]\partial L_t + [-1]\partial K_{t+1} + [1]\partial C_t$$
$$+ [0]\partial \tau_t + [(1-\alpha)\bar{L}^{1-\alpha}\bar{K}^{\alpha}]\partial Z_t + [\alpha\bar{L}^{1-\alpha}\bar{K}^{\alpha-1} + (1-\delta)]\partial K_t \quad (125)$$

Last, we turn to the capital condition. This condition has some extra future variables that we are going to have to take account of:

$$dF^K(\cdot) = [0]\partial L_t + [\beta\bar{L}^{1-\alpha}\alpha(\alpha-1)\bar{K}^{\alpha-2}]\partial K_{t+1} + \left[\frac{\beta}{\bar{C}}[\bar{L}^{1-\alpha}\alpha\bar{K}^{\alpha-1}+1-\delta]\right]\partial C_t$$
$$+ \left[\frac{\beta}{1+\bar{\tau}}[\bar{L}^{1-\alpha}\alpha\bar{K}^{\alpha-1}+1-\delta]\right]\partial\tau_t + [0]\partial Z_t + [0]\partial K_t$$
$$+ [\beta[(1-\alpha)\bar{L}^{-\alpha}\alpha\bar{K}^{\alpha-1}]]\mathbb{E}\{\partial L_{t+1}\} + \left[-\frac{\beta\bar{C}}{\bar{C}^2}[\bar{L}^{1-\alpha}\alpha\bar{K}^{\alpha-1}+1-\delta]\right]\mathbb{E}\{\partial C_{t+1}\}$$
$$+ \left[-\frac{\beta(1+\bar{\tau})}{(1+\bar{\tau})^2}[\bar{L}^{1-\alpha}\alpha\bar{K}^{\alpha-1}+1-\delta]\right]\mathbb{E}\{\partial\tau_{t+1}\}$$
$$+ [\beta[(1-\alpha)\bar{L}^{1-\alpha}\alpha\bar{K}^{\alpha-1}+1-\delta]]\mathbb{E}\{\partial Z_{t+1}\} \quad (126)$$

Given three linear conditions, we will be seeking three linear solutions for (L_t, K_{t+1}, C_t) in terms of the deviation of the fundamental state variables $\partial\bar{s}_t = (\partial\tau_t, \partial Z_t, \partial K_t)$ from their steady-state values. These equations can be written as

$$\partial L_t = D_L * \partial\bar{s}_t = [D_{L,\tau}\ D_{L,Z}\ D_{L,K}] * \begin{bmatrix} \partial\tau_t \\ \partial Z_t \\ \partial K_t \end{bmatrix} \quad (127)$$

$$\partial K_{t+1} = D_K * \partial\bar{s}_t = [D_{K,\tau}\ D_{K,Z}\ D_{K,K}] * \begin{bmatrix} \partial\tau_t \\ \partial Z_t \\ \partial K_t \end{bmatrix} \quad (128)$$

$$\partial C_t = D_C * \partial\bar{s}_t = [D_{C,\tau}\ D_{C,Z}\ D_{C,K}] * \begin{bmatrix} \partial\tau_t \\ \partial Z_t \\ \partial K_t \end{bmatrix} \quad (129)$$

Focusing on labor equation (127) for the moment, note that this equation implies that the behavior of labor is determined by three response coefficients. Since the same will be true for new capital and consumption, solving our system means determining these nine response coefficients.

We can also use these response coefficients to predict future outcomes. Hence, the future impact of an increase in K_{t+1} today on L_{t+1} tomorrow is given by $D_{L,K}$. The impact of future consumption C_{t+1} is given by $D_{C,K}$ and the impact on future capital is given by $D_{K,K}$. Realizing this, we can rewrite the capital equation as

$$dF^K(\cdot) = \left[\beta \bar{L}^{1-\alpha}\alpha(\alpha-1)\bar{K}^{\alpha-2}\right]\partial K_{t+1} + \left[\frac{\beta}{\bar{C}}\left[\bar{L}^{1-\alpha}\alpha\bar{K}^{\alpha-1} + 1 - \delta\right]\right]\partial C_t$$

$$+ \left[\frac{\beta}{1+\bar{\tau}}\left[\bar{L}^{1-\alpha}\alpha\bar{K}^{\alpha-1} + 1 - \delta\right]\right]\partial \tau_t + \left[\beta\left[(1-\alpha)\bar{L}^{-\alpha}\alpha\bar{K}^{\alpha-1}\right]\right]D_{L,K}\partial K_{t+1}$$

$$+ \left[-\frac{\beta\bar{C}}{\bar{C}^2}\left[\bar{L}^{1-\alpha}\alpha\bar{K}^{\alpha-1} + 1 - \delta\right]\right]D_{C,K}\partial K_{t+1} \tag{130}$$

Now that we have our final three-equation linearized system (124, 125 and 130), we are ready to solve for our response coefficients. We want these three equations to be zeroed out for any possible values of shock deviations and we want to pick the values of our response coefficients so that this holds. Plugging in for the endogenous changes using (127–129) gives us a matrix system of equations that boils down to nine equations in nine unknowns. Setting $\partial \tau_t = 1$ and $\partial Z_t = \partial K_t = 0$ gives us one independent three-equation system in the response coefficients for the τ shock. We can solve this for $(D_{L,\tau}, D_{K,\tau}, D_{C,\tau})$. We can proceed in a similar manner to solve for the other two sets of response coefficients. Again, each one of these sets involves only an independent three-equation system.

Remark 29. *We could have done everything in terms of a two-equation system by substituting for consumption. That would have condensed things but would come at the cost of some more intense algebra. I thought it more transparent for expositional purposes to go this route.*

Remark 30. *Because we have both K_t and K_{t+1} showing up in the Euler equation, this system has a quadratic in it. As a result, there are generally two roots, i.e., two solutions. Be careful to get the stable solution. This is the one with a response coefficient of K_{t+1} to K_t (to existing capital) that is below 1.*

A natural question at this point would be how to extend our results beyond the simple i.i.d. shock model we have considered. For example, how would we account for persistent shocks of the form:

$$\tau_t = \rho_\tau \tau_{t-1} + \epsilon_\tau,$$
$$Z_t = \rho_Z Z_{t-1} + \epsilon_Z. \tag{131}$$

Future values of the shocks only showed up in our capital condition (126). With persistent shocks, the expected future values are no longer 0, and instead are given by $\rho_\tau \tau_t$ and $\rho_Z Z_t$, respectively. Making the appropriate adjustment means adding back in the following two terms:

$$+ \left[-\frac{\beta(1+\bar{\tau})}{(1+\bar{\tau})^2} \left[\bar{L}^{1-\alpha} \alpha \bar{K}^{\alpha-1} + 1 - \delta \right] \right] \rho_\tau \partial \tau_t$$
$$+ \left[\beta \left[(1-\alpha) \bar{L}^{1-\alpha} \alpha \bar{K}^{\alpha-1} + 1 - \delta \right] \right] \rho_Z \partial Z_t \tag{132}$$

into our capital equation (129). This will change the response coefficients for these two shocks. Note, however, that this does not affect our response coefficients for capital, and allowing for persistent money growth does not affect the response to productivity and vice versa. This is all a result of the block structure of our equations.

Another approach, which is both more commonly used and arguably better, is to assume that our shocks are log-normal, which means that we do not have to worry about, for example, $Z_t < 0$. To do this, one could assume that

$$Z_t = \bar{Z} exp(z_t), \quad \text{where } z_t = \rho_z z_{t-1} + \sigma_z \epsilon_{z,t}$$
$$(1 + \tau_t) = \bar{X} exp(x_t) \quad \text{where } x_t = \rho_x x_{t-1} + \sigma_x \epsilon_{x,t}.$$

We would then assume that both of the innovations, $\epsilon_{z,t}$ and $\epsilon_{x,t}$ were standard normals. The productivity level Z_t and the money growth rate $(1 + \tau_t)$ would be log-normal, since, if we take logs, we recover normal random variables.

2. SEPARATING TREND FROM CYCLE AND BUSINESS CYCLE FACTS

Economic times series such as GDP display both a long-run trend or growth aspect and a stochastic aspect. For example, we can think of the time series Y_t as follows:

$$log(Y_t) = y_t = g_t + h_t,$$

where g_t is the growth component and h_t is the transitory or business cycle component. The simplest trend model is simply a constant growth rate, or $g_t = g^t$. This sort of trend component is very easy to estimate, since a reasonably long time series will generally lead to a very accurate estimate of the growth rate. Unfortunately, many time series do not seem to exhibit this sort of constant growth rate. Rather, they seem to go through periods of relatively high and low growth. This has led to a desire for a more flexible method of estimating the trend.

While there are many methods out there, and all of them have their drawbacks, a fairly simple method is call the Hodrick-Prescott (HP) filter. The HP method was actually invented a long time ago (first proposed by E. T. Whittaker in 1923; cf. https://en.wikipedia.org/wiki/Hodrick%E2%80%93Prescott_filter) and then reinvented for economists. But we will stick with the common jargon and refer to it as the HP filter. The filter solves for a sequence of trend vales $\{\tau_t\}$, which are the solution to the following minimization problem

$$\{\tau_t\} = \operatorname{argmin}\left(\sum_{t=0}^{T} [y_t - \tau_t]^2 + \lambda \sum_{t=1}^{T} [(\tau_{t+1} - \tau_t) - (\tau_t - \tau_{t-1})]^2 \right). \qquad (133)$$

This filter weights trying to fit the time series y_t closely vs. having only small changes in the trend growth rate. The variable λ controls the relative weight on a smooth trend. A higher value will generate a smoother trend but a less tight fit to the data series. It seems intuitive that we should have a smoother trend in high-frequency data than in a lower-frequency sample of the same data. For this reason, λ is typically taken to be 1600 in quarterly data and 6.25 in annual data.

The first-order condition for τ_t is

$$-(y_t - \tau_t) + \lambda\{[\tau_{t+2} - 2\tau_{t+1} + \tau_t] - 2[\tau_{t+1} - 2\tau_t + \tau_{t-1}]$$
$$+ [\tau_t - 2\tau_{t-1} + \tau_{t-2}]\} = 0. \qquad (134)$$

This is a linear condition, so we can solve for the trend component using a linear equation solver. This simplicity is one of the nice features of the HP filter.[4]

An early article by Kydland and Prescott does a very nice job of summarizing the basic business cycle facts from the perspective of the HP filter.[5] We reproduce some of their key findings in the following table.

All of the data reported in table 1 has been logged and detrended using the HP filter. Let us start with real output, or GDP. It is hard to interpret the volatility measure, so we will be interpreting things in terms of the other series

---

4. There are also significant drawbacks. Perhaps the best known critique of this filter is Hamilton, James D. "Why you should never use the Hodrick-Prescott filter." Review of Economics and Statistics 100.5 (2018): 831–843.

5. Kydland, Finn, and Edward Prescott. "Business cycles: real facts and a monetary myth." Quarterly Review Spring (1990): 3–18.

Table 1. KYDLAND AND PRESCOTT'S CYCLICAL FACTS

Correlations with Output

HP filter series	Volatility	$Corr(y_t,x_{t-1})$	$Corr(y_t,x_t)$	$Corr(y_t,x_{t+1})$
Real GDP	1.71	0.85	1.00	0.85
Hours (Hh Survey)	1.47	0.69	0.86	0.86
Employment	1.06	0.61	0.82	0.89
Hours per worker	0.54	0.66	0.71	0.59
GDP/Hours	0.88	0.50	0.51	0.21
Consumption	1.25	0.81	0.82	0.66
Investment	8.30	0.79	0.91	0.75
Gov. Purchases	2.07	−0.01	0.05	0.09
Exports	5.53	0.11	0.34	0.48
Imports	4.92	0.61	0.71	0.71
M1	1.68	0.35	0.31	0.22
GDP deflator	0.89	−0.64	−0.55	−0.43

volatility relative to GDP. The correlations indicate that output tends to stay above or below trend at least for several periods, so there is positive persistence in detrended output. Turn next to the employment measures. Total hours are almost as volatile as output and also show a positive pattern of comovement with output. Note that both employment and hours/employee are moving around, with more of the movement coming from employment, and that both of these positively covary, with some indication that employment follows output with a slight lag.

Turn next to output/hour, and here is our first major surprise. Output per hour is fairly volatile and positively covaries with output. This last fact is counter to a simple labor demand story, since increasing employment alone should lead to a fall in the MPL and hence a fall in output per hour. This fact will end up driving macroeconomics into the real business cycle models with their heavy dependence on productivity shocks.

We now turn to expenditures. Consumption is volatile but less so than output, while investment is much more volatile, and government expenditures are only slightly more so. Consumption and investment strongly covary with output, while government expenditures are essentially acyclical. Both exports and imports are highly volatile, but only imports strongly covary with output. This suggests that exports are not a key driver of business cycle fluctuations in the United States.

Finally, we turn to our nominal facts. The big surprise here is that the price level negatively covaries with output. This not consistent with a monetary stimulus raising prices and through that output because of the fall in real wages, a standard sticky-wage type story.

3. CALIBRATING THE GROWTH MODEL

We want to think through how we are going to put numbers into our model. One approach would be to estimate all of the parameters of the model using maximum likelihood (ML).[6] We are not going to follow this procedure and will instead calibrate the model. It is useful to understand why we are making this choice.

To put a bit of formality on the ML procedure, let $F(\theta, \{X_t\})$ denote the predicted values of our model given the parameter vector θ and the sequence of fundamental shocks $\{X_t\}$. I assume that we have direct measures of the fundamental shocks, which here are productivity and the growth rate of money. Let $\{Y_t\}$ denote the data vector. Then the additional measurement error shocks are given by

$$\epsilon_t = Y_t - F(\theta, \{X_t\}).$$

The probability of this vector of shocks is denoted by $Pr[\{\epsilon_t\}]$.[7] Maximum-likelihood estimation seeks to make the probability of these shocks as high as possible (often this is done in a relative value sense since the probability of any given realization of a continuous random variable is 0). As should be clear from this discussion, the assumed parameter vector implies the predicted outcomes $F(\theta, \{_t\})$ and hence the resulting errors $\{\epsilon_t\}$. Thus, we are associating the probability of the errors with the probability of the parameter vector.

Under the ML procedure we are seeking the parameter vector that maximizes the fit of the model and reduces the role of the measurement errors. The problem with this procedure is that the resulting parameter vector may be determined in significant part by aspects of the model that we are not confident of. For example, the model may be struggling to fit the overall volatility of labor or the correlation (or lack thereof) of labor and investment. If we think that there are other shocks, such as government spending or oil prices or interest rates, that we have left out, then this may not generate the most "believable" parameters for our model. This is why the more specification error one suspects, the less attractive ML is.

---

6. The classic example of this approach is Hansen, Lars Peter, and Thomas J. Sargent. "Formulating and estimating dynamic linear rational expectations models." Journal of Economic Dynamics and Control 2 (1980): 7–46.

7. Since the parameters typically include the variance of the measurement error shocks, this probability is really conditional on the parameter vector too.

Calibration is an alternative approach that seeks to pin down the parameters of the model by lining up the predictions of the model and the facts in the data for those predictions we feel the model is well suited to reproduce. Sometimes estimates done in other contexts are used when they seem the most relevant. Because our business cycle model is really just a growth model with productivity (and money) shocks, the literature has focused on having the model reproduce some standard long-run growth facts. This is generally done in a version of the model that is purely real (i.e., does not include a c.i.a. constraint or money).[8]

The real interest rate implied by the (detrended) model is

$$\beta = \frac{1}{1+r},$$

and since the real rate has historically been around 2%, this gives a value of $\beta = .98$. GNP in the model is the sum of payments to the two factors: capital and labor. With a Cobb-Douglas production function, the share of payments to capital is α. Measuring this in the data is a bit tricky, since some sources of income, such as sole proprietorships, include returns to both capital and labor. To get around this, one commonly just takes all of the income that we can "confidently" attribute to capital and labor and look at the shares in those data. If we do this for the period between 1995 and 2000, capital's share was roughly $1/3$ though it did fluctuate quite a bit. The private capital stock, excluding houses, is estimated at 3 times output. At the same time investment is a bit over 20% of output. This suggests an annual depreciation rate of around 7%. At a quarterly frequency, this would be around 2%. If we look at detrended total factor productivity (TFP), and estimate a simple autoregressive process of the form:

$$\log(\tilde{Z}_t) = \rho_z \log(\tilde{Z}_{t-1}) + \sigma_z \epsilon_t$$

one commonly finds values of $\rho_z = .975$ and $\sigma_z = .009$.[9]

This pins down all of our parameters except two preference parameters and the money supply process. For standard growth reasons, we are going to take the CRRA coefficient to be 1, however, in the business cycle literature it is commonly taken to be 2, so we might want to experiment a bit. The Frisch elasticity, which is $1/\gamma$, is taken to be somewhere between 0.5 and 2. So we can experiment with this one too.

8. For a great discussion of calibration in the real business cycle model, see Cooley, Thomas F. *Frontiers of Business Cycle Research*. Princeton University Press, 1995.

9. Since this is total factor productivity, and not labor-augmenting, we need to take our production function to be $Z_t(K_{t-1})^\alpha (L_t)^{1-\alpha}$.

For the money supply process, we can use Cooley and Hansen's estimate of the
money supply process for M1:[10]

$$\log\left(\frac{M_t}{M_{t-1}}\right) = .008 + .48 \times \log\left(\frac{M_{t-1}}{M_{t-2}}\right)$$

with the standard deviation of the errors being 0.009. Note that we are estimating
the TFP and money supply processes independently of the model. In so doing,
we are trying to prevent overall fit considerations from influencing the stochastic
processes I estimate for these variables. Note also, that our shocks are being done
in logs so we need to reverse this in the equations.

4. QUANTITATIVE ANALYSIS

Constructing the first-order approximation and computing it has become much
easier since the advent of an open source software code called Dynare. Dynare
works on top of Matlab to compute the solution to dynamic economic models,
simulate them, and compute the implied statistics. In the appendix I show the
mod file that I wrote in order to compute the results presented here.

The solution to the policy and transition functions of the model are reported in
table 2. To understand these results, note that a unit higher level of capital implies
that next period's capital is also higher by roughly 0.9, which is a fairly high level
of persistence. At the same time, this coefficient is below 1, so we have a stable
solution. In a similar vein, a 1% productivity shock implies that capital is higher
by 1 unit. Interestingly, a money supply shock depresses both consumption and
labor but actually increases capital expenditures.

Table 3 reports some results on the volatility of the model. These results are
very poor, in large part because the volatility of labor is very low, and that drags
down the volatility of output, consumption and capital. This low volatility was
something that was foreshadowed in our earlier analytical special case when

Table 2. POLICY AND TRANSITION FUNCTIONS

	Y	C	L	K	w	r
Constant	1.740	1.295	0.919	6.351	1.267	0.090
K(−1)	0.0436	0.099	−0.027	0.873	0.078	−0.011
z(−1)	2.251	0.866	0.339	1.385	1.0817	0.110
em	−0.072	−2.243	−0.212	2.170	0.096	−0.013
ez	2.309	0.888	0.347	1.421	1.109	0.113

10. Cooley, Thomas F., and Gary D. Hansen. "The inflation tax in a real business cycle model." The
American Economic Review (1989): 733–748.

Table 3. THEORETICAL MOMENTS

VARIABLE	MEAN	STD. DEV.	VARIANCE
Y	1.7401	0.1104	0.0122
C	1.2955	0.0787	0.0062
L	0.9197	0.0065	0.0000
K	6.3517	0.4203	0.1767
w	1.2677	0.0761	0.0058
r	0.0904	0.0021	0.0000

depreciation was 100% and labor did not respond at all to productivity shocks. The results are not so extreme here, but the overall issue still remains. Part of the problem is our assumption of log preferences over consumption, which leads to income and substitution effects canceling out, which depresses labor volatility. To match the data, we would like substitution effects to outweight income effects so that labor rises sharply during booms, something we see in the data. Kydland and Prescott in their original RBC paper do much better on this score because they assume a CRRA coefficient of 2. However, the lack of labor volatility relative to the data was present in their paper too. This led them to conjecture that there were other unmodel shocks that must account for an important chunk of labor's movements over the business cycle. Additionally, in Hansen's well-known 1985 article, he assumed that the disutility of labor was linear to further increase its response to productivity shocks.[11] For a very insightful discussion of the contribution of technology shocks and the elasticity of labor, see Aiyagari (1994).[12]

In table 4 we report the percentage variance decomposition for variables in terms of our shocks. From the table one can see that both consumption and labor effort are most strongly affected by the productivity shock; however, the impact of the monetary shock is not trivial. In particular, it accounts for 12% of the variation in labor. Given this, it is somewhat surprising that money shocks explain almost none of the movement in output. This is coming from the fact that the persistent component in money growth lowers labor but raises capital, and in this parameterization, these two effects almost completely offset one another.

Finally, we turn to the correlation results in table 5. Here we see many of the features that we saw in the data. In particular, output, consumption, labor, investment (coming through K), and productivity are highly correlated. At the same time, we see that the money shock depresses consumption and labor. This

11. Hansen, Gary D. "Indivisible labor and the business cycle." Journal of Monetary Economics 16.3 (1985): 309–327.

12. Aiyagari, S. Rao. "On the contribution of technology shocks to business cycles." Federal Reserve Bank of Minneapolis Quarterly Review 18.1 (1994): 22–34.

Table 4. VARIANCE DECOM-
POSITION IN PERCENT

	em	ez
Y	0.03	99.97
C	6.84	93.16
L	11.72	88.28
K	0.91	99.09
w	0.19	99.81
r	5.12	94.88
Z	0.00	100.00.
z	0.00	100.00
tau	100.00	0.00

Table 5. MATRIX OF CORRELATIONS

	Y	C	L	K	z	tau
Y	1.0000	0.9542	0.4892	0.9490	0.9974	−0.0059
C	0.9542	1.0000	0.4062	0.9431	0.9385	−0.2566
L	0.4892	0.4062	1.0000	0.1936	0.5453	−0.2953
K	0.9490	0.9431	0.1936	1.0000	0.9245	0.0465
z	0.9974	0.9385	0.5453	0.9245	1.0000	0.0000
tau	−0.0059	−0.2566	−0.2953	0.0465	0.0000	1.0000

is contrary to the pattern we see in the data and suggests that either our stochastic process for money does not match the data, or the way in which money operates in the model is not capturing what is going on in the data.

Let me wrap up this chapter by giving an overview of the strengths and weakness of the RBC model. One of the major contributions of the model is methodological. It showed us that there was a very rich dynamic general equilibrium structure based on the growth model that we could develop in various ways to think about business cycle fluctuations. This has led to an enormous literature that takes the basic RBC model and enriches it in many different ways, including price-setting frictions and adding multiple countries to study international business cycles, to mention just a couple. At the same time, the basic mechanism makes clear that we need other shocks besides productivity to account for the movements we see in the data. Finally, one of the major weaknesses of the model has been its inability to link productivity shocks more tightly to underlying causal shocks.

## 21

Optimal Monetary and Fiscal Policy

We have already looked at optimal monetary policy already in a model without capital. Now that we have a dynamic model with capital, we can ask about optimal monetary and fiscal policy.

1. THE LUCAS APPROACH

In talking about optimal policy, the first question is how should we be thinking about it? In particular, should we think in terms of a case-by-case (CbC) response? Or should we be trying to construct something more general? One problem with the CbC approach is that we have to think not only about what we should do but how whatever we do will affect what people expect us to do in the future. Will doing something different from before lead people to change their beliefs about how we will be conducting ourselves in this precise circumstance or in a wide variety of circumstances? This question arises because expectations are fundamental to many economic decisions, and humans are free to adjust their expectations, especially with respect to policies that the government may pursue.

For example, if we raise capital taxes today in state s, will this lead to (i) no change in future beliefs about capital taxation, (ii) the belief that capital taxes will be higher in the future if state s recurs, or (iii) raise expected future taxes in all future states? This means that a rise in current taxes today could trigger either very little response in investment from here on under the expectations in (i) or

Monetary and Fiscal Policy through a DSGE Lens. Harold L. Cole, Oxford University Press (2020).
© Oxford University Press. DOI: 10.1093/oso/9780190076030.001.0001

a sharp decline under the expectations in (iii). From this, it is easy to see that without knowing the public's expectation response, it is very hard to say what should be done.

The difficulties in pinning down future expectations led Robert Lucas to argue against this sort of CbC approach. Instead, he argued that an optimal policy should be thought of as a rule that says what the government was going to do in every state both now and in the future. This way, the commitment to the rule would simultaneously pin down what the government was going to do and what the public was going to expect the government to do.[1] This rule-based approach to policy making has become the most common approach, though recently there have been alternatives proposed that try to rationalize falling back on a more CbC basis.[2] In what comes next, we will follow Lucas's approach. In so doing, we are going to construct the "Ramsey problem", which takes a primal approach to optimal taxation.[3]

2. ENVIRONMENT

To hold down the level of complexity, we will assume that there is perfect foresight as to what will take place. Consistent with this, we will assume that the government determines all of its future policy choices and commits to these choices in the first period. Without real government expenditures (or consumption) to finance, it is pretty obvious that taxes should be 0. So, we are going to extend our basic representative agent model to include government expenditures that must be financed.

Let G denote the constant amount being financed each period. With the addition of government expenditures, the resource constraint becomes

1. Lucas, Robert E. "Econometric policy evaluation: a critique." Theory, Policy, Institutions: Papers from the Carnegie-Rochester Conference Series on Public Policy. New York: North-Holland. Trends and Impacts of Real and Financial Globalization. Vol. 29. 1983. See also Lucas, Robert E., and Thomas J. Sargent. "After keynesian macroeconomics." Federal Reserve Bank of Minneapolis Quarterly Review 3.2 (1979): 1–16.

2. For a contrary view, see Kocherlakota, Narayana R. "Practical policy evaluation." Journal of Monetary Economics (2019). Also, see Cole, Harold. "Discussion: Practical Policy Evaluation." Journal of Monetary Economics (2019), and the references therein, for a discussion of this debate.

3. We are going to skirt a number of issues in our treatment of optimal policy. For those interested in a more in-depth discussion, see Chari, Varadarajan V., and Patrick J. Kehoe. "Optimal fiscal and monetary policy." Handbook of Macroeconomics 1 (1999): 1671–1745.

$$G + C_t = [Z_t L_t]^{1-\alpha} K_t^\alpha + K_t(1-\delta) - K_{t+1}. \qquad (135)$$

The growth rate of money is now a policy choice variable of the government. We will continue to denote the money supply growth rate by τ_t but now allow it to be time-varying. With this,

$$\bar{M}_{t+1} = (1 + \tau_t)\bar{M}_t$$

We allow the government's tax policies to also be time-varying. With this, we let $\tau_{l,t}$ and $\tau_{k,t}$ denote the tax rates on labor and capital at time t. Once again, we can use the fact that labor and capital will be paid their marginal product, and hence nominal wages and capital rental prices are given by

$$w_t = P_t\left[(1-\alpha)Z_t^{1-\alpha}\bar{L}_t^{-\alpha}K_t^\alpha\right]$$
$$r_t = P_t\left[\alpha\left[Z_t L_t\right]^{1-\alpha}\bar{K}_t^{\alpha-1}\right]$$

Hence, tax revenue from labor and capital is given by $\tau_{l,t}w_t L_t + \tau_{k,t}r_t K_{t-1}$, where K_{t-1} is the beginning of period capital stock.

We are going to allow the government to also borrow and lend using pure discount bonds, just like the representative agent. We will denote the government's debt level as B_t^G and since government bonds are just like private bonds, they also receive q_t per unit sold. Now, we will need to include the government's borrowing in the market clearing condition for debt:

$$B_t^G + B_t = 0. \qquad (136)$$

Note that this change means that the representative agent can have positive or negative debt, but in equilibrium, this must be the negative of the government's position.

With these changes, the government's budget constraint is given by

$$B_t^G + T_t = \tau_{l,t}w_t L_t + \tau_{k,t}r_t K_{t-1} + q_t B_{t+1}^G + \tau_t\bar{M}_t. \qquad (137)$$

We will constrain $T_t \geq 0$ so that the government does not have access to lump-sum taxes. However, note for future reference that since raising revenue through taxes is costly, the government will never want to give anything away if it needs to raise any positive revenue. Hence, in any optimal policy, $T_t = 0$.

For simplicity, we will assume that productivity grows at a constant rate given by

$$Z_t = (1+g)Z_{t-1}.$$

Let us again make the normalization that $Z_1 = 1$, so $Z_t = (1+g)^{t-1}$.

3. HOUSEHOLD'S PROBLEM

The only changes to the household's problem come from the fact that we are allowing the government's tax policies to be time-varying. Note that the transfers always had a time-varying element whenever we were out of the steady state because tax revenue was not constant.

Given this, the household is choosing a sequence of quantities $\{C_t, L_t, M_t, B_t, K_{t+1}\}_{t=1,2}$ so as to maximize

$$\max \sum_{t=1,2} \beta^{t-1}[u(C_t) - v(L_t)] + \beta^2 V(M_3, B_3, K_3) \tag{138}$$

subject to

$$M_t \ge P_t C_t \text{ and}$$

$$P_t \left\{ \begin{array}{l} (1-\tau_l)\left[(1-\alpha)Z_t^{1-\alpha}\bar{L}_t^{-\alpha}\bar{K}_t^{\alpha}\right]L_t + \\ (1-\tau_k)\left[\alpha\left[Z_t\bar{L}_t\right]^{1-\alpha}\bar{K}_t^{\alpha-1}\right]K_t - \delta K_t \end{array} \right\}$$

$$+[M_t - P_t C_t)] + B_{t-1} + T_t$$

$$\ge M_{t+1} + q_t B_{t+1} + P_t[K_{t+1} - K_t] \text{ for all } t \le 2.$$

The consumption condition is given by

$$\beta^{t-1}u'(C_t) - P_t[\lambda_t + \mu_t] = 0. \tag{139}$$

The f.o.c.'s for labor is given by

$$-\beta^{t-1}v'(L_t) + \mu_t P_t(1-\tau_l)Z_t^{1-\alpha}(1-\alpha)\bar{L}_t^{-\alpha}\bar{K}_t^{\alpha} = 0. \tag{140}$$

The f.o.c. for capital is given by

$$-\mu_t P_t + \mu_{t+1}P_{t+1}\left[(1-\tau_k)[Z_{t+1}\bar{L}_{t+1}]^{1-\alpha}\alpha\bar{K}_{t+1}^{\alpha-1} + 1 - \delta\right] = 0. \tag{141}$$

The f.o.c.'s for money and bonds are given by

$$-\mu_t + \lambda_{t+1} + \mu_{t+1} = 0$$

and

$$-\mu_t q_t + \mu_{t+1} = 0. \tag{142}$$

Because we will assume that the c.i.a. constraint holds as an equality in each period, we again get that

$$P_t = \frac{\bar{M}_t}{C_t}, \tag{143}$$

where the numerator is the aggregate money stock at the beginning of the period and the denominator is real consumption. If we impose this in our f.o.c.'s for consumption, along with log preferences, we get that

$$\beta^{t-1} = \bar{M}_t [\lambda_t + \mu_t].$$

Note that this condition holds even though consumption may not be growing at a constant rate. This result implies that we can use a similar change in variables to help render the long-term model stationary, even though in the short term these new multipliers may be time-varying. Exploit this insight and define the following new variables using our familiar change in variables:

$$\tilde{\lambda}_t = \lambda_t \bar{M}_t / \beta^{t-1}, \text{ and } \tilde{\mu}_t = \mu_t \bar{M}_t / \beta^{t-1}.$$

If we now impose our price equation and our change in variables in our first-order conditions, we get

$$1 = \tilde{\lambda}_t + \tilde{\mu}_t.$$

If we use this too in our f.o.c. for money we get that

$$\tilde{\mu}_t = \frac{\beta}{1 + \tau_t}. \tag{144}$$

This last condition implies that $\tilde{\mu}_t$ will vary through time in response to change in the current growth rate of money, but it is stationary in the sense that it does not depend on past growth rates. Similarly,

$$\tilde{\lambda}_t = 1 - \frac{\beta}{1+\tau_t}, \qquad\qquad (145)$$

so it too will only be responding to the current monetary growth rate.

4. GOVERNMENT'S POLICY CHOICE PROBLEM

We are now in a position to state the government's optimal policy choice problem with some specificity. It is choosing a sequence of money growth rates and tax rates

$$\{\tau_t, \tau_{l,t}, \tau_{k,t}\}_{t=1}^{\infty}$$

so that the resulting competitive equilibrium maximizes the household's payoff. Note that for it to be a competitive equilibrium, the government's budget constraint (137) and all of our market clearing conditions, including (136) and

$$M_{t+1} = \bar{M}_{t+1}$$

have to hold. In addition, the household must be behaving optimally with respect to its choices. Note that implicitly we are ruling out any policy choice that does not lead to an equilibrium outcome.

4.1. Government's Policy Choice Problem Step 1

This is a ridiculously hard problem and we cannot solve it using brute force. So, we are going to try to guess what the solution looks like. In the prior consideration of optimal monetary policy, we saw that the optimal policy was to set

$$1 + \tau_t = \beta \qquad\qquad (146)$$

and that this meant that there was no monetary friction. Let's start by conjecturing that this is true here too and impose (146) as our monetary policy rule. Note that this leads to $\tilde{\mu}_t = 1$ and $\tilde{\lambda}_t = 0$ from (144 and 145).[4]

---

4. Implicitly, we are appealing to the classic result that intermediate goods or commodities should not be taxed, only final goods. In our model money is not a final good. Moreover, the labor tax and the inflation tax imply similar wedges and so taxing via money is redundant. For more on the classic result see Diamond, Peter A., and James A. Mirrlees. "Optimal taxation and public production I: Production efficiency." The American Economic Review 61.1 (1971): 8–27.

If we make use of our f.o.c. for bonds, our change in variables and our monetary policy rule (146) we get that

$$0 = q_t\mu_t - \mu_{t+1} = q_t\frac{\beta^{t-1}}{\bar{M}_t}\tilde{\mu}_t - \frac{\beta^t}{\bar{M}_{t+1}}\tilde{\mu}_{t+1} = q_t - \frac{\beta}{1+\tau} = q_t - 1, \quad (147)$$

The result that $q_t = 1$ is the Friedman rule once again, since this means that nominal interest rates are 0. This is a key result in what follows. Another important result which also follows from $q_t = 1$ and (142) is that

$$\mu_t = \mu_{t+1}.$$

If we make use of our change in variables, our monetary policy rule, and the pricing rule (143), the household's f.o.c.'s for labor and capital are now

$$-\beta^{t-1}v'(L_t) + \frac{1}{C_t}(1 - \tau_{l,t})Z_t^{1-\alpha}(1-\alpha)\bar{L}_t^{-\alpha}\bar{K}_t^{\alpha} = 0. \quad (148)$$

$$-\frac{1}{C_t} + \beta\frac{1}{C_{t+1}}\left[\left[(1-\tau_{k,t})Z_{t+1}\bar{L}_{t+1}\right]^{1-\alpha}\alpha\bar{K}_{t+1}^{\alpha-1} + 1 - \delta\right] = 0. \quad (149)$$

These conditions do look like something that would emerge from a purely real model without money.

The standard way to use conditions like (148) and (149) is to solve for the households' choices of labor and capital given taxes. But these equations also suggest another avenue. If we knew the optimal allocation variables $\{L_t, K_{t+1}, C_t\}$ we could solve for the optimal tax rates that would be consistent with these allocation variables. This alternative approach to optimal policy, solving for the optimal allocation variables rather than the policy variables and determining the policy variables residually, is called the *primal approach* and has a long history.

4.2. Government's Policy Choice Problem Step 2

So what constraints do we still need to worry about to ensure that our allocation is a competitive equilibrium, given that we are determining taxes residually in the manner just described? Certainly, we need to ensure that the resource constraint is satisfied as well as the government and the household budget constraints. There is a very old result called *Walras's law*, which notes that if the resource constraint is satisfied and all but one of the budget constraints, then the last one must also be satisfied. This means that we just need to satisfy the resource constraint and the household budget constraint and we get the government budget constraint for free.

Because the nominal interest rate is zero, we are just going to sum the household flow budget constraints across time. When we do this, nominal borrowing and money holdings largely drop out.

$$
\begin{aligned}
0 &= \sum_{t=1}^{T} \left\{ \begin{array}{l} P_t(1-\tau_{l,t})\left[(1-\alpha)Z_t^{1-\alpha}\bar{L}_t^{-\alpha}\bar{K}_t^{\alpha}\right]L_t + P_t(1-\tau_{k,t})\left[\alpha\left[Z_t\bar{L}_t\right]^{1-\alpha}\bar{K}_t^{\alpha-1}\right]K_t \\ +M_t - P_tC_t + B_{t-1} + T_t - M_{t+1} - q_tB_{t+1} - P_t\left[K_{t+1} - (1-\delta)K_t\right] \end{array} \right\} \\
&= \sum_{t=1}^{T} \left\{ \begin{array}{l} P_t(1-\tau_{l,t})\left[(1-\alpha)Z_t^{1-\alpha}\bar{L}_t^{-\alpha}\bar{K}_t^{\alpha}\right]L_t - P_tC_t + T_t + \\ P_t(1-\tau_{k,t})\left[\alpha\left[Z_t\bar{L}_t\right]^{1-\alpha}\bar{K}_t^{\alpha-1}\right]K_t - P_t\left[K_{t+1} - (1-\delta)K_t\right] \end{array} \right\} \\
&\quad + M_1 - M_{T+1} + B_1 - B_{T+1}
\end{aligned}
\tag{150}
$$

Then, note that since you cannot die in debt and do not want to die in wealth, the terminal choices of money and bonds are 0.

We want to rewrite this budget constraint in terms of allocation variables, but, importantly, we want to do so in a manner that respects the fact that the household is behaving optimally. To do this, we are going to use identities from the household's own optimality conditions, In particular, note that from the f.o.c. for consumption (139) (and given that $\lambda_t = 0$), we have that

$$
\frac{\beta^{t-1}u'(C_t)}{\mu_t} = P_t,
\tag{151}
$$

and from the household's f.o.c. for labor (140) we have that

$$
\frac{\beta^{t-1}v'(L_t)}{\mu_t} = P_t(1-\tau_l)Z_t^{1-\alpha}(1-\alpha)\bar{L}_t^{-\alpha}\bar{K}_t^{\alpha}.
\tag{152}
$$

Then, from the household's f.o.c. for capital (141), we have that the net effect of investment is zero in the above budget constraint since the gains are exactly matched by the costs,

$$
-\mu_t P_t + \mu_{t+1}P_{t+1}\left[\left[(1-\tau_k)Z_{t+1}\bar{L}_{t+1}\right]^{1-\alpha}\alpha\bar{K}_{t+1}^{\alpha-1} + 1 - \delta\right] = 0.
\tag{153}
$$

because $\mu_t = \mu_{t+1}$ when $q_t = 1$. Finally, let's make use of the fact that transfer will be zero; $T_t = 0$.

All this means that we can rewrite the above budget constraint (150) as

$$
\begin{aligned}
0 &= \sum_{t=1}^{T}\left\{ \frac{\beta^{t-1}v'(L_t)}{\mu_t}L_t - \frac{\beta^{t-1}u'(C_t)}{\mu_t}C_t \right\} \\
&\quad + P_1\left[(1-\tau_{k,1})\alpha\left[Z_1\bar{L}_1\right]^{1-\alpha}\bar{K}_1^{\alpha-1} + (1-\delta)\right]K_1 + M_1 + B_1
\end{aligned}
$$

Finally, let's make use of the fact that $\mu_t = \mu_1$ and multiply by μ_1 before using (139) to replace $\mu_1 P_1$ with the marginal utility of consumption in the first period to get

$$
\begin{aligned}
0 = \sum_{t=1}^{T} \Big\{ \ \beta^{t-1} v'(L_t) L_t - \beta^{t-1} u'(C_t) C_t \ \Big\} \\
+ u'(C_1) \Big[(1 - \tau_{k,1}) \alpha \, [Z_1 \bar{L}_1]^{1-\alpha} \bar{K}_1^{\alpha-1} + (1 - \delta) \Big] K_1 + \frac{u'(C_1)}{P_1} (M_1 + B_1)
\end{aligned}
$$

$$(154)$$

This amazing result is commonly called the *implementability condition*. Note that only initial assets show up. Other than these initial assets, all we have is the net of labor minus consumption evaluated using their marginals from the f.o.c's. All tax rates have disappeared save one, the initial tax rate on capital. This is because there is no prior cost choice to offset this gain term. The fact that this one tax rate is still here will turn out to have an important implication with respect to the initial taxation of capital.

The role of the implementability condition (154) is to ensure that the household spends all of its income. The reason for this is that the "most efficient" way for the government to pick the allocation is to have the household underspend by exactly the present value of government revenue. This would essentially be like having lump-sum taxation. Of course, no household would choose to behave in this manner; hence, we need this condition. However, the role of this condition is the reverse of the budget constraint in the household's problem. There, it is seeking to prevent *overspending* by the household, while in the government's choice problem, it will be preventing *underspending*.

Unlike the flow budget constraint, condition (154) is in the form of a present-value budget constraint. This is because we are not seeking to constrain the spending of the household on consumption and new capital to equal its income in each period. Rather, we are seeking to constrain the overall level of spending and are allowing the government and the household to borrow and lend to each other.

4.3. Government's Policy Choice Problem Step 3

We are now ready to formulate the government's choice problem. Since we have already determined monetary policy, what remains is fiscal policy. Since we are following the primal approach the government is directly choosing the initial tax rate on capital $\tau_{k,1}$ along with the allocation, which here is the sequence of consumption, labor, and capital levels $\{C_t, L_t, K_{t+1}\}$, and then inferring labor and capital taxes using (148 & 149). Since we are assuming that the only thing the government cares about is the welfare of the representative agent, its objective is to maximize the payoff to this agent, which is given by (138). The constraints on the government's choice of the initial tax rate and allocation consist solely of the resource constraint in every period (135) and the implementability condition (154), which is a single condition.

If we form the Lagrangian, where the multiplier on the resource constraint is $\beta^{t-1}\lambda_t$ and the multiplier on the implementability constraint is given by μ, we get

$$\mathbb{L} = \max\min \sum_t \beta^{t-1}\left\{u(C_t) - v(L_t) + \lambda_t[(Z_t L_t)^{1-\alpha} K_t^{\alpha}\right.$$

$$\left. + K_t(1-\delta) - K_{t+1} - G - C_t]\right\}$$

$$+ \mu \sum_{t=1}^{T}\left\{ \beta^{t-1}v'(L_t)L_t - \beta^{t-1}u'(C_t)C_t \right\}$$

$$+ \mu\left\{u'(C_1)\left[(1-\tau_{k,1})\alpha[Z_1\bar{L}_1]^{1-\alpha}\bar{K}_1^{\alpha-1} + (1-\delta)\right]K_1 + \frac{u'(C_1)}{P_1}(M_1 + B_1)\right\}$$

$$\tag{155}$$

If we take the derivative with respect to the initial tax rate on capital to form the f.o.c., we get

$$\mu u'(C_1)\left[(1-\tau_{k,1})\alpha[Z_1\bar{L}_1]^{1-\alpha}\bar{K}_1^{\alpha-1}\right]K_1 = 0. \tag{156}$$

This condition seems hard to interpret at first, because it implies that the implementability condition cannot bind; in other words, $\mu = 0$. But if this is the case, then we are back to a pure social planning problem and there is no distortion from taxation. How can this one tax rate solve all of the problems of taxation for us? There is only so much capital and the return to it is bound to be limited. Even if we set the tax rate to 100%, how can this remove all future problems associated with taxation? This is because we can set the tax rate to be much more than 100%; we can essentially increase $\tau_{k,1}$ to be 100 or 1000 or whatever we need. If we tried to do this in the future, no one would choose to hold capital, but in the first period, households start with a fixed amount of capital and cannot change that. Thus, the initial tax on capital acts as a lump-sum tax and the message here is that *lump-sum taxes do not cause efficiency problems*, and hence, we should just use that tax to do everything.

Still, this result seems fishy since if the household could, it would want to destroy its capital stock if we set the tax rate too high. To get around this issue one commonly argues that there is some plausible upper bound on capital taxation.

In that case, the optimal choice here is to set the capital tax to a level high enough to cover all of the government's expenses now and forever, or to the upper bound, depending on which is the smaller of the two.

Let us next take the first-order condition with respect to consumption. This is given by

$$u'(C_t) - \lambda_t + \mu\{u'(C_t) + u''(C_t)C_t\} = 0. \tag{157}$$

This condition is pretty difficult to interpret, especially since it involves the second derivative of the utility function. However, there are two key feature to note here. The first is that if consumption ever becomes constant as $t \to \infty$, which means that we converge to a steady state, then λ_t becomes constant. This cannot happen here with positive growth and $g > 0$. But it could happen in the special case of $g = 0$.

The second key feature emerges if we make a standard assumption, and assume we have CRRA preferences over consumption. When this is true, it implies that $u''(C_t)C_t = -\gamma u'(C_t)$, and hence, this condition becomes simply

$$(1 + \mu[1 - \gamma])u'(C_t) = \lambda_t. \tag{158}$$

Next, let's take the derivative with respect to capital at time t. The capital we are choosing only shows up in the resource constraint, and this implies that the first-order condition is

$$-\lambda_{t-1} + \beta\lambda_t\left[\alpha Z_t L_t^{1-\alpha} K_t^{\alpha-1} + (1-\delta)\right] = 0. \tag{159}$$

If we then use (158) we recover a very familiar equation for the optimal choice of capital

$$-u'(C_{t-1}) + \beta u'(C_t)\left[\alpha Z_t L_t^{1-\alpha} K_t^{\alpha-1} + (1-\delta)\right] = 0. \tag{160}$$

This is the same condition we see in a model without any capital taxation. Moreover, when we look at the level of capital taxation implied by (149), we find that $\tau_{k,t} = 0$ for all $t > 1$. This is considered the fundamental result in Ramsey taxation.[5]

---

5. This result was first developed by Chamley, Christophe. "Optimal taxation of capital income in general equilibrium with infinite lives." Econometrica: Journal of the Econometric Society (1986): 607–622.

Remark 31. *I want to mention one complication that we are ignoring. Because first period consumption C_1 is being distorted, this implies that the intertemporal rate of substitution between period 1 and period 2 is also being distorted; i.e., $\beta u'(C_2) u'(C_1)$. This in turn will affect the tax rate we derive in from our allocation in period 2, $\tau_{k,2}$. Any limitation on this tax rate can bind and hence distort the consumption level in period 2. But this distortion will impact on the marginal rate of substitution between periods 2 and 3, perhaps leading to the period 3 tax limit binding and so forth. Surprisingly, it is possible for this binding pattern to continue way, perhaps infinitely, into the future.*[6]

5. OPTIMAL POLICY IMPLICATIONS

We can now sum up the three major implications our analysis has suggested:

1. Monetary policy should operate so as to make the nominal interest rate equal to 0.
2. Capital taxes should initially be quite high.
3. After that, capital taxes should be zero.

I said that our result suggests these findings because I really did not prove that the Friedman rule was optimal. Rather I showed that with the Friedman rule, we got back to something that worked like a purely real model without money. Given that, we then analyze the optimal labor and capital tax rates. That is a serious caveat. In addition, I really only proved that capital taxation is zero in the steady state, and in a growing economy with CRRA preferences, given that monetary policy follows the Friedman rule. However, these results are more general than this would suggest. See Chari and Kehoe (1999) for more.[7]

The key feature driving the optimal tax result is that in a steady state or along a balanced growth path, capital becomes infinitely elastic with its after-tax return pinned down by the marginal rate of substitution

$$\frac{\beta u'(Cg)}{u'(C)}.$$

6. See Straub, Ludwig, and Iván Werning. Positive long run capital taxation: Chamley-Judd revisited. No. w20441. National Bureau of Economic Research, 2014. See also Chari, Varadarajan V., Juan Pablo Nicolini, and Pedro Teles. Optimal capital taxation revisited. mimeo, Federal Reserve Bank of Minneapolis, 2016.

7. Chari, Varadarajan V., and Patrick J. Kehoe. "Optimal fiscal and monetary policy." Handbook of Macroeconomics 1 (1999): 1671–1745.

This in turn is a function of three exogenous variables: the discount rate β, the growth rate g, and the CRRA curvature parameter α. Other models, such as the overlapping-generations model in which the real interest rate is not so starkly pinned down, do not have quite this same sharp implication for taxation.

The fact that we initially tax capital very heavily and thereafter not at all means that optimal policy tends to have the government raising a lot of revenue early on, and then saving much of this revenue and using it to pay for expenditures down the road. This is clearly not much like what we see in reality with the heavy use of public borrowing.[8]

Another feature to note here is that if the government was ever allowed to reconsider its optimal policy rule, it would very much like to do so if this came as a complete surprise to the representative agent. This is because it could use this opportunity to impose a second nondistortionary levy on capital, exactly as it did in the first period. This fact means that the optimal tax policy we have constructed here relies very heavily on the fact that the government has committed itself to its optimal policy rule.[9]

8. For more on where the optimal taxation literature leads us in practice, see Mankiw, N. Gregory, Matthew Weinzierl, and Danny Yagan. Optimal Taxation in Theory and Practice (June 11, 2009). Harvard Business School BGIE Unit Working Paper No. 09–140.

9. See Kydland, Finn E., and Edward C. Prescott. "Rules rather than discretion: The inconsistency of optimal plans." Journal of Political Economy 85.3 (1977): 473–491. Trying to analyze policies without commitment is a much more difficult enterprise. A famous example of this sort is Lucas Jr, Robert E., and Nancy L. Stokey. "Optimal fiscal and monetary policy in an economy without capital." Journal of Monetary Economics 12.1 (1983): 55–93.

## PART 4

Reviews

## 22

Math Reviews

The course will be concerned with using models to think about how the world works and what the optimal government choices are in terms of monetary and fiscal policy. We will assume that individuals are rational, which we will take to mean that they have a well-defined payoff function that they are seeking to maximize. This will imply that we are making extensive use of basic optimization theory. In addition, we will have to think carefully about how these individuals make their optimal choices in the face of uncertainty. As a result, we will also be using basic probability theory to an extensive degree. In this section we provide a short review of this material.

These reviews are meant to be very basic refreshers. For those needing or wanting more, I would suggest the following additional sources: For more on calculus, go back to your college/high school textbook, or look at Serge Lange's *A First Course in Calculus*. For more information on optimization theory, a great place to start is Avinash Dixit's *Optimization in Economic Theory*, (first or second edition) from Oxford University Press. For more on statistics and inference, I would suggest Silvey's *Statistical Inference*. All of these books can be bought used.[1]

---

1. Lang, Serge. *A First Course in Calculus*. Springer Science & Business Media, 2012. Dixit, Avinash K., and John JF Sherrerd. *Optimization in Economic Theory*. Oxford University Press on Demand, 1990. Silvey, Samuel David. *Statistical Inference*. Routledge, 2017.

1. OPTIMIZATION REVIEW

Our models will feature individuals and agents who seek to maximize their payoff. The payoff is a ranking of the set of possible outcomes from best to worst. Constraints then determine which elements of the overall set of possible choices are feasible for the agent. Their problem is to pick the best element in the set of feasible choices. We will represent preferences over outcomes with a function. This function will tell us the numerical value associated with different outcomes and the ranking is implied by these values. For example, the payoff or utility from a consumption vector c is given by the function $U(c)$ which maps from the space of possible consumptions, C, to the real line. A higher value such as $U(c_1) > U(c_2)$ means that c_1 is preferred to c_2.

For another example, assume that the individual cares about consumption and labor effort, with more consumption making him better off and more labor effort making him worse off. Then the utility function U will map from the set of possible consumptions, C, and the set of possible labor efforts, L, to the set of possible payoffs, which will be elements of the real line, R. We denote this by $U : C \times L \to R$. Because consumption is a good thing, the marginal impact of an increase in c will be positive, while l will be negative.

All of the possible consumption c and labor effort l choices, which we denote by $(c, l) \in C \times L$, will not necessarily be feasible. We construct the set of feasible choices by imposing a constraint. A typical constraint would be a budget constraint

$$c \leq w * l.$$

The set of feasible choices would then be given by $\{(c, l) \in C \times L : c \leq w * l\}$

For another example of a constraint, assume that there were two types of consumption, A consumption and B consumption, which we denote by c_a and c_b. Then a budget constraint over these two types of consumption would be

$$p_a c_a + p_b c_b \leq y.$$

Nonlinear constraints often arise in production economies For example, assume that output is produced with labor l and capital k, and that this output can be used either for consumption c or next period's capital k'. Then a typical nonlinear budget constraint would be

$$f(k, l) \geq c + k'.$$

We will characterize (i.e., describe) the optimal actions of our agents, households, firms, and so on, by solving their optimization problem. This optimization will typically consist of an objective function, a choice set, and a constraint that limits the choice set further. For example: (i) max U by choosing values of c and l that satisfy the budget constraint, or (ii) max U by choosing values of c_a and c_b that satisfy the budget constraint.

We will assume that the functions are nice in the following sense. First, they will in general be continuous and smooth. A **smooth function** is one that changes continuously. This will mean that such a function is differentiable (more on this later).

With respect to preferences, we will assume that they are concave so that positive amounts of all goods are preferred to consuming simply one good or the other. A function U is said to be **concave** if for any two consumption points (c_a, c_b) and $(\bar{c}_a, \bar{c}_b)$ and any λ between 0 and 1, when we define the consumption point $(c_a^\lambda, c_b^\lambda)$ by

$$c_a^\lambda = \lambda c_a + (1-\lambda)\bar{c}_a$$
$$c_b^\lambda = \lambda c_b + (1-\lambda)\bar{c}_b$$

then,

$$U(c_a^\lambda, c_b^\lambda) > \lambda U(c_a, c_b) + (1-\lambda)U(\bar{c}_a, \bar{c}_b).$$

Note that this does not imply that equal amounts of the two goods are preferred. In fact, the individual may have a distinct preference for one or other of the two goods. However, completely extreme consumption bundles are not desirable. Here are some examples of concave functions:

- Example 1:

$$U(c_a, c_b) = c_a^{1/2} + c_b^{1/2}$$

- Example 2:

$$U(c_a, c_b) = \log(c_a) + \log(c_b)$$

Before turning to optimization we want one other key definition. A set G is said to be **convex** if c and $c' \in G$, then $\lambda c + (1-\lambda)c' \in G$ for any $\lambda \in [0,1]$.

We turn next to optimization. Assume that c is a vector, F is a concave function, and the set of feasible choices G is convex. Then, if we are not at an optimum, we can always improve locally by moving toward the optimum. To see this, assume that $F(c') > F(c)$, and both c' and c are in G. Then for any $\lambda \in [0,1]$, the fact that G is convex implies $\lambda c + (1-\lambda)c' \in G$ if $c', c \in G$. And since F is concave, $F(\lambda c + (1-\lambda)c') > F(c)$. Hence, we can always find a local improvement (i.e., λ close to 1), which is feasible if we are not at the global max. Also, by the same logic, a local max is also a global max. This is why we often make these assumptions.

A one-dimensional choice problem is one in which the choice variable, say, x, is a scalar.

$$\max_{x} F(x).$$

If F is a concave function then there is one optimal choice, though it could be at the extremes. Concave functions are hump-shaped and have only a single hump. The top of the hill is flat and concave. This is true even in the multidimensional context. To utilize this fact, we next define tangency and derivatives.

Tangency and Local Peaks: The **slope** of a line between two points x and y:

$$\text{slope} = \frac{F(y) - F(x)}{y - x}.$$

A **tangent line** meets but does not pass through a curve or surface. If the surface is curved, this will mean that it will meet at a single point if a sufficiently small interval is considered. This occurs because the tangent line replicates the slope of the curve at the meet point. Because the top of the hill is flat, local peaks (and troughs) have a tangent line with slope = 0.

Derivatives: The derivative is the slope of the line around the point x, or the slope between x and y as y approaches x:

$$\lim_{y \to x} \frac{F(y) - F(x)}{y - x}.$$

In other words, it is the slope of the tangent line to the point.

1.1. Derivatives

Figuring out the derivative of different functions typically boils down to knowing some key derivatives and then using them to build up to the derivative of the function in question. To see how this is done, and to understand exactly how the derivative was determined, we work out a couple of key examples.

Example 2. *Start with the equation of a line*

$$y = A + Bx.$$

We want to know how y changes with x. The old-fashioned answer is the slope coefficient B. We ask that question again armed with calculus. The derivative of y with respect to x is given by

$$\lim_{h \to 0} \frac{A + B(x + h) - (A + Bx)}{h} = \lim_{h \to 0} \frac{Bh}{h} = B.$$

Comfortingly we get the same answer. So a linear relationship has a constant derivative that is given by the slope.

Example 3. *The derivative of x^2 is the solution to*

$$\lim_{h \to 0} \frac{(x+h)^2 - x^2}{h} = \frac{x^2 + 2xh + h^2 - x^2}{h}$$
$$= \lim_{h \to 0} (2x + h) = 2x.$$

This is a relationship we were all forced to memorize long ago. Here we see that it has a very simple basis. Note however that, unlike the linear relationship, the value of the derivative depends on where we are examining it (i.e., it depends on x).

Example 4. *What about the derivative of a quadratic function? Start from the relationship*

$$y = A + Bx + Cx^2.$$

We want to know what the derivative of y is w.r.t. x. This is given by

$$\lim_{h \to 0} \frac{A + B(x+h) + C(x+h)^2 - (A + Bx + Cx^2)}{h}$$
$$= \lim_{h \to 0} \frac{Bh + C(2xh + h^2)}{h} = B + 2Cx + \lim_{h \to 0} Ch = B + 2Cx.$$

So the derivative of a quadratic, which is the sum of a linear and a squared term, is simply the sum of the derivatives of the pieces, and these pieces are just the two expressions we derived previously.

This result is very general. The derivative of the sum of two functions is the sum of the derivatives:

$$\lim_{h \to 0} \frac{[F(x+h) + G(x+h)] - [F(x) + G(x)]}{h}$$
$$= \lim_{h \to 0} \frac{[F(x+h) - F(x)] + [G(x+h) - G(x)]}{h}$$

1.2. Derivatives and Continuity

We can think of the derivative coming either from above or below. Consider $y < x$ and take the limit as

$$\lim_{y \to x} \frac{f(x) - f(y)}{x - y} = f'_-(x).$$

This is the derivative coming from below or from the left. Similarly, we can define the derivative coming from above or the right as $y > x$

$$\lim_{y \to x} \frac{f(x) - f(y)}{x - y} = f'_+(x).$$

When $f'_+(x) = f'_-(x)$ then we say that the derivative of the function exists at x. Clearly for the right- and left-hand side derivatives to be finite, we need the function f to converge to $f(x)$ at x. In addition, we need the local slope to be converging to a common value, which means that the function cannot have a kink at the point x. In other words, it must be sufficiently smooth at x.

1.3. The Chain Rule

We often have to deal with functions that are themselves dependent on another function. For example $y = f(u)$ where $u = g(x)$. Putting this together we have that $y = f(g(x))$ so y is really a function of x. How can we think about the slope of y w.r.t. x? Formally this is given by

$$
\begin{aligned}
\frac{\Delta y}{\Delta x} &= \lim_{h \to 0} \frac{f(g(x+h)) - f(g(x))}{h} \\
&= \lim_{h \to 0} \frac{f(g(x+h)) - f(g(x))}{g(x+h) - g(x)} \frac{g(x+h) - g(x)}{h} \\
&= \left(\lim_{h \to 0} \frac{f(g(x+h)) - f(g(x))}{g(x+h) - g(x)} \right) \left(\lim_{h \to 0} \frac{g(x+h) - g(x)}{h} \right) \\
&= f'(g(x))g'(x).
\end{aligned}
$$

The last step makes use of the fact that the limit of the product is equal to the product of the limits. To flesh out this key result, we turn next to a simple example.

Example 5. *Consider two linear functions of the form*

$$F(G) = A + B * G,$$
$$G(x) = C + D * x.$$

The composite function is then given by

$$F(x) = A + BC + BDx,$$

so the derivative of F w.r.t. x is BD.

1.4. More on Derivatives

Example 6. *A common function that we might need to differentiate is an inverse relationship like $1/x$. The derivative is given by*

$$\lim_{h \to 0} \frac{1/(x+h) - 1/x}{h} = \lim_{h \to 0} \frac{\frac{x-(x+h)}{x(x+h)}}{h} = \lim_{h \to 0} \frac{\frac{-h}{x^2+xh}}{h} = \lim_{h \to 0} \frac{-1}{x^2+xh} = \frac{-1}{x^2}.$$

To get this result, we cross-multiplied by the two denominators in the upper expression, then multiplied above and below by $1/h$ and finally just evaluated things at the limit.

The examples we have considered so far have all been fairly easy. Unfortunately, that is not generally the case. Just to close this discussion out, we consider a couple of harder examples.

Example 7. *What is the derivative of e^x? Consider the more general problem of the derivative of a^x w.r.t. x. This is the solution to*

$$f'(x) = \lim_{h \to 0} \frac{a^{x+h} - a^x}{h} = a^x \lim_{h \to 0} \frac{a^h - a^0}{h} = a^x \lim_{h \to 0} \frac{a^h - 1}{h}.$$

Next, notice that if we evaluated the derivative of $f(x) = a^x$ at $x = 0$, then we would get

$$f'(0) = \lim_{h \to 0} \frac{a^{0+h} - a^0}{h} = \lim_{h \to 0} \frac{a^h - 1}{h}.$$

So, we can rewrite our original expression as

$$f'(x) = a^x f'(0).$$

To make forward progress from here, we resort to a special case. It turns out the e can be determined in a vareity of ways, and one of them is

$$\lim_{h \to 0} \frac{e^h - 1}{h} = 1.$$

So, IF $a = e$, then we know the answer.

$$\frac{d}{dx} e^x = e^x.$$

One more case is that of natural logs. Start from the definition of an inverse function. We say that $f(x)$ and $g(x)$ are inverses of each other if

$$g(f(x)) = x.$$

That is, g undoes whatever f did to x. Then use the chain rule to get that

$$g'(f(x))f'(x) = 1,$$

so

$$f'(x) = 1/g'(f(x)).$$

So, at each point g' undoes the slope effect of f'. Now, $\ln(x)$ and e^x are inverses of each other by construction. So,

$$\ln(e^x) = x.$$

Then, using the chain rule

$$\frac{d}{dx}\ln(e^x) = \left[\frac{d}{da}\ln(a)|_{a=e^x}\right]\left[\frac{d}{dx}e^x\right] = 1$$

and hence

$$\left[\frac{d}{da}\ln(a)|_{a=e^x}\right][e^x] = 1 \Rightarrow \left[\frac{d}{da}\ln(a)|_{a=e^x}\right] = \frac{1}{e^x}.$$

From this it follows that

$$\frac{d}{da}\ln(a) = \frac{1}{a}.$$

Here are some examples of derivatives we will use:

Table 1. SOME USEFUL DERIVATIVES

$$x^{1/2} = \frac{1}{2x^{1/2}} \qquad x^\alpha = \alpha x^{\alpha-1} \qquad \log(x) = \frac{1}{x}$$
$$-e^{-\alpha x} = \alpha e^{-\alpha x} \qquad a^x = a^x * \ln(a)$$

1.5. Approximating Functions

When we seek to approximate a function $F(x)$ using only local information around the approximation point $\bar{x}$, we are seeking an approximating function that shares the features of the original function as closely as possible. So, it would be natural to ask that it equal the function at $\bar{x}$. It would also be natural to have its slope be the same as the function at $\bar{x}$. Going further, we might want the change in the slope at $\bar{x}$ to be the same and so forth. It is natural to do this approximation using a polynomial since under appropriate assumptions (smoothness and bounded variation), a function can be arbitrarily closely approximated by a sufficiently high degree polynomial. Also, polynomials distinguish sharply the various elements of the intercept, slope, change in the slope, and so forth.

So starting from our function $F(x)$ and our polynomial $P(x)$, where

$$P(x) = \sum_{j=0}^{N} A_j \times (x - \bar{x})^j$$

we have a sequence of requirements:

$$F(\bar{x}) = P(\bar{x}) = A_0$$

$$\frac{1}{dx} F(\bar{x}) = \frac{dP}{dx} P(\bar{x}) = A_1$$

$$\frac{1}{dx^2} F(\bar{x}) = \frac{dP}{dx^2} P(\bar{x}) = 2 \times A_2$$

$$\frac{1}{dx^3} F(\bar{x}) = \frac{dP}{dx^3} P(\bar{x}) = 3 \times 2 \times A_3.$$

For this reason we end up with an approximating expression that looks like

$$P(x) = F(\bar{x}) + \frac{F'(\bar{x})}{1}(x - \bar{x}) + \frac{F''(\bar{x})}{1 \times 2}(x - \bar{x})^2 + \frac{F'''(\bar{x})}{1 \times 2 \times 3}(x - \bar{x})^3 + \ldots$$

This type of approximation is commonly called a *Taylor approximation*.

A special example that has some independent interest is taking a high order Taylor approximation to the function e^x, which we often use in compounding or growth circumstances. Note that

$$\frac{1}{dx^n} e^x = e^x.$$

Then, if we approximate around $x = 0$ where $e^0 = 1$, we get the following expression

$$e^x \approx \sum_{j=0}^{N} \frac{1}{j!} x^j,$$

where $j! = j \times j - 1 \times j - 2 \times \ldots \times 1$ and is call j factorial.

We can also use Taylor approximations to learn about functions around their maximum and minimum points. If we start from a first-order approximation, it is easy to see that at a maximum or a minimum

$$F'(\bar{x}) = 0.$$

If we want to distinguish between maximum and minimum, we need to use a second-order approximation, and it is easy to see that at a maximum

$$F''(\bar{x}) < 0.$$

With more complex problems, we have to extend our approach to allow for multiple variables. Consider a **multivariate function** $F(x_1, x_2, ..., x_n)$. Then, let the vector

$$x = \begin{bmatrix} x_1 \\ x_2 \\ \vdots \\ x_n \end{bmatrix},$$

and denote the argument of F, hence $F(x)$. So notationally things look the same. Then, for the analog of the derivative, let $\nabla F(\bar{x})$ denote the gradient vector or

$$\nabla F(\bar{x}) = \begin{bmatrix} \frac{dF(x)}{dx_1} \\ \frac{dF(x)}{dx_2} \\ \vdots \\ \frac{dF(x)}{dx_n} \end{bmatrix},$$

and let the second-order term be given by

$$\nabla^2 F(\bar{x}) = \begin{bmatrix} \frac{d^2 F}{dx_i dx_j} \end{bmatrix}.$$

Then, the second-order approximation is given by

$$F(x) = F(\bar{x}) + \nabla F(\bar{x})^T (x - \bar{x}) + \frac{1}{2}(x - \bar{x})^T \nabla^2 F(\bar{x})(x - \bar{x}).$$

where T denotes the transpose

$$\nabla F(\bar{x})^T (x - \bar{x}) = \sum_{i=1}^{n} \frac{dF(x)}{dx_i}(x_i - \bar{x}_i).$$

If we write this out in more standard notation,

$$(x - \bar{x})^T \nabla^2 F(\bar{x})(x - \bar{x}) = \sum_{j=1}^{n} \sum_{i=1}^{n} \frac{dF(x)}{dx_i}(x_i - \bar{x}_i)\frac{dF(x)}{dx_j}(x_j - \bar{x}_i)$$

At a maximum
$$\nabla F(\bar{x}) = 0,$$

and
$$\nabla^2 F(\bar{x})$$

is negative semi-definite.

The optimality condition $\nabla F(\bar{x}) = 0$ can be written out as

$$\frac{d}{dx_i}F(x) = 0 \text{ for each } i = 1, ..., n.$$

This gives us n equations in n unknowns. So we can readily solve for the x that satisfies this condition.

One issue is that there may be more than one x or point at which the vector of first partials is zeroed out. However, if F is concave and G (the choice set) is convex there will be one and only one solution. Note that we are only worrying about single deviations. Any combination of dx_i and dx_j is approximately

$$\frac{dF(x)}{dx_i}dx_i + \frac{dF(x)}{dx_j}dx_j.$$

If $\frac{dF(x)}{dx_i} = \frac{dF(x)}{dx_j} = 0$, there are no profitable deviations, and if this isn't true, then there always are.

1.6. Optimization with Constraints

Consider the following maximization problem

$$\max_{x,y} f(x,y),$$

subject to
$$g(x,y) = c.$$

If we consider adjusting x and y to satisfy the constraint, then locally the constraint implies

$$g_x dx + g_y dy = 0,$$

or

$$dy = \frac{-g_x}{g_y} dx.$$

Using this fact, we think about a variation in x inducing an appropriate variation in y. Hence at an optimum

$$f_x + f_y \left(\frac{-g_x}{g_y} \right) = 0$$

$$\implies \frac{f_x}{f_y} = \frac{g_x}{g_y}.$$

Lagrangians: Consider forming the Lagrangian

$$L = f(x,y) + \lambda g(x,y) - \lambda c,$$

and differentiating with respect to x, y, and λ to get

$$f_x + \lambda g_x = 0$$

$$f_y + \lambda g_y = 0$$

$$g(x,y) = c.$$

Note that if we eliminate λ from the first two equations we get our optimality condition from our original statement of the problem. Note also that the third equation is simply our constraint.

Formally, the **Theorem of Lagrange** states that if at the solution x^*, the vector of first partials of the constraint function g has nonzero derivatives for each choice variable, then there will exist a multiplier λ such that

$$\nabla f(x^*) + \lambda \nabla g(x^*) = 0.$$

The reason that things break down if this isn't true is that there is no way to locally price a deviation if $\partial g(x^*)/\partial x_i = 0$.

So far, we have dealt with equality constraints of the form $g(x,y) = c$. What about an inequality constraint of the form

$$g(x,y) \le c?$$

This can be handled by first adding a dummy argument z and changing the constraint to

$$g(x,y) + z = c$$

where z is constrained to be nonnegative. Then the Lagrangian becomes

$$L = \max_{x,y,z} \min_{\lambda} \; f(x,y) + \lambda \left[c - g(x,y) - z \right].$$

When we take the f.o.c. w.r.t. z we get that

$$-\lambda \le 0 \text{ and where this must be strict if } z > 0.$$

The weak inequality follows from the nonnegativity constraint on z. This implies that $\lambda \ge 0$ with this form of an inequality constraint.

We can informally state the **Kuhn-Tucker Theorem**, which is the formal basis for Lagrangian theory, as follows. Assume we have a maximization problem that has two constraint: an equality constraint and an inequality constraint. Assume that this problem is given by

$$\max_{x} f(x)$$

subject to

$$g(x) = 0 \text{ and}$$

$$h(x) \le 0.$$

We are assuming here that x may be a vector. The constraint with the function g is an equality constraint, while that with the function h is the inequality constraint. Then, under some fairly standard conditions on f, g, and h, there exists a vector choice variables x^* and vectors of multipliers λ and μ such that

$$\nabla f(x^*) + \lambda \nabla g(x^*) - \mu \nabla h(x^*) = 0$$

and

$$\mu \nabla h(x^*) = 0.$$

This last condition is called the *complementary slackness condition*, and it says that either $h(x^*) = 0$ so the constraint may bind; in which case the vector of multipliers μ can have nonnegative elements wherever this is true. But wherever the constraint does not bind, that is, $dh(x^*)/dx_j < 0$, it must be the case that $\mu_j = 0$.

To understand the role of the multiplier a bit more, consider the following simple maximization problem where x is one-dimensional,

$$\max_x f(x).$$

If f is monotonically increasing, then the solution is to set $x = \infty$. Now add in a constraint

$$\max_x f(x) \text{ s.t. } x \leq y.$$

The solution is trivial: make x as large as possible since f is increasing in x. So, the solution is $x = y$. But go ahead and form the Lagrangian

$$L = \max_x \min_\lambda f(x) + \lambda[y - x].$$

Then note that the slope of L w.r.t. x is given by

$$f'(x) - \lambda.$$

So, the solution for x is to increase x up until this slope is equal to zero. λ is acting as the price of increasing x. The right price is when

$$\lambda = f'(y).$$

In this case, the constraint will be satisfied. Note that in this case, $y - x = 0$ and the value of λ doesn't affect L. If $\lambda \neq f'(y)$, then the value of L can be increased by changing x. So, λ is not minimizing L. This is why we are always working in the opposite direction with the multiplier as in the original problem. We are trying to construct the smallest possible penalty that will prevent you from violating the constraint in a maximization problem, and the biggest possible penalty in a minimization problem.

Consider next the following example with two constraints:

$$\max_{x,y} f(x,y) \text{ s.t.}$$
$$x \leq A$$
$$y \leq B$$

If f is increasing in both x and y, we again know the answer: Set $x = A$ and $y = B$. If we form the Lagrangian we get that

$$L = \max_{x,y} \min_{\lambda,\mu} f(x,y) + \lambda\left[A - x\right] + \mu\left[B - y\right].$$

The f.o.c.'s include

$$f_x - \lambda = 0$$
$$f_y - \mu = 0.$$

We also know what the right values of the multipliers are $f_x(A,B) = \lambda$ and $f_y(A,B) = \mu$. So, what is going on here is that λ is the "price" of being able to have a bit more x and μ is the "price" of a bit more y. These prices are being chosen so that you are just on the constraint.

One last important point about Lagrangian multipliers is that they "price" a relaxation of the constraint. Consider our simple one-dimensional choice problem

$$L = \max_{x} \min_{\lambda} f(x) + \lambda\left[y - x\right],$$

and note that

$$\frac{dL}{dy} = \lambda = f'(y).$$

This makes sense since at the margin, when we increase y, we get $f'(y)dy$ as the increase in the objective.

2. INTEGRATION

The definite integral of a function is the area under the function over a certain interval. For example, if we wanted to know the area of a wall which had height $f(x)$ at the point x, for x taking on values in a certain interval then area of the interval is the "sum" of all the points in the interval times the height of the wall. We can approximate this sum by taking a grid of values on the interval $[x_0, ...x_T]$ and then computing

$$\sum_{j=0}^{T}(x_{j+1} - x_j)f(x_j).$$

Unfortunately, the answer here will vary with the grid and also with which side we approximate from; in other words, we could have done

$$\sum_{j=0}^{T}(x_{j+1} - x_j)f(x_{j+1}).$$

The problem arises because the function f is not constant over these intervals, and hence, if we change the grid or change which side we approximate from, we get a different answer. If the function is continuous, then as the grid becomes arbitrarily fine, both the r.h.s. and the l.h.s. approximations will converge to the Riemann integral.

We can compute approximate integrals by using the grid approach so long as we have a "sufficiently" fine grid. The appropriate fineness is tied to the smoothness of the function we are integrating w.r.t. since the key is that it does not vary much over our intervals.

If we define the function $F(x)$ as the area of the wall over the interval $[0,x]$ where the height is $f(x)$, we can ask what the change in the area is if we change x by a small amount. This is the derivative of F or

$$lim_{h\to0}\frac{F(x+h)-F(x)}{h} = lim_{h\to0}\frac{f(x)\Delta h}{\Delta h} = f(x).$$

This illustrates that differentiation is the reverse of integration.

3. LINEAR APPROXIMATING MODELS

Our fundamental model can be thought of as consisting of two vector equations. The first is the law of motion for our shocks,

$$x_t = Ax_{t-1} + B + C\varepsilon_t.$$

The second is our economic condition which can be thought of as an expectation condition,

$$E\{F(x_t,y_t,x_{t+1},y_{t+1})|x_t\} = 0,$$

where y_t consists of the endogenous variables at time t, and we are forming expectations about both the endogenous and the exogenous variables at time $t+1$.

We are going to linearize our economic equation around the steady state of our model. The steady state is computed assuming that the innovations, ε_t, are equal to zero, so $x = B/(1-A)$. At the steady state $y_t = y_{t+1} = y$. Hence, our equation becomes

$$F(x,y,x,y) = 0.$$

This is a vector equation, so if there are n components in y, we are solving a system of n nonlinear equations in n unknowns.

We are going to linearly approximate our economic condition around the steady state. To do this we are taking a Taylor first-order approximation to F. This yields

$$F(x_t, y_t, x_{t+1}, y_{t+1})$$
$$\approx F(x, y, x, y) + F_1(x, y, x, y)(x_t - x) + F_2(x, y, x, y)(y_t - y)$$
$$+ F_3(x, y, x, y)(x_{t+1} - x) + F_4(x, y, x, y)(y_{t+1} - y)$$
$$= F_1(x, y, x, y)(x_t - x) + F_2(x, y, x, y)(y_t - y)$$
$$+ F_3(x, y, x, y)(x_{t+1} - x) + F_4(x, y, x, y)(y_{t+1} - y).$$

If we plug this approximation back into our economic condition, we get that

$$E\{F(x_t, y_t, y_{t+1}, x_{t+1}) | x_t\}$$
$$\approx F_1(x, y, x, y)(x_t - x) + F_2(x, y, x, y)(y_t - y)$$
$$+ F_3(x, y, x, y)E\{(x_{t+1} - x)\} + F_4(x, y, x, y)E\{(y_{t+1} - y)\}.$$

Note something very important here. First, because we are approximating around the steady state, $F_i(x, y, x, y) = 0$, which is a nice simplification and also will tend to yield an accurate approximation if our model variables stay close to their steady-state values. Second, the coefficients $F_i(x, y, x, y)$ (actually vectors of coefficients because x_t and y_t will have more than one element) are known and not random. Third, while x_t and y_t are stochastic, they are known at time t, and hence the expected value is equal to the actual value. Fourth, the only expectational variables we end up having to worry about are x_{t+1} and y_{t+1}, but they come in linearly, so we only care about their expected value at time t. This is often called *certainty equivalence*, in that we end up treating the expected values of the random variables as if they were the known values. Fifth, this is a linear system, and hence, it will have a linear solution for y_t (and y_{t+1} by extension).

To facilitate working with this linear system, we are going to make a change in variables and think of our stochastic system as involving deviations of x_t from x and y_t from y. To do this denote

$$\tilde{x}_t = x_t - x,$$
$$\tilde{y}_t = y_t - y.$$

Then, note that our two conditions become

$$\tilde{x}_t = A\tilde{x}_{t-1} + C\varepsilon_t$$
$$F_1(x, y, x, y)\tilde{x}_t + F_2(x, y, x, y)\tilde{y}_t + F_3(x, y, x, y)E\{\tilde{x}_{t+1}\} + F_4(x, y, x, y)E\{\tilde{y}_{t+1}\} = 0.$$

The expected value will be given by

$$E\{\tilde{x}_{t+1}|\tilde{x}_t\} = A\tilde{x}_t.$$

The solution for our endogenous variables will take the form

$$\tilde{y}_t = D\tilde{x}_t$$

Hence,

$$E\{\tilde{y}_{t+1}|\tilde{x}_t\} = E\{D\tilde{x}_{t+1}|\tilde{x}_t\} = DA\tilde{x}_t.$$

This yields the linear equations we need to solve for the values of the matrix D,

$$F_1(x,y,x,y)\tilde{x}_t + F_2(x,y,x,y)D\tilde{x}_t + F_3(x,y,x,y)A\tilde{x}_t + F_4(x,y,x,y)DA\tilde{x}_t = 0$$

for all possible values $\tilde{x}_t$. Because this equation has to be zero for every possible value that the vector x_t can take on, we can treat each component that affects $\tilde{x}_t$ separately. Thus, if $\tilde{x}_t$ has two components where $\tilde{x}_t = [\tilde{x}_{1,t}, \tilde{x}_{2,t}]$. Then plug in $[1,0]$ to get the first set of equations, and $[0,1]$ to get the second set. The number of equations in each set will be the number of elements in y_t, and the number of sets will be the number of elements in x_t. This will correspond to the number of elements in the matrix D that we are solving for. So, our system is well defined.

4. PROBABILITY THEORY REVIEW

Probability is a way of expressing the likelihood that an event will occur or has occurred. The probability of an event A is represented by a real number in the range from 0 to 1 and written as $\Pr(A)$. An impossible event has a probability of 0, and a certain event has a probability of 1. However, the converses are not always true: probability 0 events are not always impossible, nor are probability 1 events certain. There is a rather subtle distinction between "certain" and "probability 1."

The opposite or complement of an event A is the event $[\text{not } A]$ or A^C; its probability is given by $\Pr(A^C) = 1 - \Pr(A)$. As an example, the chance of not rolling a 2 on a six-sided die is $1 - (\text{chance of rolling a six}) = 1 - 1/6 = 5/6$.

If both the events A and B occur on a single performance of an experiment this is called the intersection or joint probability of A and B, denoted as $\Pr(A \cap B)$. If two events A and B are independent, then the joint probability is $\Pr(A \cap B) = \Pr(A)\Pr(B)$. For example, if two coins are flipped the chance of both being heads is $1/2 \times 1/2 = 1/4$.

The probability of events A or B occurring is denoted by $\Pr(A \cup B)$. If the events are mutually exclusive then $\Pr(A \cup B) = \Pr(A) + \Pr(B)$. However, if they are not mutually exclusive, then we are in essence double counting the event that both A and B occur, and hence, $\Pr(A \cup B) = \Pr(A) + \Pr(B) - \Pr(A \cup B)$.

Conditional probability is the probability of some event A, given the occurrence of some other event B. Conditional probability is written $\Pr(A|B)$, and is read as "the probability of A, given B." It is defined by

$$\Pr(A|B) = \frac{\Pr(A \cap B)}{\Pr(B)}.$$

For example, the likelihood of rolling a 2 on a six-sided dice is $1/6$. However the conditional probability of rolling a 2 given that the value of the dice was less than or equal to 3 is

$$\frac{1/6}{3/6} = \frac{1}{3}.$$

If we use our conditional probability result, we can derive Bayes' rule. To do that, start by noting that

$$\Pr(A|B)\Pr(B) = \Pr(A \cap B) = \Pr(B|A)\Pr(A).$$

This implies that

$$\Pr(A|B) = \frac{\Pr(B|A)\Pr(A)}{\Pr(B)},$$

which gives us a simple way of computing one conditional probability from the knowledge of the other. This formula is used a lot in statistical updating.

A random variable is a way of assigning a real number to each possible event, for example, the temperature tomorrow at noon. The set of events is all possible things that can happen tomorrow, and for each of those events we have a temperature reading. A random variable has an associated *probability density* which gives the probability of a particular value and a *probability distribution* which gives the probability that the random variable is less than or equal to some value. Let x denote a random variable and $G(x)$ its distribution. Then, $G(\bar{x}) = \Pr\{x \leq \bar{x}\}$ and its density is $g(x) = dG(x)/dx$ if x is continuous, and is equal to $G(x_j) - G(x_{j-1})$ where x_{j-1} is the next lower value of x. The *expected value* is almost surely (i.e., with probability 1) the limit of the sample mean as sample size grows to infinity. Note that this is not the most likely value, and may even be impossible—like having 2.5 children. We denote the expected value of x by $E\{x\}$, and it is given by

$$E\{x\} = \int_x xg(x)dx$$

if x is continuous, or

$$E\{x\} = \sum_x xg(x)$$

if it is discrete. The conditional expectation of a random variable is the expected value of x given that it takes on the value in the set A only. This is given by

$$E\{x|A\} = \sum_x x\Pr(x|A) = \sum_{x\in A} x\frac{g(x)}{\sum_{x\in A} g(x)}.$$

For example, the mean of a six-sided dice is

$$\frac{1+2+3+4+5+6}{6} = 3.5$$

and the conditional mean given that the die roll was less than or equal to 3 is

$$[1+2+3]\frac{\frac{1}{6}}{\frac{1}{6}\times 3} = \frac{1+2+3}{3} = 2.$$

The normal (or Gaussian) distribution, is a continuous probability distribution that is often used as a first approximation to describe real-valued random variables that tend to cluster around a single mean value. The graph of the associated probability density function is "bell"-shaped, and the probability density is given by

$$f(x) = \frac{1}{\sqrt{2\pi\sigma^2}}e^{-\frac{(x-\mu)^2}{2\sigma^2}}$$

where μ is the mean and σ^2 is the variance. The distribution with $\mu = 0$ and $\sigma^2 = 1$ is called the standard normal. We often write $x \sim N(\mu,\sigma^2)$ to denote that x is a normally distributed random variable with mean μ and variance σ^2.

A log-normal distribution is a probability distribution of a random variable whose log is normally distributed. A variable might be modeled as log-normal if it can be thought of as the multiplicative product of many independent random variables each of which is positive. The density is given by

$$g(x) = \frac{1}{x\sqrt{2\pi\sigma^2}}e^{-\frac{(\ln x-\mu)^2}{2\sigma^2}}.$$

To understand why we have an x in the denominator, assume that x was log-normally distributed, and let its distribution be given by $G(x)$. Note that if x is log-normally distributed, then

$$G(x) = F(\ln(x)),$$

where F is the distribution function for the normal. From the definition of the distribution function, the density $g(x)$ must satisfy

$$G(x) = \int_0^x g(x)dx.$$

and

$$F(\ln x) = \int_{\ln(0)}^{\ln(x)} f(\ln(x))d\ln(x)$$

$$= \int_{\ln(0)}^{\ln(x)} f(\ln(x))\frac{dx}{x}$$

since if $y = \log(x)$, then $dy = dx/x$, and hence $xdy = dx$.

5. TIME SERIES REVIEW

Macroeconomic data typically come to us in the form of time series. For example $\{x_t\}_{t=1}^T$ and $\{y_t\}_{t=1}^T$. These data often exhibit both short-term and long-term fluctuations. Short-term fluctuations die out after enough time. Long-term fluctuations do not die out. We can think of short-term fluctuations as coming from business cycles and long-term fluctuations as coming from growth shocks. We are interested in both types of fluctuations.

Here are some basic time series statistics that we use to characterize series behavior:

- The average value (or mean) of a series is given by

$$E(x_t) = \frac{1}{T}\sum_{t=1}^T x_t$$

- The variation in a series is measured by the variance

$$var(x_t) = \frac{1}{N} \sum_{t=0}^{T} (x_t - E(x_t)))^2$$

standard deviation

$$sd(x_t) = sqrt \left[\frac{1}{N} \sum_{t=0}^{T} (x_t - E(x_t)))^2 \right]$$

- Time series exhibit comovement patterns which we measure in two basic ways covariance

$$cov(x_t, y_t) = \frac{1}{N} \sum_{t=0}^{T} (x_t - E(x_t))) (y_t - E(y_t)),$$

correlation

$$corr(x_t, y_t) = \frac{cov(x_t, y_t)}{sd(x_t) * sd(y_t)}.$$

Some basic facts about these statistics

- Series are independent if $cov(x_t, y_t) = 0$.
- The variance of independent series is additive

$$var(x_t + y_t) = var(x_t) + var(y_t).$$

- The variance is nonlinear in the scale

$$var(Ax_t) = A^2 var(x_t).$$

- The standard deviation is linear in the scale

$$sd(Ax_t) = Asd(x_t),$$

but $sd(x_t + y_t) \neq sd(x_t) + sd(y_t)$.
- The correlation is independent of the scale

$$corr(Ax_t, y_t) = corr(x_t, y_t)$$

  - the correlation takes on values between -1 and 1 with 0 interpreted as uncorrelated, > 0 positively correlated and < 0 negatively correlated.

5.1. Caution: Hard to Work with Trends

- Assume that $x_t = gt + \varepsilon_t$, where $\varepsilon_t \sim N(0, \sigma)$ and $g > 0$.
- $E(\varepsilon_t) = 0$, but $E(x_t) = gt$, hence

$$E\left\{\frac{1}{T}\sum_{t=1}^{T}x_t\right\} = \frac{1}{T}\sum gt,$$

  which is going to infinity if $g > 1$ and going to $-$infinity if $g < 1$.
- The sample variance is a mess

$$\frac{1}{T}\sum_{t=1}^{T}(x_t - mean(x_t))^2$$

  and the shocks are getting small if $g > 1$ or very large if $g < 1$

$$\frac{\sigma^2}{gt}$$

- But the detrended variance is ok

$$\tilde{x}_t = x_t - gt = \varepsilon_t.$$

Lesson: Detrend before doing time series computations.

## 23

Python and Dynare Code

In this chapter I include a number of examples of our programs in Python 3 and our business cycle code in Dynare. The Python code is designed to work in conjunction with the Anaconda installation of Python 3+ and its various packages. I am assuming that anyone using this section is either familiar with Python or learning it elsewhere.[1]

An important word of caution in reading this code. The typesetting language I used to create this book, Latex, is pretty insistent about how it wants to interpret certain characters. This is generally great when you want to create mathematical expressions, but it is a problem when you are trying to render code exactly. This means that certain little errors creep in here. For example, it is tricky to render certain characters like underscore or uparrow. I tried to clean everything up, but there may still be a few errors induced by this.

1. SS1 CODE

This is the Python version of the code from 1.2 on page 28.

```
import numpy as np # import numpy as np because later you use np
def Labor(ta,Z,Be,gam,alp):
```

---

[1]. In learning Python, I found the following resources to be very helpful: First, *Learning Python*, 5th edition, by Mark Lutz. Second, the Python Youtube video by Giraffe Academy.

Monetary and Fiscal Policy through a DSGE Lens. Harold L. Cole, Oxford University Press (2020).
© Oxford University Press. DOI: 10.1093/oso/9780190076030.001.0001

```
    l = Be*(Z**(1-alp))/(1+ta)
    l = l**(1/(alp+gam))
    return l
Z = 1
Be = .98
gam = .5
alp = 2
TA = np.arange(1, 2.05, 0.05) # arange in python generates arrays without
the end point
Results = np.zeros((len(TA),5))
counter = 0
for i in range(len(TA)):
    Results[i,] = [Z, TA[i], gam, alp,Labor(TA[i],Z,Be,gam,alp)]
print(Results)
import matplotlib.pyplot as plt
plt.plot(Results[:,1],Results[:,4]) # index in python starts from 0
plt.xlabel('growth rate of money τ')
plt.ylabel('labor')
plt.title('Steady State Labor Effort vs. Inflation')
plt.show()
```

2. VELOCITY CODE

This is the Python version of the code from 1.2 on page 42.

```
from scipy.optimize import fsolve
import numpy as np
def VelEQ(X,params,tau,kap):
    L, mu, lamda = X
    alph, gam, beta, Z = params
    Er1 = ((Z*L)**(-alph))*kap*Z*L - (mu + kap*lamda) # consumption
foc
    Er2 = (L**gam)*kap*L - mu # labor foc
    Er3 = (1+tau)*mu/beta - mu - lamda
    return Er1, Er2, Er3
alph = 2
gam = .5
beta = .98
Z = 1
```

```
tau = 1
params = [ alph, gam, beta, Z]
X = [.75, .5, .5]
TA = np.arange(0, 2.05, 0.05) # arange in python generates arrays without
the end point
Results1 = np.zeros((len(TA),6))
Results2 = np.zeros((len(TA),6))
counter = 0
for i in range(len(TA)):
    kap1 = 1
    L, mu, lamda = fsolve(VelEQ, X, args=(params,TA[i],kap1))
    Results1[i,] = [kap1, TA[i], Z, gam, alph,L]
    kap2 = .5
    L, mu, lamda = fsolve(VelEQ, X, args=(params,TA[i],kap2))
    Results2[i,] = [kap2, TA[i], Z, gam, alph, L]
print(Results1)
print(Results2)
import matplotlib.pyplot as plt
plt.plot(Results1[:,1],Results1[:,5],Results2[:,1],Results2[:,5]) # index in
python starts from 0
plt.xlabel('growth rate of money tau')
plt.ylabel('labor')
plt.title('Steady State Labor Effort vs. Inflation with two different kappas')
plt.show()
```

3. ELASTIC MONEY DEMAND CODE

This is the Python version of the code from 3 on page 45.

```
import numpy as np # import numpy as np because later you use np
    Labor(ta,Z,Be,gam,alp,phi):
    fac = (1+phi*(1+ta))**gam
    fac = fac*(1+phi)
    l = (Be/(1+ta))/fac
    l = l**(1/(alp+gam))
    return l
Z = 1
Be = .98
gam = 1.5
```

```
alp = 1
PH = np.arange(0.0, 1.05, 0.05) # arange in python generates arrays without
the end point
Results = np.zeros((len(PH),5))
counter = 0
for i in range(len(PH)):
    ratio = Labor(.1,Z,Be,gam,alp,PH[i])/Labor(0,Z,Be,gam,alp,PH[i])
    Results[i,] = [PH[i], Z, gam, alp,ratio]
print(Results)
import matplotlib.pyplot as plt
plt.plot(Results[:,0],Results[:,4]) # index in python starts from 0
plt.xlabel('phi')
plt.ylabel('ratio of real balances')
plt.title('Impact of phi on change in real balances')
plt.show()
```

4. STOCHASTIC 1

This is the Python version of the stochastic model code from 2.2 on page 65.

```
from IPython import get_ipython
get_ipython().magic('reset-sf') # spyder remembers any created variable
unless cleared
import numpy as np # import numpy as np because later you use np
import random # will use a random number generator
# define some of our parameters
Z = 1
M = 1
Be = .98
gam = 1.5
alp = 1
tm = .1 # mean of the money growth rate
gm = 1.02 # mean of the productivity growth rate
def Labor(ta,Z,Be,gam,alp):
    l = Be*(Z**(1-alp))/(1+ta)
    l = l**(1/(alp+gam))
    return l
Results = np.zeros((30,8))
for i in range(30):
    ta = random.uniform(tm*.5, tm*1.5)
```

```
    grow = random.uniform(gm*.95, gm*1.05)
    Z = Z*grow
    M = M*(1+ta)
    L = Labor(ta,Z,Be,gam,alp)
    Results[i,] = [i,ta, grow,Z,M,L,Z*L,M/(Z*L)]
print(Results)
import matplotlib.pyplot as plt
plt.plot(Results[:,0],Results[:,3]) # index in python starts from 0
plt.xlabel('growth rate of money τ')
plt.ylabel('labor')
plt.title('Stochastic Path for Productivity')
plt.show()
plt.plot(Results[:,0],Results[:,4])
plt.xlabel('growth rate of money τ')
plt.ylabel('labor')
plt.title('Stochastic Path for Money')
plt.show()
    plt.plot(Results[0:29,0],Results[1:30,7]/Results[0:29,7])
plt.xlabel('growth rate of money τ')
plt.ylabel('labor')
plt.title('Stochastic Path for Inflation')
plt.show()
print('Correlation between Inflation and Output Growth')
print(np.corrcoef(Results[1:30,7]/Results[0:29,7],Results[1:30,6]/
Results[0:29,6]))
print('Correlation between Inflation and Money Growth')
print(np.corrcoef(Results[1:30,7]/Results[0:29,7],Results[1:30,4]/
Results[0:29,4]))
```

5. MONTE CARLO CODE

This is the Python version of the Monte Carlo simulation code from 3 on page 67.

```
#!/usr/bin/env python3
# -*- coding: utf-8 -*- """ Created on Sat Apr 6 12:00:45 2019
@author: colehl
# This program does a Monte Carlo simulation to compute the distribution
of
# long-run correlations within our model
```

```
from IPython import get_ipython
get_ipython().magic('reset -sf') # spyder remembers any created variable
unless cleared
import numpy as np # import numpy as np because later you use np
import random # will use a random number generator
import matplotlib.pyplot as plt
# define some of our parameters
Z = 1
M = 1
Be = .98
gam = 1.5
alp = 1
tm = .1 # mean of the money growth rate
gm = 1.02 # mean of the productivity growth rate
def Labor(ta,Z,Be,gam,alp):
    l = Be*(Z**(1-alp))/(1+ta)
    l = l**(1/(alp+gam))
    return l
# Storing the correlation results
MCsize = 100
MCResults = np.zeros((MCsize,4))
for j in range(MCsize):
    Results = np.zeros((30,8))
    Z=1 # reset initial Z for each MC
    for i in range(30):
        ta = random.uniform(tm*.5, tm*1.5)
        grow = random.uniform(gm*.95, gm*1.05)
        Z = Z*grow
        M = M*(1+ta)
        L = Labor(ta,Z,Be,gam,alp)
        Results[i,] = [i,ta, grow,Z,M,L,Z*L,M/(Z*L)]
    YY = Results[10:30,6]/Results[0:20,6]
    grY = np.array([np.log(y)/10 for y in YY]) # though does not change the
result, convert list to array before combine it with other arrays in line 75
    YY = Results[10:30,7]/Results[0:20,7]
    grP = np.array([np.log(y)/10 for y in YY])# though does not change the
result, convert list to array before combine it with other arrays in line 75
    XX = np.array([Results[10:30,2], grY, grP])
    corrXX = np.corrcoef(XX)
    MCResults[j,] = [j, corrXX[0,1], corrXX[0,2], corrXX[1,2]]
plt.figure(1)
```

```
plt.hist(MCResults[:,1:3]) # plot the histogram
# indent matters in python though not in matlab, with the indent, this line
will be run inside for j in range(MCsize) loop
# in python, indexation 1:2 of array give you only the column indexed by
1; 1:3 gives you columns 1 & 2
plt.figure(2)
plt.hist(MCResults[:,3]) #
print(MCResults)
print("of MCResults, corr of money-ouput money-price ouput-price : ")
print(np.mean(MCResults[:,1:4], axis = 0))
print(np.std(MCResults[:,1:4], axis = 0))
```

6. NEW KEYNESIAN SCATTERPLOT

```
#!/usr/bin/env python3
# -*- coding: utf-8 -*-
""" Created on Sun Jun 2 04:56:27 2019
@author: colehl
"""

# This code is designed to compute simple scatterplots of our expectational
Phillips
# Curve from the New Keynesian model.
from scipy.optimize import fsolve
import numpy as np
import matplotlib.pyplot as plt
# Our fundamental parameters
beta = .98
gam = .5
rho = .95 # markup parameter
taubar = .1
sig = .03 # std parameter money process
def Labortar(beta, gam, rho, taubar):
fac = rho*beta / (1+taubar)
Lbar = fac**(1/(1+gam))
return Lbar
def Laboract(epsil, Lbar, sig, taubar):
labor = (1 + (sig*epsil)/(1 + taubar))*Lbar
return labor
Lbar = Labortar(beta, gam, rho, taubar)
```

```
# We want to draw some random variables from the standard normal
distribution
    EPs = np.random.normal(0, 1, 50)
    Laborarray = np.array([])
    Moneygr = np.array([])
    for i in range(len(EPs)):
    result = Laboract(EPs[i], Lbar, sig, taubar)
    Laborarray = np.append(Labor_array, result)
    Moneygr = np.append(Money_gr, 1+taubar+sig*EPs[i])
    plt.figure(1)
    plt.scatter(Moneygr,Labor_array,color="black")
    plt.xlabel('growth rate of money')
    plt.ylabel('labor')
    plt.title('Scatter Plot with IID Money Growth')
    plt.savefig('NKscatterplot.png', format='png', dpi=1000)
    print(Lbar)
```

7. DYNARE CODE

% This is s Dynare mod file for our Business Cycle Model from 1 on page 203.

```
    var Y C L K w r Z z tau;
    varexo em ez;
    parameters rhoz rhom beta delta gamma alpha lambda;
    alpha = 0.33; % capital share
    delta = 0.07; % depreciation rate
    beta = 0.98; % discount rate
    rhoz = 0.975; % persistent prod shock
    rhom = 0.48; % persistent money shock
    gamma = 0.5; % Frisch elasticity parameter labor
    model;
    r = alpha*Z*K(-1)^(alpha-1)*(L)^(1-alpha); % real capital return
    w = (1-alpha)*Z*K(-1)^alpha*L^(-alpha); % real labor return
    L^gamma = (beta/(1+tau))*w/C; % labor condition
    1/C=beta*(1+tau)/(1+tau(+1))*(1/C(+1))*(r(+1)+1-delta); % capital
condition
    C + K = Y + (1-delta)*K(-1); % consumption condition
    Y = Z*(L)^(1-alpha)*K^(alpha); % output definition Z = exp(z); % overall
productivity level
    z = rhoz*z(-1) + ez; % productivity shock process
```

```
tau = exp(rhom*tau + em) -1; % money shock process
end;
steady_state_model;
Z = 1;
tau = 0;
r = 1/beta + delta -1;
w = (1-alpha)*(alpha/r)^(alpha/(1-alpha));
L = ((( (alpha/r)^(alpha/(1-alpha)) - delta*(alpha/r)^(1/(1-alpha))))^
(-1)*beta*w )^(1/(gamma+1)));
K = L*(alpha/r)^(1/(1-alpha));
Y = L^(1-alpha)*K^(alpha);
C = L^(1-alpha)*K^(alpha) - delta*K;
end;
steady;
shocks; var ez; stderr 0.009;
var em; stderr 0.009;
end;
check;
stoch_simul(order=1) ;
```

CPSIA information can be obtained
at www.ICGtesting.com
Printed in the USA
BVHW031725171021
619083BV00003B/89